Forbidden Fruits

Forbidden Fruits
Taboos and Tabooism in Culture

Edited by Ray B. Browne

Bowling Green University Popular Press
Bowling Green, Ohio 43403

Copyright © 1984 by Bowling Green University Popular Press

Library of Congress Catalogue Card No.:

ISBN: 0-87920-255-8 Clothbound
      0-87972-256-8 Paperback

Dedicated to

William T. Jerome III
and
Stanley K. Coffman Jr.

Who dared challenge the taboos

CONTENTS

Introduction

Don't Touch, Don't Do, Don't Question— Don't Progress

Ray B. Browne

The philosophy of checks and balances in nature, the belief that if a god created evil he also created good to balance it, though timeless, was well articulated in the transcendental philosophy of Ralph Waldo Emerson in his poem "Compensation" and his essay of the same name. In the essay he outlined the notion: "An inevitable dualism bisects nature, so that each thing is a half, and suggests another thing to make it whole." This attitude is basic to human nature and the actions of men and women throughout history; it has been and continues to be the very basis for much of folk—that is "primitive" in its original sense—culture in its broadest definition. As such it has had a controlling influence on much human behavior and development, by manifesting itself in tabooed and approved attitudes and actions.

The early, primitive, manifestations of the dualism are obvious: day and night, hot and cold, dry and wet, summer and winter, God and Satan, knowledge and ignorance, intelligence and stupidity, sin and innocence, sex and chastity, etc.; and of inclusion and exclusion, the allowed and the forbidden.

Throughout human experience the pendulum of attitudes and behavior has swung back and forth between the extremes, depending largely on basic and primitive impulses. As people have felt secure the pendulum has been inclined to hover on the positive side, with the light, the happy, the free. Contrariwise, as people have been individually or collectively insecure, lonely, threatened, they have tended to drive the pendulum to the negative, dark side of existence and to emphasize the forbidden, if for no other reason than to placate the evil forces and thereby to improve the situation in life. Just as there is joy and happiness in the freedom of thought and action in living, there can be comfort, or pretended comfort and (perhaps perverse) joy in the things one cannot do. There can be personal and collective power and pleasure in denying the flesh and spirit; such an attitude is prohibiting "sins of the flesh" or of the

1

spirit, fearing the dangers of too much liberty or joy. What it really means, however, is that people are afraid to let loose of the ballast of the traditional, of the past, of the status quo. People will go so far as to create or recreate the past in order to have this bulwark to cower behind. As Eric Hobsbawm states in *The Invention of Tradition*, this re-creation represents a growth industry in present-day society: " 'Invented tradition' is taken to mean a set of practices, normally governed by overtly or tacitly accepted rules and of a ritual or symbolic nature, which seek to inculcate certain values and norms of behavior by repetition, which automatically implies continuity with the past."

This attitude has taken its form in the shape of individual, collective or national denial, as in a family denying its members pleasures because abstinence is thought to be healthy, virtuous or otherwise desirable; of groups (political, religious or otherwise) dedicating their members to the purposes of denial; of nations directing the energies of their members toward some limited or general "puritan" or "spartan" goals, as the early American Puritans, the present-day (1984) "Moral Majority" or perhaps even more dangerous national purposes as in the fundamentalism of present-day Iran. Such taboos must have or must have had some merit in the past, so the reasoning for their continuance goes; they have borne the test of time and workability and have proved themselves pragmatically.

Generally speaking, however, taboos are a kind of camera-aperture which allows the actions and attitudes of light and action onto the film of social and cultural development as experience and intelligence allow, bringing new attitudes and actions as the film has been perfected to accept the panorama of life. The film and the camera, as with all technology, improve slowly but surely, curiously perhaps at the same time both impeding development of all possibilities as the size of the aperture and the speed of the shutter are incapable of allowing the full scope of life to be exposed, yet inevitably bringing some advancement and some new development even as it excludes much. Thus the camera (and the taboos) act as conservators of culture of filming the past and some of the present but not always accepting all of the present or much of the future.

This is perhaps not the place to advance and develop new theories about the nature and importance of taboos. They are, clearly deep-set, powerful and complicated, and are described and analyzed in the essays contained in this volume.

It *is* the place, however, to suggest that like all deep-set, powerful and complicated sets of attitudes and behavior, taboos are far too important and far-reaching to leave unexamined. Taboos are the ghosts of history, or as Charles Dickens might have said, the attitudes and actions of time past; they are the power of our ancestral behaviors, which still haunt and control much of our present and to a large extent direct and control our future. It is therefore especially important that in the middle of the eighth decade of the 20th century we examine the whole concept because of the feeling of religious, financial, technological, esthetic insecurity currently gripping the nation which makes us come up with curious and possibly aberrational attitudes and behavior.

These attitudes and styles of behavior should be modified and controlled by the so-called intellectuals, the thinkers, in our society, who should be the leading edge of the knife that cuts the taboos and releases the winds of irrationality. Yet it is perfectly clear that the intellectuals who deny having taboos or who minimize the power of taboos to influence their attitudes are in fact strongly influenced by the rituals and prohibitions inherent in taboos. These influences are sometimes unconscious, sometimes deliberate and used for nefarious purposes. Sometimes the cutting edge that should free us from the bonds of taboos is turned in against us all and draws blood.

Of all the intellectuals that should lead the march against the inhibiting forces of taboos, academics should be foremost. Sometimes they are, especially in the sciences. Most breakthroughs in the advancement of pure science, in medicine, for example, have been made in academic environments. These breakthroughs have brought new environments in human culture and have "advanced" the human situation in the physical world.

But men and women do not live by science alone. There is a much stronger "intellectual juice" which controls that energy of society. This is the cultural humanities, which are perhaps more important than the scientific, for without the directing force of the humanities—the philosophies which interpret and add meaning and understanding to life—the scientific advances might well drive human society upon the beach of sterility and self-destruction. It is, then, a matter of the lens of the humanities, to revert to this figure of speech, improving its shutter speed and developing capacity fast enough to modify or break the taboos and thus to accommodate the necessary changes of life.

The world may be, as Daniel J. Boorstin argues in his book *The Image: A Guide to Pseudo-Events in America* (1961), expecting too much out of society and therefore creating celebrities to try to fill the aching void. But the world also expects too *little* out of society and allows the survival of taboos, and other cultural anchors, to drain the blood from reality and keep the individual and collective bodies of society less strong than they might otherwise be.

To modify the insightful words of the 19th century British author George Gissing: "It is because nations tend to [follow taboos] that mankind moves so slowly; it is because individuals have a capacity for better things [for breaking taboos] that it moves at all."

A people or a nation can be no more advanced than its taboos. In other words, a people is no better than the taboos it keeps.

What are the humanities that academics should espouse, and what are the main taboos that prevent academics from espousing them? We should examine these two questions separately and in some detail.

The humanities are those elements in life which tend to "humanize" us and tie us together in some kinds of societies. The humanities are attitudes and characteristics in a culture that people inherit from the past, use in the present and pass on to the future. They are the cultural aspects which distinguish the human being from other animals, the human society from other societies.

Since the humanities are consciously or unconsciously inherited, intellectuals often rely too much on the humanistic statements of the past (often dim and primitive past) and to slight the importance of the present in definitions and attitudes. Most academics pay slavish respect to the "masters" of the past, especially if they wrote in Classical languages—Plato, Cicero, Homer, etc.—and even our own masters of the past—Jefferson, Emerson, Thoreau, etc. Thus, for example, the National Endowment for the Humanities, a weak and flexible reed subject to the political whims and prejudices of the political party in command in Washington, after the election of Ronald Reagan in 1980, reversed the working definitions of the humanities that had been in place for four years and outlined different areas and approaches that had been declared outmoded and misguided under the previous Administration. The new philosophy took curious turns. For example, in the announcement of the National Endowment for the Humanities for the summer seminars and institutes of 1984 the wisdom of Plato and Cicero—quoted in Greek and Latin for the enlightenment and humiliation of the high school teachers it was directed at—was cited as the guiding principles that would govern the choice of subjects in the humanities and the direction in which they should be developed. It seems strange indeed that in 1983 at a time when money is tight in government as well as academia that vital "humanities" subjects would be those such as "Shakespeare: The State of the Art," or "An Institute on Homer's *Odyssey*."

Such abuse of definition, and of history, flies in the face of the obvious. There have been great and profound thinkers since the Ancients, since Shakespeare, whose wisdom, like everything else, has increased with time and distance. Yet many humaninists, like the people who proposed and chose the institutes for the NEH, ignore the evident.

For example, Richard Hoggart, a British observer of the human situation, is well worth citing for his timely comments. He and many others insist on the usefulness of the contemporary and the universal in casting light on our individual and collective lives and society. Hoggart observed that "Literature at all levels has the unique capacity to increase our understanding of a culture." He also observed in a larger context: "The closer study of mass society may make us have sad hearts at the supermarket, but at the same time it may produce an enhanced and tempered sense of humanity and humility, instead of the sense of superiority and separateness that our traditional training is likely to have encouraged." He might have added, the sense of superiority and separateness that many academic humanists hold and want to encourage and perpetuate.

Isaac Sequira, an Indian scholar who studies the situation in his country with its more than 1500 languages and dialects, thinks that the popular humanities must be used as the only common language in that country if there is to be any kind of unity achieved there.

Leslie Fiedler, an acute American critic of the contemporary scene, pushes this reasoning to its logical conclusion and believes that the popular humanities may achieve man's greatest challenge, that of uniting all mankind into a brotherhood.

Robert Coles, psychologist and Pulitzer Prize winner, insists on humanizing the humanities: "The humanities," he says, "belong to no one kind of person; they are part of the lives of ordinary people, who have their own various ways of struggling for coherence, for a compelling faith, for social vision, for an ethical position, for a sense of historical perspective." In other words, everybody has a right to pursue the humanities in his or her own way toward his or her highest understanding and appreciation of the human situation.

Many intellectuals—especially academics—however, apparently do not grant this right. Academics, especially those who are the self-appointed custodians of the value and wisdom of the conventional humanities—devote more time to protecting what they have learned than in developing or enriching it.

Many tend to be rather open-minded while they don't know much and don't have much to defend. But as they develop they tend to become proprietary and protective. They are inclined to make it their purpose to learn facts rather than to develop the ability to interpret and understand. They often make knowledge an end in itself, a substitute for action and the pursuit of wisdom.

With such an attitude, it should come as no surprise that some academics—who should be radical in approaching new ideas and new ways of investigating them because the movement of progress though not steadily so and though history may seem to repeat itself is irreversibly forward—are unduly conservative. In their minds it is safer and less taxing to restir the cold ashes of yesteryear and yestercentury than to build new fires to enlighten the present or to dream of seeing into the future. Academics pay lip-service to new curricula, for example, to new academic configurations, to new concepts of administration, to advanced technology. Yet often the whole action amounts merely to pouring old wine into new plastic bottles: business as usual, with only cosmetic changes. In failing to carry out the mandate that has always flown on the flags above and been chiseled on the doorways of libraries, labs and classrooms of so-called advanced education—learning is too exciting and valuable not to be pursued with unrelenting vigor and imagination—many academics often turn the back of boredom and self-satisfaction on newness and indeed manage to make sow ears out of purses.

Thus there is little surprise that the curse of taboos hangs close to academia. Probably thus it has always been, with some notable exceptions, but thus it does not always have to be. A slight shift in thinking and attitude, a slight recalibration in the realization that in this world few laws involving the human mind and imagination are immutable, a slight acceptance of the value of the unimpeded imagination will break the shackles of taboos and open up new vistas.

Perhaps not every book can perform the miracle of freeing and stimulating the human mind. But such is the humble intent and purpose of this volume. It is hoped that this examination of some dozen different kinds of taboos will demonstrate that contrary to some aspects of conventional wisdom and propaganda, no taboos are holy, and all should examined. It is suggested that just outside the tabooed land there are wonderful aspects of life swelling with the potential of new insights, new understandings and new joys.

We sell ourselves short if we ignore these new aspects.

SHH! Don't Touch!

Thoughts on the Tabus of Cultural Institutions

Fred E.H. Schroeder

It was a crisp January day in Philadelphia, so my privately conducted tour of Independence Mall Park seemed especially exclusive. My tour guide was John Cotter, one of the deans of historical archaeological studies in the United States, and a man who although technically retired from the National Park Service had worked intimately with research and interpretations of this most historic of historic shrines. It was not tourist season, nor even seasonable for touring, so there was no one else around as we approached the Liberty Bell. "Touch it," John said. "Go ahead." Gingerly I did so. "Thump it," he said. "Ring the Liberty Bell." I did, and I assure you that more happened to me than to the Liberty Bell. The privilege, I learned, was not mine alone: *anyone* can touch the Liberty Bell, thereby violating the cardinal tabu of museums DO NOT TOUCH. We are all invited to take liberties with the Liberty Bell.

Generally we consider tabus as irrational proscriptions, deeply ingrained traditions that once may have had reasonable meanings that have long since worn away leaving a residue of ritual behavior. The tabus of our western high-cultural institutions, however, are notably rational, and the departures from the tabus are also rational, for the most part. DO NOT TOUCH in museums and gardens and QUIET in libraries and concert halls are restrictions that are almost as easily explained as DO NOT TURN and CAMPFIRES PROHIBITED. The principle is simple. By accepting small restrictions on our absolute liberty, everyone gains in freedom to share in the benefits of the institution. The silence of a library guarantees an atmosphere conducive to study, reading and uninterrupted thought; the protection of the objects in museums from wear and breakage guarantees that they can be enjoyed by others in the future. Q, one would think, E.D.

Not quite. Some of the restrictions and prohibitions are mere tabus, for example the rule in symphony halls that silence is to be

7

maintained between movements in musical pieces. Many of us writhe in the memory of enduring the silent censure of an audience of a thousand when our unsophisticated pleasure gave way to forbidden applause after a spirited scherzo. And yet, any casual musicologist has read of nineteenth-century audiences whose intermovement applause forced composers and conductors to repeat an attractive second movement entirely before being allowed to continue to the end of the work. In recent years this tabu has been lifted; judicious intermovement applause is the ultimate of sophistication. Another example suggests further that silence tabus are cultural traditions. Some years ago I was attending a concert at Carnegie Hall. I was enjoying an aesthetic orgy, but in front of me was a gentleman who was enjoying the concert even more: *he* had a bag of roasted chestnuts, and he was clearly, like me, a provincial visitor enjoying the Big Apple's mis-en-scene to the very core. Yet he had unpardonably violated the tabu, because of cultural ignorance of the tradition that in America symphony concerts are abstracted auditory experiences. On the other hand, I recall the embarrassed horror I felt at my first jazz concert (Dave Brubeck and Gerry Mulligan) when the audience, more sophisticated than I, interrupted the actual performance to applaud each break.

A final musical anecdote. The Met was on tour in Chicago, and an uncle of mine with wealthy connections who was amused by his aesthete nephew's tastes had procured for me a box seat for one production, and the following night a seat second row center for *La Boheme*. There I sat in my tan houndstooth high-school graduation suit, surrounded by tuxedos, furs, diamonds, pearls and Italians, my immediate neighbor being a venerable diva of the Golden Years of the old Chicago Lyric Opera. It was a stellar performance: Siepi, Valdengo, de los Angeles and Tagliavini. The final duet was moving; my neighbor was moved all the way to tears, nay, she blubbered, gasped and wailed, completely drowning out Tagliavini's coos. But her noise was an Italian tribute.

Silence is not a universal common courtesy; it is a relative thing, a culturally determined and culturally variable tabu.

The ritual characteristics of the silence tabu in libraries are not of the same kind as the concert hall. Libraries set a high premium on quiet whether they are research libraries, school libraries or public libraries (with the exception of children's departments, more of which later). The tabu is international and library users need hardly fear that their habits of whispering, murmuring and pussyfooting will be out of place in Rangoon, Heisinki or Caracas, or, if transported by time machine to ancient Alexandria, that the

The urge to touch objects of art for reasons elevated or base as old art itself. This painting is well out of reach in the Metropolitan Museum of Art.

tabu would be lifted. One even wonders if the Alexandrian Library burned because no one shouted "Fire!" My quip is probably as old as the Alexandrian Library, because the ritual aspect of this tabu is reflected in the pervasive pattern of jokes, cartoons and anecdotes that surround libraries and librarians. The tabu is universal and rational, but the absorption of the tabu into the personalities of librarians (both in reality and in popular image) goes beyond reason. The image of the old maid librarian, her grey hair pulled back into a bun, severely shushing noisy children is all that a cartoonist needs to set the stage. Even attractive Marian the

The exhibit of furs at the Anchorage Museum invites touching, but this young man chooses to walk blithely by.

librarian in *The Music Man* gains her dramatic strength from being straitlaced in social relationships if liberal in mind, and paired off with a bellicose traveling salesman. One of my favorite scenes from the old *Batman* television series showed Batman and Robin in hot pursuit of The Riddler and The Penguin. The villains run into the public library, so the dynamic duo have no choice but to follow sedately, on tiptoe, and whisper to the librarian at the desk: "Did you see two men run in here?" "I don't believe so," she replies. "How would I recognize them?" "By their garb," Batman explains. "One is wearing a green leotard with a yellow question mark on the chest; the other wears a tuxedo, top hat and a long cigarette holder."

A demonstration of traditional tortilla preparation at San Antonio's Museum of Texan Cultures has great multisensory potential.

Thoughtfully, the librarian touches her pencil to her lips and reviews the patrons she has noticed. "No," she answers quietly. "I don't think I've seen them." High adventure in a library is no excuse for relaxing a tabu that protects readers from unseemly interruption nor exotic visitors from expulsion, so long as they are quiet.

An even more pointed example of the power of the silence tabu in libraries occurred in Duluth in 1981. The police were pursuing a fugitive from justice who ran into the public library. Uniformed police surrounded the building, and the library director was notified that only unobtrusive plainclothesmen were entering the building. Their instructions: "When you find him, overpower him. *Quietly.*" It

A "try on" exhibit at the Please Touch Museum in Philadelphia invites a tactile experience that goes beyond finger-tip touching.

was done, and only a few people in the crowded building saw a handcuffed man being ushered past the checkout counter. "See," one librarian remarked quietly to an amazed person, "that's what happens when you don't pay your book fines."

Tabus of silence in cultural institutions are both reasonable and useful, but as all the above anecdotes might indicate, they can also become heavy crosses to bear for the professions, especially for those in the professions of a liberal cast of mind who want to enlarge the audiences and the benefits of their institutions. I feel certain that my chestnut-cracking klutz at Carnegie Hall never went to another symphony concert, for I neglected to mention that I shushed him.

Library schools are plagued with the silent image that continues to attract a preponderance of wallflower bookworms and antisocial misfits when what the profession needs is self-confident persons who can interact with a broad public with helpful encouragement rather than with forbidding exclusiveness. The children's departments of libraries were probably the leaders in breaking the tabu. My father, who later was a member of the city library board, never forgot or forgave the treatment he received probably around the year 1906. He had requested some book, and after weeks of waiting, the book was in. Delightedly, he threw his cap into the air. The librarian promptly took the book away from him and refused him library privileges. The librarian, Miss Nettie Watts, continued to terrorize children for the next forty-five years, although she had been rusticated to remote branches of the library by the 1930s to make room for the children's department at Main to flower and change.

The change, I think, came about from the realization that the tabu was not the reason for a library, but that the underlying purpose of the library was to encourage reading. So story hours were initiated for preliterate children. The tabu was broken, but even more important was the recognition that multi-sensory cultural experiences enhance learning. Now the evidence is overwhelming that this goes beyond enhancement; it is essential to complete intellectual and social development in human beings. Many children, we learn, are denied such necessary stimulation in their homes, not to mention the poverty of home reading material, and libraries are one of several cultural institutions that strive to provide material for enrichment of minds and homes. Thus, at a library such as the Duluth Public Library, there are not only books and story hours, puppet shows and music, but children can check out toys and games along with their books, and they can Dial-A-Story from home. Moreover, the services extend to adults who can borrow sculptures, framed pictures and video and audio recordings. Nevertheless, each service meets some resistance: to some QUIET means not only silence in the library rooms, but the silence of the printed page as well.

For, unlike museums, libraries only *implied* the touch-tabu. In museums, the liberalizing of the tabu parallels that in libraries. Touching the Liberty Bell, however, is of a somewhat different order, because the Bell is an object of reverence. The conventional tabu could be justified to preserve the Liberty Bell for future generations, but the tabu is also an instrument of awe, a separation from sacred things to preserve not themselves but their sacredness.

Which makes the relaxation of the tabu even more interesting. The greatest concession that the National Park Service made in 1976 must have been a concession to Today, for posterity is going to inherit a worn-out bell. True, it is a sturdy artifact, and it will take a heap of touching and thumping to wear it down, and in the interim it will even benefit from the sort of polish we have all seen on bronze breasts and penises in art museums, but wear it will, if the liberal policy persists into the Tricentennial. Yet, curiously, except for blind persons one can hardly come up with an educational rationale for touching the Liberty Bell. Bells are not tactile experiences. They are auditory, and I think that the public would much rather hear the old cracked bell than feel it—if historic re-enactment and multi-sensory education were our purposes in lifting the tabu.

But they aren't. Touchers of the Liberty Bell are not learners; we are communicants. Which is why I said that more happened to me than to the Liberty Bell when I touched it. The frustration of the communicant denied access to the object is extreme, as in the Country Music Hall of Fame where worshippers strive to kiss Elvis Presley's Cadillac. Such an impulse I haven't succumbed to, but I recall being disturbed by the tabus in the Baseball Hall of Fame upon seeing that the home plate of Ebbett's Field is displayed on the floor, with a protective barrier around it. This is all wrong, I thought, homeplate is to be stepped on, not looked at. What difference if it wears down? Is the Blarney Stone diminished by centuries of lips? Is the Capitol in Washington less because the steps are worn? Quite the contrary. They are enhanced by the tokens of wear that deepen our communication with generations of others like us.

So, in museums, the object of reverence is a special case for the touch tabu. Art objects such as paintings are often somewhat objects of veneration, but since they were designed as visual artifacts, never intended to be fingered, and extremely vulnerable to surface damage that would severely and often irreparably alter their worth—aesthetic, communicatory and monetary alike—the tabu is necessary and proper. Drawings and prints are even more delicate and almost all decorative art objects such as glassware, ceramics, silverware, needlepoint and draperies are properly tabued. However, the last examples, fabrics, present a genuine problem: women. Denying most women the tactile experience with fabrics is real impoverishment. The statement I suppose is sexist; after all some men do tailoring, knitting and needlepoint and many women are not seamstresses or even care about clothing, drapes and tableclothes. But speaking as a rare man who enjoys shopping in department stores, I have always marvelled at how women feel compelled to touch material as part of the evaluative experience. Often in a yardgoods department one will see a woman cruising an aisle looking at fabrics while lightly running her fingers along other bolts that she may not even be looking at. The essential point to recognize here is that she is not indulging in wanton whimsy, but *reading* in the fullest sense: *to read* in Anglo-Saxon was not merely to convert literal symbols into meanings, but to advise, counsel and guess. Men (or at any rate American men) are not immune to the need for tactile testimony, especially regarding wood and metal. Probably the most ingrained of the masculine needs to touch is the kinesthetic, to *heft* objects, to try their weight and mass. Women are not necessarily uninterested, but once again, if you watch people in a department store, it is the men who make the characteristic up-and-down hefting motion with overcoats, crystal and cameras, while their female companions will read the first with fingertips and the latter probably with eyes alone.

When we observe gender-differentiated behaviors, it is certain that childhood training is indicated: girls are trained with an emphasis on fine muscle control, boys with am emphasis on large muscles. Strangely enough, in America this has not been fostered in formal elementary education in classroom activities; the effects result from informal home training and examples and from sanctions of ridicule from older children, peer models, and eventually from advanced formal education and vocational training.

Museum education programs are largely aimed at the elementary age children. And, just as in libraries, this is where most has been done to liberate visitors from the tabus. Also in common with other formal primary education, there is no conscious program to fix gender-differentiated behavior in the museum activities. All the tots fingerpaint, or arrange weeds, or play colonial roundgames, or sample a Chinese soup or tell what they think is going on in a picture. True, there are some activities such as dressing like an Arabian boy or girl or re-enacting the play activities of Indian children that necessitate sex-roleplaying.

But the important thing here is the immense range of sensory experiences that are provided for children in a museum. Look back at the examples in the paragraph above and ask yourself how many of these things have been available to you as an adult, in a museum setting. Generally they are tabu. Now ask yourself, how many of these things do you *want* to do in a museum. If my experience and observations have any validity, the odds are that you don't really want to do any of these. The tabus are fully integrated into us.

Denial of sensory stimulation is a mark of adulthood. The five senses, if would seem, are for kids. Recently, for example, I toured the Governor's Palace at Colonial Williamsburg. The actress tour-guide involved us from time to time in not-too-threatening roleplaying—we were a group of citizens presenting a petition to the governor (and a devil of a time we had with it; we had to go through the whole house to get any satisfaction)—and we were invited to practice "making a leg" or "ducking a curtsey" to the servants we would encounter. Thirty adults, and I was the only male to play the game. Two women curtsied. And my playing the game is an exception that proves the point, for I used to be an elementary school teacher, I am a museum consultant who regularly gets behind the scenes where the anointed may sometimes touch, and I am accustomed to performing before audiences. Oh. By the way: do not touch the wall-coverings or sit on the furniture in the Governor's Palace.

In Philadelphia there is a museum with the engaging name of the Please Touch Museum. Needless to say it is for children, although the children must be accompanied by adults. A delightful playpen—which unfortunately must charge an admission fee that practically guarantees that multisensory experiences and relaxation of the tabus are a privilege for the privileged—it does make an interesting laboratory for observing the tabu in action. Most of the parents sit or stand and watch their children touching and with "only" children it's a bit like Miss Havisham in *Great Expectations* telling Pip to "Play, boy." The museum is called Please Touch, but adults know tabus too well to be caught at it. Strangest of all, it really is an institutional tabu, because not only do adults regularly handle merchandise in department stores and other shops, but generally speaking, adults are perfectly responsible touchers. As any retail store clerk knows, it's the teenies and their ice cream cones and bubble gum and tussling that endanger, not the adults.

Nevertheless, museums are finding many ways of providing multisensory experience for adults. The key seems to be placing the experiences into a voluntary setting rather than forcing participation. Although most people are unaware of this, it is one of the *educational* virtues of museum shops that touchable replicas bearing price tags and relevant craft kits are available for normal adult consumer behavior. Restaurants such as that of the Boston Museum of Fine Arts feature menus to interlock sensations of taste, odor and texture with certain exhibits, and of course museum programs that offer films, lectures and demonstrations to explain or enhance art exhibits are common, as are auditory concerts and recitals in exhibit halls. Notice, however, that while these may be somewhat multisensory, most call for passive participation and don't call for touching.

Multisensory for adults often means multimediation, but the mediation usually is limited to our long distance senses of sight and sound. The touch tabu remains. But there are exceptions, particularly the Exploratorium of San Francisco where the entire museum is developed along lines of inquiry, experiment and exploration. Science museums like the Museum of Science and Industry in Chicago have been in the total sense experience business for a long time, for I recall as far back as the early nineteen forties the workable models to demonstrate principles of physics as well as the tour of a "coal mine." Natural history museums, on the other hand, often still adhere to the tabu policy, and it is only in recent decades that most zoos have "petting zoos"—for children, of course. But then, if you've petted a goat once in your life, maybe that's all you need.

Until recently, historical museums maintained the tabu, but in the many agricultural museums like Cooperstown, or village reconstructions like Old Sturbridge Village, or "living history" museums like the Living History Farms of Des Moines, adult visitors are given some opportunities for tactile learning. Again they are usually voluntary experiences and always limited, with the possible exception of Plimmouth Plantation where you can lie on the beds, if you want to try. After all, none of the artifacts here are historically old or one of a kind, and the Plimmouth folks are going to be re-enacting seventeeth-century repairs and replacement of worn or broken things anyway, so why tell visitors from "the future" not to touch? Even so, for me, it doesn't seem right, not because it's a museum, but because the "residents" of Plimmouth so thoroughly act their parts that I feel like a *guest*. And I know how to act and how not to act in other folks' homes. But that's another tabu.

A touching exhibit that is both commendable and curious in the light of my exploration of touch tabus is a room in the University of Pennsylvania Museum that is designed for the blind. A dozen or so objects (I recollect a stringed instrument made from a tortoise shell and a small baroque bronze among them) are attached firmly to chest-height pedestals. There is a continuous guide bar connecting the objects, thereby making it easy for the blind visitor to move along. A commendable exhibit, but as I say, it is curious as well because it would appear that until museum personnel were obliged to consider handicapped access, they had largely gone on the unquestioned assumption that the no-touch tabu was rational rather than traditional. And yet, if the objects now don't need to be tabued for the blind, why have they so long been tabued for everyone? It does seem that we are talking about sensory handicaps either way. The blind have been denied sight by illness or accident; the sighted have been denied touch by cultural tabu.

Yet I am going to advocate the *virtues* of the tabus of cultural institutions, and only because of the previously mentioned reasons of preservation and allowing for others' enjoyment. For the concert hall, the library, the shrine and the museums are havens of decency in a world of turmoil where one of the most precious and rare of liberties is possible, that of contemplation. All that the tabus require is conventional decorum; observe the decorum, and your mind can be at liberty, even to be revolutionary. The library, as the late and lamented director of the Tulsa Public Library, Allie Beth Martin, said, is *The Neutral Corner* where thoughts are free as long as actions are decent, while the self-restraint we exercise in museums reminds us of the touching awareness of the old man in E.A. Robinson's poem that in our fragile world, "most things break."

Centers, Interiors and Edges:
Taboos and Taboo-Breakers in Architecture

Dennis Alan Mann

In the spring or early summer of each year many large cities in America produce a showcase of the latest in home design and furnishings offered by the homebuilders in the area. These annual extravaganzas normally entice tens and sometimes hundreds of thousands of curious people to tour the best that the homebuilding industry has to offer. These model homes represent innovative design, quality construction and fashionable decor along with the latest trends in energy saving technology. I've been a keen observer of the home show in my area, called "Homerama," since 1965. Although the styles of the homes have changed over the years, the interest and enthusiasm of the public in these shows as a source for aesthetically acceptable ideas has remained constant. During the two weeks that the show is open to the public, lines of eager people await their chance to critically study the smartly decorated living rooms, dining rooms and bedrooms of the most popular styles of the day. This ritual occasion, like department store fashion shows which reveal the latest trends in clothing, serves to solidify the aesthetic and architectural standards of a major segment of the American public.

Meanwhile the profession of architecture has its own annual fashion shows known as "Design Award Programs." The most watched program, the one most anticipated by the young and trendy architects, is the *P/A* Awards. *P/A* stands for *Progressive Architecture*, one of the more popular trade journals among architects. January 1983 marked the 30th year that the most illustrious members of the architectural profession have convened to present first awards, awards and citations to projects which they feel represent the highest level of quality and originality and which embody concerns for the aesthetic and formal aspects of architecture. But more importantly the *P/A* design awards are awaited with eager anticipation by those architects and students in architecture school who are interested in avant-garde issues. Close observation of student design work after the appearance of the January *P/A* issue in the design studios shows the obvious influence of the award winners.

Both cases point out that what is acceptable in architecture and what is popular varies with the point of view. In fact, these two examples symbolize one of the major debates in architecture today. At issue is the basis upon which architectural form is generated. Should architectural form reflect the values of the center of American society—the normative values? Should architectural form reflect the values of the establishment? Or should architectural form push the edge of the envelope by reflecting the avant-garde values? Of course no one single position can be justified. A strong case can be built for each position. Furthermore, each position— center, interior and edge—has its own canons, its own dogma and its own taboos.

When society was simply structured and static, taboos were understood by everyone. They referred to a large variety of prohibitions which had ritual significance. Taboos carried on the accumulated wisdom of generations by controlling the impact of the future on the present. Breaking a taboo often brought about punishment, danger or in extreme cases ostracism from society. Taboos were important because their goal was to *preserve the status quo*. Norman Farberow points out that taboos, "the permitted and the prohibited, the do's and the don't's, are developed by society for its members out of self-preservative, tradition-enhancing motives."[1] This is an important concept to keep in mind as I examine taboos as they apply to the architecture of the center, interior and edge of society. Still, what is meant by preserving the status quo in a society which is not only dynamic but also pluralistic? What might be interpreted as a taboo for one segment of society might be perfectly acceptable for another segment. It might even be perceived as a measure of social or economic standing.

For example, in Columbia, Maryland, a residential haven for mainly upper-middle class and upper-class families located between Washington and Baltimore, a series of covenants and architectural reviews have been established to control the aesthetic quality of each neighborhood. Television antennae are prohibited as are chain link fences and green astroturf lawns, steps and front porches. *Wall Street Journal* reported that "boat trailers parked in the driveway are taboo."[2] In a less affluent neighborhood in another part of the country, the size of the TV aerial, the use of astroturf or recreation vehicles parked in the driveway are items which advertise the success of the homeowner. The "good taste" of Columbia, regulated

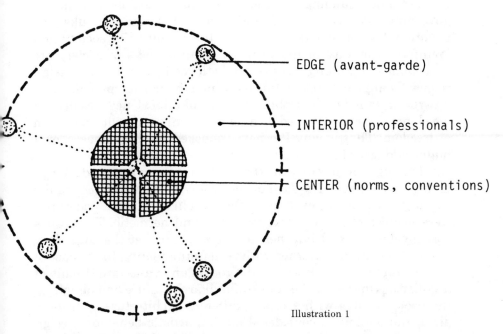

EDGE (avant-garde)

INTERIOR (professionals)

CENTER (norms, conventions)

Illustration 1

by law, would be seen as anti-social or snobbish behavior by someone in another suburban area. Taboos can be imposed either by covenant or by conformity.

Popular architecture and popular values are best exemplified by the home show. Establishment architecture is best exemplified by the work of the large commercial architectural firms. Avant-garde architecture is best represented by the design award programs which honor projects *prior* to their ever having been constructed. When each of these architectures is examined in light of the taboos that govern their design, a new perspective of American architecture is established.

Center, Interior and Edge

First, imagine all of society as reduceable to a circle. (illustration 1). All the buildings constructed by that society can be distributed somewhere within that circle. Remember, buildings reflect the values of society since they are constructed to satisfy the needs, desires and aspirations of the institutions of that society. Those buildings which gravitate to the center of the circle would reflect the normative and traditional values of society. Popular architecture and the homeshow fit there. This central position is best described by Umberto Eco when he points out that conventional building "accepts without question the norms governing society...."[3] These types of buildings, like the traditional suburban house, satisfy the demands of society and "reinforce the way of life to which the members of society are accustomed."[4] Zoning codes, aesthetic convenants and design review boards concretize taboos which in earlier periods were unwritten canons. Homeshow houses, like most new residential developments are regulated by a sense of conformity within a realm of freedom. That is why I'm never shocked by these houses, or, I might add, ever inspired by them.

The edges of the circle are the location of the avant-garde. When Irving Howe wrote *The Idea of the Modern*,[5] he characterized the avant-garde artist as existing at the margin of society. Modernists were iconoclastic, alienated, monastic and hermetic. Their work was mysterious and impenetrable. By existing at the edge, they found themselves concerned with re-defining reality. In the case of architecture Eco has described the goal of an avant-garde architect as "dispens[ing] with the conventional architecture and oblig[ing] the people to live with a totally different architecture."[6] Probing along the borders is considered normal artistic behavior. Design award programs seldom honor conventional solutions. That would be taboo among creative people. Students in architecture school would never copy a successful solution to a building problem. That would be taboo. Students are rewarded for being original and for imitating the type of behavior that they understood the early modernists to have displayed. Along the edge we might find the Plocek House by Michael Graves, the Daisy House by Stanley Tigerman or the Frehley House by George Ranalli (illustration 2). Among the avant-garde nothing is taboo except complacency, expediency and convention.

In the area between the center and the edges lies the interior, the domain of the commercial practice of architecture. These professionals, in their role as agent of the client, apply knowledge, judgment and skills to satisfy the needs and demands of their client. Professional services are marketed to directly benefit a client. Professionals are expected to establish a relationship of "trust" with their clients, show "impartiality" in judicial matters, and demonstrate "disinterest" in financial matters.[7] The basic foundation for the establishment and maintenance of a sound profession is a set of ethics within which a professional is expected to operate. This set of policies, both broad and specific, written and unwritten, can be interpreted as taboos. To practice outside these ethics marks one as a renegade. Those who choose to break these

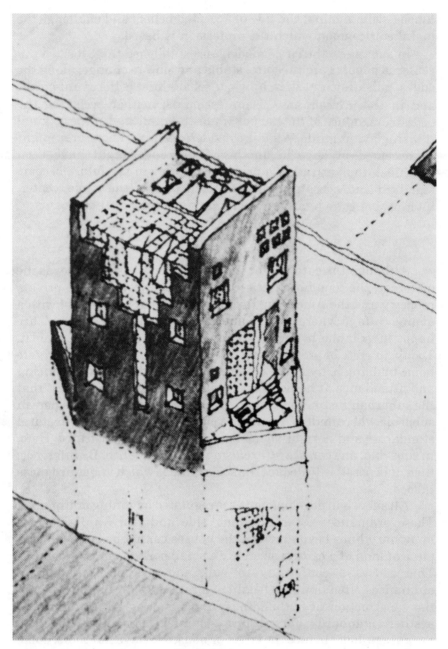

Illustration 2

Sketch of the Frehley House by George Ranalli, Architect. Won a citation for architectural design, 27th annual *P/A* awards, January 1980.

taboos swim against the tide of accepted beliefs and challenge the moral edifice upon which the profession is based.

In summary, the circle model has established three loci. In the center is popular architecture, stable and slow to change; along the edges, pulsating and stretching our sensibilities is the avant-garde; and in the interior are the professionals, neither accepting the pedestrian values of the hoi polloi nor the challenge of the original thinking avant-garde. What is considered a taboo in one area might be accepted practice in another. What once might have been unethical, thus taboo, to a professional may in the future become standard and accepted practice. Each part of the circle, center, interior and edge has its own standards and its own taboos.

Center Taboos

Although the catalyst for the development of suburbia was the motorcar, the foundation existed in the American right to private property and the American dream of that small plot of land with a quaint cottage where "Molly and me and baby makes three" are happy in their blue heaven, as the popular song of the thirties said it. Today, in spite of present high interest rates and a slack in private home-building activity the dream has not faded. Creative financing and attendance at homeshows is enough evidence to suggest that the suburban instinct may only be in hibernation. And it is here in suburbia where middle American tastes, aesthetic and architectural standards[8] and normative behaviors are best demonstrated. Here, in suburbia, one can see *by exclusion* all that is taboo. By inference, then, it is possible to deduce the social values which undergird these taboos.

All suburban developments are regulated by zoning ordinances. These ordinances establish front, side and rear yard setbacks; imaginary lines beyond which the houses cannot be built. Given a piece of land of a certain size, only a small portion of it is buildable. This causes a conformity in bulk and location. In addition, ordinances often limit the height of a residence, the use of fencing, the construction of outbuildings, and in many cases define the aesthetic standards. For instance, some developments do not allow the garage doors to face the street or houses to have flat roofs. Some developments regulate these standards through design review boards. These boards will examine a builder's drawings prior to construction to determine whether the plans will fit into the pre-established stylistic range. These architectural zoning ordinances concretize taboos. There have been numerous court cases which extend the police power of the state beyond that of protecting the general health, safety and welfare of people to include aesthetic considerations. One such case is worth noting.

In a 1970 Missouri case an appellate court overturned a lower court which had ruled that a building permit should be issued to build a highly modernistic residence of pyramid shape sporting a flat top and triangular windows and doors in a residential neighborhood of conventional two-story houses. A permit had earlier been denied by the architectural review board. The following quote, by attorney Robert Manley, summarizes the appellate court decision:

> The appellate court reversed the trial court and overruled the *Magidson (State ex rel Magidson v. Henze*, Missouri 1970) case, pointing out that the argument that the ordinances were based entirely upon aesthetic factors ignored the proviso that unsuitable structures had to be detrimental to the stability of value and the welfare of the surrounding property, structures, and residences, and to the general welfare and happiness of the community. The court stressed that the aesthetic factors to be taken into account by the architectural board were not to be considered alone, but was only one factor which should be considered along with the effect that the proposed residence would have upon the property values in the area. The court said that in this time of congested urban areas it is in keeping with the ultimate idea of general welfare that the architectural board preserve and protect existing areas in which structures of a general conformity of architecture have been erected.[9]

There has been litigation involving improper signage, clotheslines, exterior architectural appeal and functional plans, and changes in the historic or architectural character of neighborhoods protected by overlay zoning ordinances. As long as the courts can judge that it has been more than aesthetics that is being regulated, like the general welfare as measured by the maintenance of property values, then the rulings have been upheld.

There are also the unwritten laws. Fronts of houses and their landscaping are aimed at the public while the rear of the house is made private for the homeowner. Here we find the plastic wading pool, the barbecue pit on the brick patio, the ersatz barn-cum-storage shed, and the prefabricated children's play set. When was the last time you saw a vegetable garden in the front of a suburban house? Hundreds of dollars and weekends of sweat are devoted to the front yard while the backyard goes neglected. Even the garage has been domesticated.[10] Once the garage was relegated to the outermost corner of the lot. Now it has taken its place right up front with the main entrance, fully integrated into the facade of the house.

All in all, the homeshow itself is still the most conclusive evidence of lifestyle taboos which exist in the center of my model. In the past the most radical or revolutionary houses, whether in style, use of materials, internal layout or form and proportion, have been the last to sell. Although they create attention during the show, it is mostly curiosity. After all the other houses have sold, the odd-one stands alone, unsold and unappreciated. Interestingly enough, 1983's "Homerama" in Cincinnati had only traditional houses. Yet this is the age of space travel, the computer and instant communication. Marshall McLuhan told us years ago that we live in a global village; Buckminster Fuller referred to the earth as a spaceship; artificial hearts and genetic engineering will soon become common practice and the six-million dollar man, though probably undervalued, is more of a probability than a fantasy. But in 1983 the award for the best contemporary house in Homerama went to the "Whisperwood" (illustration 3), a house which blended rich traditional character flavored with soft contemporary styling.

Finally, it must be pointed out that taboos, especially at the center, are status items. A bass boat and trailer in the sideyard, a 4x4 wheeler in the driveway, or a mobile home parked outside is taboo in an affluent neighborhood but they can be status items in less-well-to-do areas. Allowing a front lawn to go natural rather than contracting with Chemlawn is taboo in an upper income suburb but normal among the ecology-minded. Aluminum or vinyl siding, insulbrick or cyclone fences are the order of the day in a lower middle-class neighborhood but absolutely taboo in a more affluent area where natural, rather than artificial, materials are demanded.

It is the center which forms the stable part of society. Change is slow to occur and taboos dominate. Without the center and its conservative attitude, rituals and taboos, the interior and the edges would be less apparent.

Interior Taboos

Professions connect the center to the edges. As the model demonstrates there are many paths from the center to the circumference. Each path represents a different professional role. In the architectural profession the architect acts as an agent of the client by contractual arrangement. The field of ethics helps to define this relationship. Not so very long ago ethics as *codified taboos* clearly delineated what the proper behavior for an architect was if he was to be accepted as a professional by his colleagues and by society.

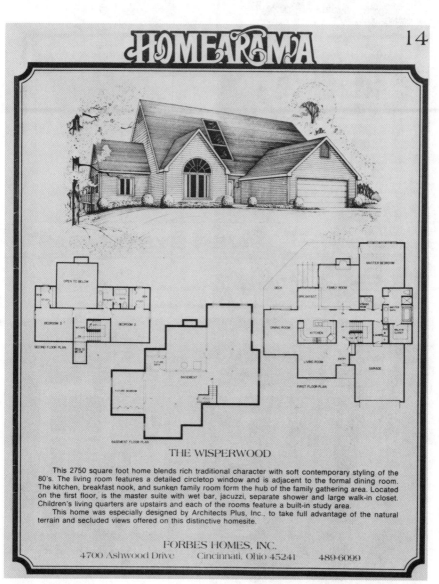

Illustration 3

Illustration 4

For instance, the American Institute of Architects (AIA) published as recently as the 1970s *The Standards of Professional Practice* which spell out quite clearly what an architect could or could not do and remain within the ethical boundaries of the profession. Among the bold type list of fifteen "Mandatory Standards," the following are noteworthy:

1. An Architect shall not render professional services without compensation.
2. An Architect shall not knowingly compete with another Architect on a basis of professional charges . . . .
3. An Architect shall not engage in building contracting.
4. An Architect shall not knowingly injure falsely or maliciously the professional reputation, prospects or practices of another Architect.
5. An Architect shall not use paid advertising, nor use self-laudatory, exaggerated, or misleading publicity.
6. An Architect shall not solicit, nor permit others to solicit in his name, advertisements or other support toward the cost of any publication presenting his work.

All these conditions, among others, have been overturned in various court cases. Many, like the establishment of a mandatory fee schedule, were declared violations of the Sherman Antitrust Act because they fixed prices. Others, like the architect acting as a contractor (builder), competing with other architects on the basis of fee, or advertising the services of a firm were interpreted by the Attorney General or the courts as a restraint of free trade and a violation of antitrust legislation. The AIA ultimately abandoned its mandatory code of ethics and professional conduct at a national convention in Cincinnati in 1980. It was replaced by a voluntary statement of ethical principles which would not be enforced by the Institute. The coup-de-grace for the mandatory standards occurred when the AIA settled a $5 million lawsuit arising out of a controversy between two architects, one of whom had "supplanted" the other *without written notice*, then a violation of the mandatory standards. The AIA settled for $700,000 but the impact on ethics was far greater. No longer could these taboos be legally enforced. Architects could now act as builders and developers, they could advertise (illustration 4), they could be publicly critical of one another's work and they could mercilessly compete for work in the open marketplace.

Surely professional societies exist to perpetuate professionals and protect their own self interests. They also exist to maintain a set of standards which they believe to have ethical value. So, in spite of the fact that these standards are changing, they still serve as the basis for the taboos which permeate the profession. As I have already pointed out, taboos can be understood in a positive manner as a stabilizing influence and a moral deterrent. In the case of the profession of architecture taboos exist to promote the aesthetic, scientific and practical efficiency of practitioners. These taboos are organized around what architects perceive to be responsibilities to the client, to professional associates and to the public.

For example, an architect establishes a relationship of trust with his client. He must preserve the confidence of the client and at no time discuss with others privileged information given to him by the client. The architect must always act in the best interest of the client. For a commercial architect, one working within the establishment, it would be taboo to promote personal aesthetics *at the expense* of the client. Architects are also obligated to improve the human environment through their work. Licensing examinations are set up to preserve the health, safety and general welfare of the public. In addition, architectural education promotes the importance of "contextual design"—the philosophy that buildings should contribute positively to their immediate environment through shape, scale, proportion, regulating lines and use of materials. Self-referential buildings are often criticized in the architectural press. In the area of professional responsibilities the architect must show impartiality. In this judicial function it is unethical to favor the client over the builder, the user over the client or the builder over a materials supplier. The architect is the person in the middle and is expected to act fairly.

Ethics are changing in many professions today. Philosophers have been invited into many medical centers to discuss the ethical issues that have arisen out of abortion, organ transplant surgery and genetic research. Old taboos are falling by the wayside as the content, context and practice of professions change. Certainly new taboos will arise. They always have. If we abide *strictly* by a definition of taboo which suggests that the violation of a taboo brings about automatic danger, punishment, sanctions or penalties then equating ethics with taboos would be naive. But now that mandatory ethical standards have disappeared from the practice of architecture and are in question in other professions, it will be interesting to follow them underground. Since professions are fundamentally conservative, perpetuating their own self-interests then the function of taboos in protecting and enhancing those interests will remain, albeit in another form.

Edge Taboos

It is the edges of the circle that allow the circle itself to be defined. In my model the edge is not constant nor is it symmetrical with the center. Sometimes one part of the arc is being pushed while another part is being pulled. Edges are not safe places to be. They are wrought with danger, frustration and lack of recognition. People on the edge are vulnerable. Tom Wolfe in *The Right Stuff* refers to test pilots who "push the outside of the envelope." Pushing the outside means probing the outer limits by defining the capacities of man and machine. This is the role of the avant-garde, the advance guard, those self-chosen few who elect to probe the edge by dragging society into the future through the insights that their work provides. These are the taboo-breakers, the makers of glass houses, the anti-rational mannerists, the revolutionaries, the utopians and the visionaries, to name only a few. Taboo-breakers embrace heresies and jolt our sensibilities into seeing other points of view. For the avant-garde it is taboo not to be a taboo-breaker.

Progressive Design (P/A) magazine's design awards are a rich source for avant-garde architects who usually break rank with accepted conventions (illustration 5). The comments by those who review the submissions, called jurors, reinforce the idea that the most significant projects are those that exist along the edge. It should be pointed out that all the projects submitted to *P/A* for consideration must be real projects but not yet constructed. One thread that runs through many of the comments of the jurors is that the large commercial firms are less interested in testing new ideas than small firms. Tom Beeby said in the 29th annual *P/A* award issue:

> Another paradox of today seems to be the incredible schism that exists between the large commercial work done by big firms and the more self-conscious artistic work being done by small practitioners.[11]

Translated to suit the thesis of this essay, this statement by Beeby magnifies the difference between the interior and the edge. Large commercial work is done by corporate establishment firms—play-it-safe firms, as I call them. Small artistic work is done by avant-garde firms—the type in which Tom Beeby has a leadership role. In the 27th awards issue, Robert A.M. Stern remarked that many of the submissions were disappointing, uninteresting and mechanical. He remarked that:

Progressive Architecture

January 1982

Illustration 5

29th annual P/A Awards

> What the subject of architecture *is* either takes a longer time to filter to the big offices, or they resist it because it's a change they don't want to get involved in; probably both are true.[12]

Most of the jurors look for new ideas and most establishment offices do not supply them. Only the small offices, those that survive hand-to-mouth, are willing to break established formal taboos. From an historical stand-point this was certainly true with the modern movement in architecture and with modernism in general. Modern art has never been well-received by the public and modern artists have not been known to be conservative or conformists. They have a dream of a better world and they see their work as a means of reaching it. Selling out to the establishment or going commercial are taboo activities if an avant-garde architect expects to retain the respect of his peers and retain his position at the edge of the circle.

All disciplines have their innovators, inventors and orginators as well as their conservators. But at the edge, the rules of the game are different. Old paradigms are unacceptable because they hinder innovation. New paradigms need to be developed. Any taboos which might stand in the way must be dispensed with, made to appear foolish, trivial, backward and superstitious. Taboo-breaking behavior is nurtured in educational programs in architecture which teach students to question everything and accept nothing as given. No ideas are sacred. Traditional ways of solving problems only constrain an active and imaginative mind. If the world is to be made more beautiful, more efficient, more humane, more energy-conscious or whatever the agenda happens to be, then no present codes of behavior should be protected. Creative people must be free spirits.

Today the discipline of architecture is changing so rapidly that even the edge is difficult to define. For instance, when Robert Venturi wrote *Complexity and Contradiction in Architecture* he swept away the taboos against using historical precedents. Those taboos had been a basic canon of the modern movement. Christopher Alexander's work with "pattern language," begun in the late 1960s made it possible for users to become directly involved in creating their own environments. Even research in architecture has emphasized post-occupancy evaluation studies based on empirical research methodology. These studies focus primarily on evaluating user behavior in recently constructed buildings and comparing that behavior to assumptions that were being made while the building was being designed. Research in architecture was generally a taboo area as architects saw themselves as artists.

The edge is a dynamic area where the only taboo is the acceptance of things as they are rather than as they might be. At the edge the only rule is that there are no rules.

Conclusions

Uncovering the taboos in architecture has at least one very important by-product. That by-product is the identification of a number of role-models that exist within the profession of architecture. This is particularly significant for students of architecture who can be shown that they have some choice in the direction that their careers take. These role models have surfaced as a means of serving the unique needs of different segments of society. They also contribute in a number of ways to the discipline of architecture. If the model of society that I have used to illustrate taboos has any pedagogical value, then it should be possible to characterize professional roles for the center, interior and edge. These role-models clearly distinguish between each pair of roles and establish the kind of behavior expected from each.

The role-model which serves the center is the *Normative* model. Here the architect would aim at understanding existing codes of behavior, traditional building solutions and conventional methods of building. There would be no desire to change people through architecture but merely to reinforce a life-style which is deemed desirable by a majority of the public. Legal clinics and public health clinics are excellent models in other professions for this type of service.

There are two role-models which are appropriate to the interior of the circle. The first is the *Establishment* model. Large commercial firms serve this model. Their clients are generally large organizations which represent the most powerful and prestigious institutions of our society; institutions like Government, Education, Religion and Business/Finance. The philosophy of the Establishment firms is to serve the present and future needs of their clients while at the same time making their clients aware of the latest advancements in building technology, space-planning and construction management. These corporate firms engage in the same type of business practices as their clients. In addition to the Establishment model, the interior of the circle also houses the *Transactional* model. The basic philosophy of this model is that of exchange. Here, the architect identifies his agenda and helps the client to identify his own agenda. If they share enough, if their separate agenda overlap enough, then a transaction may occur. All professionals have an agenda which owes some allegiance to their discipline. But naturally the client is less concerned with the discipline of architecture than with his own direct needs. Clear, open and direct communication between the architect and the client allows this model to provide satisfaction to both parties.

There are many role-models that exist along the edge. As we move from the unity of the center to the chaos of the edge we discover more and more viable role-models. I have written earlier of the *Avant-garde* architect. In addition to this role-model there is the *Revolutionary* model, the *Utopian* model and the *Visionary* model. Here, each architect dreams of a different future but their methods for achieving that future vary. Each model can be active or passive, each uses visual images and a written rationale to promote their ideas, and each professes that a better world will result from their beliefs. Architectural history and theory is rich with the important contributions that these architects have provided.

Some role-models are more permanent than others. Those that are the most stable have the most taboos while those that are the most evanescent have little time or opportunity to establish taboos. Yet no human being can be a totally free spirit unhampered by any fear or any self-protective tendency. Even the most independent architect has some inhibitions and these he protects with taboos.

Notes

[1]Faberow, Norman L. (ed.) *Taboo Topics*, Atherton Press, 1963, pp. 1-2.
[2]*Wall Street Journal*, Nov. 29, 1982. Article by Frank E. James.
[3]Eco, Umberto, "Function and Sign: Semiotics of Architecture," *VIA 2*, Publication of the Graduate School of Fine Arts, University of Pennsylvania, 1973, p. 145.
[4]Ibid., p. 145.
[5]Howe, Irving, ed., *The Idea of the Modern in Literature and the Arts*, Horizon, 1977.
[6]Op. cit., Eco, p. 145.
[7]Goldman, Alan, *Moral Foundation of Professional Ethics*,
[8]See "Architectrue, Aesthetics and Pluralism: Theories of Taste as a Determinant of Architectural Standards," Dennis Alan Mann, in *Journal of Popular Culture*, XIII: 4, Spring 1980, pp. 701-719.
[9]Manley, Robert E. and Fischer, Timothy, A., *The Effect of Aesthetic Considerations on the Validity of Zoning Ordinances; The Status of Aesthetic Land Use Controls in Ohio*, The Cincinnati Institute, 1974, pp. 13-14.
[10]See *The Necessity for Ruins*, J.B. Jackson, Univ. of Mass., Press, 1980, "The Domestication of the Garage."
[11]*Progressive Architecture*, Jan. 1982, p. 109.
[12]*Progressive Architecture*, Jan. 1980, p. 87.

Beauty Secrets:
Tabooing the Ugly Woman

Jane E. Caputi

For a man, there is nothing more depressing than an ugly woman.
Georges Bataille[1]

George Masters is a make-up man *extraordinaire*—a professional designer of the female face and figure—recently acclaimed for his miraculous transformation of Dustin Hoffman into Dorothy Michaels in *Tootsie*. Journalist Paul Galloway, reciting Masters' accomplishments, includes his "enhancing the looks of some of the world's best-known, wealthiest and beautiful women." After dropping some twenty names ranging from Rita Hayworth, the Duchess of Windsor and Marilyn Monroe through Bo Derek, Nancy Reagan and Jane Fonda, Galloway comments:

> This is just a partial list. I still am most impressed with his transformation of Lynda Bird Johnson in the '60s when she was dating George Hamilton; making her almost beautiful was both a humanitarian act and a public service.[2]

This is self-serving and sexist humor. Few would so complacently pick on the face of the father, Lyndon Baines Johnson. He was, after all, a man and generally safe from such snide attacks. Of course, when someone did just that, the sexual animosity was unmistakable.

In that singular document *The SCUM Manifesto* (1967), Valerie Solanas took pains to distinguish her proposed organization from traditional women's rights groups. She wrote, "If SCUM ever marches, it will be over LBJ's stupid, sickening face; if SCUM ever strikes, it will be in the dark with a six inch blade."[3] The political bias here is evident and to most sensibilities outrageous. Yet Galloway's humor—although all too common, suitable for the daily paper, and cloaked in the praise of women's beauty—is reflective of equally intense biases and hatreds.

Women are everywhere proclaimed and praised to be the beautiful sex; this is one of the most effective and encompassing of sexual stereotypes. Yet the underside of that apparent compliment is a most unflattering fixation on female appearance and a fear and hatred of all that can be construed as ugly in a woman. Such ugliness, we are repeatedly told, is depressing, distressing and even socially dangerous. Hence, the cleaning up of Lynda Bird Johnson's image could be spoken of as a "humanitarian act" or a "public service." This taboo governing female appearance is most emphatic in the symbolic worlds of celebrity, fashion, pornography, film and television, There, "beautiful" women are accorded the awe of a fetish, while the "ugly" are blatantly subjected to what Gaye Tuchman has termed "symbolic annihilation"—the trivialization or condemnation of a group accomplished by its systematic exclusion in the imagery of the mass media.[4]

Such annihilation is obvious in any of the slicker fashion or pornographic magazines—mass forms and institutions predicated upon this myth of female beauty and devoted to its propagation. In these, an extremely narrow aesthetic censors out any (in reality the vast majority) who do not conform to their specifications of height, weight, facial and racial characteristics. Edna Woolman Chase, a long-time editor of *Vogue*, recalled:

> Once Vogue showed two or three dresses for stout women, but we were so shaken by the experience that we haven't repeated it in fifty-seven years.[5]

The trauma here is one induced by taboo violation; its intensity indicates the seriousness of what is basically an ideological trangression.

The obsession with female appearance and resultant standards of beauty (with thinness as a prime example) have as much to do with fascism as with fashion—that is, with politics as well as aesthetics. Even the most seemingly innocuous fashion imagery can be seen to uphold the standards of a fascist art form, displaying what Susan Sontag described as a "utopian aesthetics—that of physical perfection ... forbidden to show bodily imperfection."[6] Yet no one is born with some innate sense of what constitutes good looks, bodily perfection or who should have these in the greatest measure. Instead, these are acquired tastes; they shift through time, are learned through socialization, and are precisely political. Accordingly, we are judged not only by how well we ourselves fit the culturally approved standards, but by how well we have internalized these and made them our own. A Stanford-Binet I.Q. test from 1960 makes this abundantly clear.

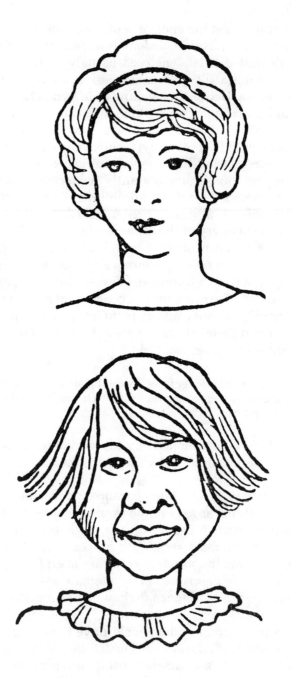

"Which is prettier"? (Stanford-Binet, 1960)

The Fair Sex

Why does a beautiful girl need an I.Q. to say I do?
                    20th Century popular song[3]

Drawings of two women illustrate an intelligence test question which asks, "Which is prettier?" The figure at the top is demure and properly feminine. Her features are regular and bland and her hair has been styled. The face shows evidence of make-up. Her eyes are cast downward and to the side. The figure at the bottom, however, presents a totally different aspect and mood. Her hair is coarse and unattended; even worse, facial hair can be seen on her cheeks. Her nose is large and so are her lips. She looks directly into the eyes of her beholders. *"Which"* (we might also note the use of the inanimate pronoun), then, "is prettier?" All those who don't want to put their intelligence on the line would quickly choose the figure at the top Yet how fair is such a test and what does this question really measure—our intelligence or our internalization of a cultural bias? Also, is its function not only to test, but also to teach us that very bias, for this simple set of images very effectively conveys some basics of sexism and racism as they are intertwined with the larger cultural stereotyping of beauty. These include:

1. *The image of the beautiful woman functions as an icon or symbol for the beliefs and values of the core culture:* Our culture worships itself in its myth of physical perfection as dramatized by celebrities, fashion models, sports heroes and movie stars. These types are the modern equivalent of more traditional action-oriented heroes. But the *look* of such figures in this image-ruled world is as critical to analyze as were the *deeds* of the former types. Film theorist Bela Balazs has commented:

> The physical incarnation of the hero or heroine is beauty of a kind which exactly expresses the ideologies and aspirations of those who admire it. We must learn to read beauty as we have learned to read the face.[8]

Historically we know that in Nazi Germany the stereotypic blue-eyed blonde was the fashion dictate for purely ideological reasons; that was a system in which, "Outward appearance was always stressed as a sign of the correct racial soul."[9] Yet how qualitatively distinct is that attitude from the more submerged one in America whereby outward appearance is taken as the first and sometimes the only indicator of one's racial or sexual acceptability.

Furthermore, what ideologies are revealed by our standards of *ugliness* as well as of beauty?

When Black Liberation in the 1960s first coined the slogan, "Black is Beautiful," it was a response to years of racist conditioning that black features were in and of themselves displeasing. In August 1968, the *Thunderbolt,* an extremist anti-black newspaper, stated quite baldly, "Most white men are not attracted to Negro women because they are ugly."[10] Certainly, one of the more effective methods of transmitting racism is to fuse some racial traits with ugliness while exalting others as the epitome of earthly beauty. American racism can be discerned in both the absence of any celebrated images of colored beauty and in the ceaseless procession of clone-like blue-eyed blondes from Farrah Fawcett and Cheryl Ladd to cover-girls Cybil Sheppard, Cheryl Tiegs and Christie Brinkley. This type is celebrated in annual models because it represents an idealized racial and sexual symbol. That is also why those particular looks are stereotyped and finally perceived by nearly all to actually *be* beautiful. For without the symbolic overlay, these stars and supermodels might seem as forgettable, featureless and interchangeable as Barbie dolls, as indistinct as our correct answer in the I.Q. test. And what conclusions can we draw regarding her memorable, if wrong, counterpart? She is obviously of an unspecified, but (because of the association with ugliness) strongly disfavored ethnic origin; her nose, lips and hairiness all point in that unmistakeably racist direction.

To return to Balazs' point, ideologies certainly can be discerned in cultural representations of beauty, but to further that analysis we should inquire as to why the symbolic burden of beauty falls primarily upon the "heroine" and not the hero, the female and not the male.

2. *Women are the pretty sex*: It is hardly likely that the imagery of the test question could be sexually reversed, that there be drawings of two men with the same query, "Which is prettier?" Even if we substituted the word *handsome,* the situation would remain absurd. In our culture looks are not supposed to be a primary concern of men. Handsomeness might be a side-effect of masculinity, but it is certainly not a necessary or definitive attribute. Prettiness and the primacy of appearance are, however, considered to be eminently feminine traits. In 1852, *Godey's Lady's Book* offered this dictum: "It is a woman's *business* to be beautiful,"[11] that is, her obligation and sexual occupation. Indeed if she is to get and remain beautiful it will also be a lifelong *preoccupation.*

As the beautiful sex, women are expected to relinquish their claims to vast fields of human endeavor; the first of these is intelligence and creativity. The negative correlation of beauty to brains is everywhere propagandized. Oscar Wilde once flattered his own sex by noting, "No woman is a genius; women are a decorative sex." Rooted in the myth of female beauty is the stereotype not only of the dumb blonde but also the companion belief in the general intellectual inferiority of women. Rather than create great works of art, women are expected to regard themselves as works of art—to sculpt their bodies, develop their breasts, paint their faces and invent an image of themselves as their supreme aesthetic expression.

Two centuries ago, Mary Wollstonecraft wrote, "Taught from infancy that beauty is women's sceptre, the mind shapes itself to the body, and roaming round its gilt cage, only seeks to adorn its prison."[12] Taught the role of the beautiful sex, dressed for the part, and reviled if they refuse it, women are still named as vain, superficial, narcissistic and frivolous when they enact it. These acquired traits, however, have some very non-frivolous functions. Helene Roberts has commented:

> The narcissistic ideal is for women to become lost in a trancelike fixation on their own images in the mirror, engrossed in what they see there, while the real world, man's world of science and finance, politics and government, revolves on its own axis, without them.[13]

The second field that must be surrendered is worldly power. Whereas women's sexual charm is centrally located in their physicality, men's chief allure emanates from their work, achievements, wealth and social station—essentially from their power. Consider the cultural dramas of *Dallas* and *Dynasty*. Both J.R. Ewing and Blake Carrington command interest and sex-appeal not because they are blondes or brunettes or change their clothes every five minutes, but because they are set up as the potentates of vast financial empires.* Beautiful women form just another part of their holdings.

Finally, the stereotype of feminine beauty designates women as sex objects *par excellence*, not only in the eyes of men who behold them but also in their own eyes. Fashion becomes a social master and the female body and all that is considered to be wrong or ugly about it becomes a woman's enemy and obsession for life.

---

*Correspondingly, Bobby Ewing's beauty only contributes to his status as the young, softer and weaker brother, while Alexis Colby's power, combined with her dark beauty, confirms her as the archetypal wicked witch.

3. *Submission is beautiful and feminine beauty is submissive*:
Marabel Morgan wrote in her best-seller, *The Total Woman*, "It is
only when a woman surrenders her life to her husband, reveres and
worships him, and is willing to serve him, that she becomes really
beautiful to him."[14] Beauty here is unmistakably in the eye of the
beholder; and that eye belongs to an overseer.

In the imagery of the I.Q. test, it is crucial to note that the
prettier picture has cast her eyes demurely to the side while the
fearsome woman gives a direct and unwavering gaze. This is a
classic instance of body language. Averted eyes signify submission
while the direct stare indicates equal status and a challenge. What
we learn from this test is that a component of feminine prettiness is
a willingness to submit. Companion traits include passivity,
vulnerability, fear and weakness. All these liabilities are found to be
desirable, erotic and beautiful in women and are coded into the
norms that say men must be older, taller, larger, stronger and more
experienced than the women who attract them and that women
must be younger, smaller, thinner, weaker and more naive than the
men they are seen with.

Frankly, the entire relation between women and fashion is one
of dominance and submission. If the basic purpose of fashion is to
make women beautiful, i.e., pleasing to men, it may well be that the
individual and shifting styles—be they long skirts or short, thinness
or plumpness—are themselves secondary. What is primary is a
common symbolic denominator of submission.* Submission is the
background attraction factor in female fashion and it is this factor
that imbues any style with its fundamental sex-appeal. Such a
dynamic is revealed by the language itself.

The Fashionable Woman

ARTIST MAKES REPORTER A WOMAN.
Headline for Paul Galloway's story on George Masters

One is not born, but rather becomes a woman.
Simone de Beauvoir[15]

Indubitably, women are the fashionable sex. Yet, although
easily overlooked, the word *fashion* is not only or even primarily a
noun or adjective. It is also a verb and it is the verb form that reveals
its character. As verb *fashion* means "to make; shape; mold;
contrive." Hence, the fashionable woman is the one who can be most

---

*The equivalent factor in male dress is *uniformity;* the paradigm for one is a slave, for the other a
soldier.

easily shaped, most effectively made, unmade, made-up and made-over. When one absorbs the meaning and function of this word as a verb, a previously undetected history of fashion becomes apparent. This is not the history of costume, but of creation.

In many of the earliest creation mythologies, a god takes a bit of clay or mud and fashions it into a suitable shape, usually somewhat after his own image, blows a little life into the figure and sets it on its way. The story of Pandora is one such myth and a staple of Western culture. Most of us are familiar with the version promoted by Hesiod in *Works and Days.* According to this, there were no women at all on Earth during the Golden Age, but Zeus planned to send a great evil to mankind, enlisting the aid of Hephaestus, the craftsman god. Hephaestus took clay and "moulded an image, in form of maiden fair." Then Athene and some other goddesses bedecked, bejeweled and arranged her. The beautified creature is then given "as a gift and sorrow to covetous man."

But Jane Ellen Harrison, the great Cambridge classical scholar, looked into this story and found it to be essentially a theological expediency, a reworked version of an older myth which arose in response to what she termed "a social shift from matrilinear to patrilinear conditions." For originally, Pandora had been the primary Cretan deity. The name itself means "All-Giver," the one who distributed the gifts of the Earth to humanity, *not* one who was herself given as a gift. But to suit the new order, the former deity was transformed into something of a mannequin or living doll. Harrison explains:

> On the Bale Cylix in the British Museum the birth of Pandora, or rather her fashioning is depicted .... So she who made all things, gods and mortals, is unmade and remade and becomes the plaything of man, his slave, his lure, dowered only with bodily beauty and with a slave's tricks and blandishments.[16]

This myth precisely establishes the connection between the fashioning/making process and that of fashion/beautifying—complementary methods in the social construction of women. We might also note that when the two converge, *forming* has frequently become *deforming.*Take, for example, two classic styles: bound feet and corseted waists.

For nine centuries in China (ending only with the 1949 revolution) female footbinding was the mandatory and definitive beauty ritual for women. Only those peasants who had to work were spared this practice which left the less fortunate, but truly fashionable woman with three inch putrescent stubs. The doctored feet leaked pus, reeked of rotten flesh, and had to be kept wrapped and hidden in bandages. Nevertheless, these ceremonial wounds were fetishized as the supreme expression of beauty and given such deceptive names as "lotus feet."[17]

Tight lacing of a corset produced the mandatory hourglass figure for 19th century American women. Yet at the same time it interfered with the oxygen supply and frequently caused hazardous compression of the vital organs and displacement of the ribs. Fashionable customs such as foot-binding or corseting not only re-shaped the female body, but crippled and constrained it in the process.[18] Thus beauty could be found in a useless three inch foot or a breathless sixteen inch waist. Then, the finished or fashioned body could be used as "proof" that women were the "weaker" sex. Modern updates of such rituals include dieting which not only minimizes female presence and bodily strength but can be a slimness until death,[19] as well as various forms of cosmetic surgery, a branch its practitioners refer to as the "most creative."[20]

Andrea Dworkin has pointed out that ideal female beauty often requires the mutilation of the natural body.[21] Even short of this extreme, the coveted look is usually a determined denial of the natural body. It is found in a carefully composed mask, a rigorously watched weight; it is literally made-up, precisely *glamorous* in that word's literal sense of witchcraft or a magical and deceptive illusion.[22] The general insinuation is that women bewitch, charm and enchant men with their beauty, but this is almost purely a reversal. It is women themselves who are hexed by this stereotype.

Although idols and models of women are everywhere—sex symbols, objects and goddesses—and although fashion and the cult of feminine beauty purportedly exist to celebrate the beauty of women, the actual cumulative effect is to convince most women that they are hopelessly hideous, fat, hairy and futile. Paging through the magazines, most of us know that we look nothing at all like the young, thin and lovely creatures that populate the front pages—never did and never will. But, tucked away in the back are the realistic, recognizable and frightening images—the one-pagers that visually and verbally berate us. "How do you look from behind?" one leers, playing self-appointed rear-view mirror. "Take a look for yourself, because your closest friends won't tell you."

If not the behind, almost any other part can be served up for selective female self-hatred: miniature breasts, little bumps on the thighs, big noses, limp hair. It is supposedly normal for men to fetishize the female body, favoring some choice part and declaring themselves "leg-men" or "tit-men." This fragmentation is bad enough, but what is worse is that women have learned to do likewise to themselves. Only women themselves often *loathe* the selected part, if not the whole body. One hospital administrator interviewed in *Ms.* gave voice to this collective trauma: "Basically, growing up was the dilemma of trying to decide what about me was the ugliest."[23] She also spoke of her "fear of fat" and the "fear of being a monster."

Her fear is not unfounded for behind all the lip-service to female charm is the inescapable inference that women in their natural state are flawed or monstrous, that beneath the mask of beauty is a barely caged beast.* It is really only the made-up woman, concocted in the culture's imagination and fabricated by cosmetics, treatments and rituals who is the "true" beauty. Christian Dior, one of the modern masters of female design, exemplifies the fashion animus. A 1955 article in *Colliers* discussed his work and influence:

> The greatest of M. Dior's virtues, of course, is his burning desire to make all women beautiful. "My desire," he says, "is to save them from nature."[24]

Who, however, will save us from M. Dior, for the fashioning process results in the creation not of beings but of things, objects—precisely sex objects.

Sex Objects

> *Snow-white was already dead when the heroic prince fell in love with her. "I beseech you," he pleaded with the 7 dwarfs, "to give it to me, for I cannot live without looking upon Snow-white." It awake was not readily distinguishable from it asleep.*
>
> **Andrea Dworkin**[25]

> *A thing of beauty is a joy forever.*
>
> **John Keats**

At first it might be thought that the modern term *sex-object* refers to someone who is the object or aim of another's sexual desire. This, however, is only a partial and secondary meaning. A modern

---

Malleus Maleficarum (1484) handbook of the European witchcraze put it this way: "You do not know that woman is the Chimaera, but it is good that you should know it; for that monster was of three forms; its face was that of a radiant and noble lion, it had the filthy belly of a goat, and it was armed with the virulent tail of a viper.... A woman is beautiful to look upon, contaminating to the touch, and deadly to keep."

Heinrich Kramer and James Sprenger, *The Malleus Maleficarum*, trans. with an introd. and notes by Montague Summers (London: John Rodker, 1928; rpt. New York: Dover, 1971).

understanding of *sex-object* must include the notion of the woman
as a sexual object or thing. The first place a woman confronts herself
as an object is as an image, an object of sight, someone who is
transformed into something to be looked upon, reviewed, displayed,
scrutinized and surveyed. She learns this status through the
personal ritual of mirror-gazing, through interpersonal harassment
and surveillance on the streets (euphemistically called "girl-
watching")[26] and through all the mass forms and rites which
confirm the status of woman as spectacle—fashion, pornography,
cheesecake, the sexual sell, pin-ups, centerfolds, beauty contests,*
and strip shows—just some of the many ways that men manage to
keep on eye on women.

Good Looking

*If she had her choice of an Oscar or a high fashion magazine cover, she'd
take the cover.*
Lee Majors on Farrah Fawcett (then his wife)

In ideal cultural form, men act as heroes; in ideal cultural form
women appear as models.[27] Art historian John Berger, in an
analysis of the visual dynamics of sexism, has written that how a
woman appears to others, especially men, is of crucial importance
for what is normally thought of as the success or failure of her life:

To be born a woman has been to be born within an allotted and
confined space, into the keeping of men .... *Men act* and *women
appear.* Men look at women. Women watch themselves being
looked at. This determines not only most relations between men
and women, but also the relation of women to themselves.[28]

Berger's conclusions stem largely from his study of European
oil painting and, as he indicates, many of those established
conventions have continued into the medium of photography and
advertising imagery. The era in which the term *sex-object* has
become commonplace is also the era in which women, perhaps more
than any other class of individuals, are relentlessly pictured by
photography. Susan Sontag has commented:

To photograph people is to violate them, by seeing them as they

---

*The first Miss America pageant was held in 1921, a year after women constitutionally won the
right to vote. Historian Lois Banner avers that this event ritualized the notion that women's
primary goal should be the pursuit of beauty and marked a "victory of fashion over feminism."
See Lois Banner, *American Beauty* (New York: Knopf, 1983), p. 16.

never see themselves, by having knowledge of them they can never have; it turns people into objects that can be symbolically possessed.[29]

The two modes of photography that best exemplify this critique are fashion and pornography—the major manufacturers of images of women—and two structurally similar forms. Each is a complementary outpost on one sexual taboo. While pornography exposes the unclothed, fashion focuses on the clothed. Pornography poses and selectively undresses; fashion poses the selectively dressed. The subject matter of each is the fetishized female body. Each manufactures fantasies for a sexually dangerous society. Women look and learn from fashion journals—*Glamour, Vogue, Mademoiselle;* men do the same with *Penthouse, Playboy, Hustler.* Although segregated from each other, and nominally distinct, fashion differs from pornography in much the same way as the women's toilet differs from the men's.

Living Dolls

A doll I can carry, the girl that I marry must be.

Irving Berlin.

I'd rather have a paper doll to call my own than a fickle-hearted real live girl.
The Mills Brothers

...the pornographic object's most quintessential form [is] the pornographic doll. Pornography is replete with images and evocations of the "doll," an actual plastic copy of a woman, made to replace a woman, and to give a man pleasure without the discomfort of female presence.

Susan Griffin[30]

The commingling of fashion and pornography has become increasingly conspicuous in the past decade as the more daring photographers spike their fashion shots with sado-masochism, kinky sex, overt objectification, and desperation.[31] One of the most flagrant of these is Helmut Newton, a regular contributor to French and American *Vogue* as well as *Oui* and *Playboy.* One of Newton's trademarks, along with the use of prosthetic props, scenes of sexual slavery and ritual murder, is the photography of wax mannequins as if they were live women. Edward Behr, an editor of European *Newsweek*, introduces one of Newton's books, *Sleepless Nights*:

> But above all here is a man who loves women so passionately, so completely that he has to carry this love to its ultimate conclusion. Look, he says, in a brace, a plaster cast, even in an artificial limb, she remains beautiful and desirable. And since

models and mannequins are objects to be manipulated at will, why not attempt the final manipulation, the mingling of real life and wax models? Do we really know the difference—not only here but in real life?[32]

As such photography suggests, not only submission and deformation can be "beautiful and desirable," but also catatonia and lifelessness. Furthermore, as Behr so delightedly concedes, the boundaries between real women and their images are being intentionally and successfully confused. Such techniques abound in the photography of Newton and Guy Bourdin. For illustrations see Bourdin's photo essay "Woman Now" in *Vogue*, August 1979, pp. 109-113 and Newton's "Saint Laurent—*rive gauche*" in *Vogue*, Sept., 1982, pp. 205-211.

In other areas of the fashion world, women work as "living dolls," freeze models who stand in stores and pretend to be mannequins. One of them, Beverly Kadow, remarked: "It's just great fun to hear people arguing about whether or not you're real ... that's the nicest compliment a freeze or robot model can get."[33] On the other side of the mirror, mannequin manufacturers are just as seriously concerned with how *real* their objects will appear. In a *New York Times* article we learn that "a good mannequin is first molded in clay by a sculptor who usually demands a live subject." It then gets a series of beauty treatments—bedecking, arranging, etc., reminiscent of Pandora. Department store designers keep three hundred or so of these around, collections that they term "stables" or "harems," for most of these dummies are "females." Robert Benzio of Saks explains that he rarely uses male mannequins because "they never look real."[34] Women apparently are more successful as fakes because the feminine ideal is so exactly one of objectification and artifice. Finally it becomes explicit that along with passivity, vanity, etc., *unreality* is another feminine trait and that women have been slotted into the position, not only of the second sex, but of the symbolic sex.

The Symbolic Sex

I never understood it—this sex symbol—I always thought symbols were those things you clash together! That's the trouble, a sex symbol becomes a thing. I just hate to be a thing.
                                                                Marilyn Monroe (1962)[35]

Marilyn. She's gone. *Marilyn was, as she said herself, a sex symbol.* She died young and remains eternally young, a symbol preserved by death. (emphasis mine)*
                                                                Bert Stern (1982)[36]

*Stern expediency eraces Monroe's expressed hatred for the mass appreciation of her self as symbol.

Man would have nothing to lose, quite the contrary, if he gave up disguising woman as a symbol.

Simone de Beauvoir[37]

When Paul Galloway referred to the beautification of Lynda Bird Johnson as a "humanitarian act," he obviously meant humanity to be male, indirectly exemplifying what Simone de Beauvoir recognized as a general cultural taboo on women.

In *The Second Sex*, de Beauvoir develops the concept of the female as "other." Citing recurring attitudes in male philosophies such as this from Aristotle—"The female is a female by virtue of a certain lack of qualities; we should regard the female nature as afflicted with a natural defectiveness," or from Thomas Aquinas who pronounced woman to be an "imperfect man," an "incidental being," de Beauvoir concludes:

Thus humanity is male and man defines woman not in herself but as relative to him ... she is simply what man decrees; thus she is called "the sex," by which is meant that she appears to man as a sexual being .... She is defined and differentiated with reference to man and not he with reference to her. She is the incidental, the inessential as opposed to the essential. He is the Subject, he is the Absolute—she is the Other.[38]

In that dialectic which names man as subject and woman as other, man becomes not only the self, the essential, but also the real. Consequently, woman becomes the inessential, the object, the unreal or the symbolic sex. Whether as virtue or vice, used to sell consumer goods or even to critique the world that industrialism and advertising have made (McLuhan's *Mechanical Bride*), the image of woman is used everywhere as the primary stuff of symbolism in this culture. James Laver, an historian of fashion, has commented, "Woman is the mould into which the spirit of the age pours itself."[39] This final appropriation of woman as receptacle and image encapsulates the cultural directive that reduces the female to the symbolic. Thus, images and sex symbols are encouraged to proliferate, but the reality of women—and all that that might include—is characterized as boring, ugly or perverse and is tabooed.

In the symbolic world, male villains can be ugly and are almost always less attractive than the hero (who can himself be fairly ordinary). But the more evil a woman is, the more spectacularly gorgeous she is, the more deadly her beauty is made to appear.[40] Beauty is her token whether she is good or bad, villain or victim. So comprehensive is this directive that in the real world—man's world—female reality can simply become so drab and so plain as to be *invisible*, even alien. For a vivid example of this see James Tiptree Jr.'s astonishing short story, "The Women Men Don't See."[41]

But as the symbolic and usually all too visible sex, women are available as ever-ready targets, scapegoats, symbolic victims, a role that is only supported by the myth of their beauty. Andrea Dworkin gives her version of the sexual dialectic:

> Where he is erect, she is supine. Where he is awake, she is asleep. Where he is active, she is passive. Where she is erect, or awake, or active, she is evil and must be destroyed . . . . She is desirable in her beauty, passivity and victimization. She is desirable because she is beautiful, passive and victimized.[42]

Thus, along with submission, vulnerability,* deformation and lifelessness, victimization becomes one of those beautiful and sex-linked traits.

The link between the myth of feminine beauty and the reality of women's victimization by men was encapsulated in David Berkowitz's boast, "I only shoot pretty girls."[43] During 1977, Berkowitz as the bogie-man Son of Sam effectively established a reign of terror over New York City in his campaign to "shoot pretty girls." As Pam McCallister pointed out, *Max Factor* cosmetics opted to capitalize on this mass sex crime by introducing a product called "Self-Defense" (a facial moisturizer), using an ad campaign which read:

> *WARNING*
>
> *A PRETTY FACE*
> *ISN'T SAFE*
> *IN THIS CITY.*
> *FIGHT BACK*
> *WITH*
> *SELF-DEFENSE.*

Both campaigns—the sex crime and the advertising—linked desirability with vulnerability and operated on the assumption that prettiness functions as an irresistible target for male violence (an assumption which also guides many formulaic defenses of rape). Moreover, McCallister argues that the overall use of women as

---

*Photographer Bert Stern had this to say about Marilyn Monroe: "There have been many beautiful women since Marilyn Monroe. But who is there that has her total magic? Nobody has that vulnerability anymore." The loss of her vulnerability is mourned far more than the loss of her life.

spectacles encourages the belief that women form an interchangeable class, malleable objects that can be used to fit any man's sexual fantasy.[44]

Even more than Berkowitz, the career of another mass sex-killer, Ted Bundy, illuminates the possible consequences of this cultural dynamic. Although convicted of three murders in Florida and suspected of many more in other states, Bundy has never confessed. He did, however, agree to speculate in the third person about the mental state of such a killer. During his conversations with two journalists, Bundy kept referring to the victims as "symbols" and "images," terms that were not immediately clear to his listener, Stephen Michaud. This exchange ensued:

> "Victims," I said. "You indicated that they would be symbols and image. But I'm not really sure. Images of what?"
> "Of women," he exclaimed. "I mean of the idealized woman. What else can I say?"
> "A stereotype?"
> "No. They wouldn't be stereotypes necessarily. But they would be reasonable facsimiles to women as a class. A class not of women per se, but a class that has almost been created through the mythology of women and how they are used as objects."
> Would there be a standard of beauty or attractiveness? I wondered, thinking of the range in the victim's appearances.
> "Everyone," Bundy answered huffily, "has his standards."
> He said that a distinctly unattractive, overweight, or otherwise unappealing woman wouldn't be a candidate.[45]

Bundy further referred to the fascination of "possessing them physically as one would possess a potted plant, a painting or a Porsche. Owning, as it were, this individual."

Of course all women, regardless of their appearance, have been candidates for sexual violence, but Bundy, Berkowitz, and others like them, epitomize a stereotypic and symbolic form of male sexual violence and although they are the extreme, they nevertheless should be seen as the logical products of a sexually dangerous society, a patriarchal culture which promotes an inanimate view of women and which actively prefers symbols of women to women themselves. This sexual preference is brilliantly parodied by Ira Levin in his 1973 novel *The Stepford Wives*. More often, however, it is propounded with utter seriousness.

One example of this is Bert Stern's account of his photographic sessions with Marilyn Monroe just weeks before she died. In a forthcoming book (excerpted in *Vogue*), he confesses his expectations and fantasies of Monroe and his dream of shooting her nude. Stern reports that he not only succeeded in getting her nude, but that she then wanted to make love to him. This modern prince, however, rejected his no longer symbolic or sleeping beauty. He explains:

> My desire for her was too pure, it bordered on awe. To make love to her would have been too much ... and not enough.

For making love to her—despite his requisite lip-service to her ultimate desirability—was not at all what Stern really wanted. He did want to possess her, but not in that sticky, intimate, physical form; rather, he preferred a symbolic possession. And, according to him, he got just that:

> I saw what I wanted. I pressed the button, and she was mine ....
> My love affair with Marilyn had been photographic. It had all the energies a love affair should have and none of the problems.[46]

Although an ecstatic and energizing experience for Stern, it (if true) probably left Monroe only with a familiar and deepening alienation. Like the pornographic doll described by Susan Griffin, human sex-symbols can also be manufactured and symbolically possessed. And as a replacement for female reality (even with the actual woman right there) such symbols can "give a man pleasure without the discomfort of female presence," for such presence would no doubt be perceived as active, unerotic, problematic, frightening and *ugly*.

Beauty Secrets

> *Being an incomplete female, the male spends his life attempting to complete himself, to become female. He attempts this by constantly seeking out, fraternizing with and trying to live through and fuse with the female, and by claiming as his own all female characteristics— emotional strength, and independence, forcefulness, dynamism, decisiveness, coolness, objectivity, assertiveness, courage, integrity, vitality, intensity, depth of character, grooviness, etc.—and projecting onto women all male traits—vanity, frivolity, triviality, weakness, etc. It should be said, though, that the male has one glaring area of superiority over the female—public relations. (He has done a brilliant job of convincing millions of women that men are women and women are men.)*
> **Valerie Solanas SCUM Manifesto**

> *The most beautiful women in this room are men. There is no one more feminine than a drag queen.*
> **Niles Rogers of the group Chic.**

When Paul Galloway interviewed George Masters, he also requested that Masters perform one of his miraculous transformations on him, making the male reporter into a "woman." Galloway later raved:

> The guy's a genius .... I went to the mirror. I looked pretty terrific myself. I don't want to sound conceited or kinky, but I might even lust after somone like me.

The article is illustrated by before and after pictures so that we too can witness and marvel at this miracle.

One beauty secret already disclosed is that men frequently do not desire the real-life (even if beautiful) woman, but are more interested in possession of the symbol. Another well-kept secret is that feminine beauty (although supposedly the manifestation of woman's natural propensity) is actually a male fantasy. For women are not only a symbolic sex, but also a socially constructed one. This is exactly de Beauvoir's point when she writes, "One is not born, but rather becomes a woman." This also is exactly the meaning of the myth of the fashionable woman and the institution of fashion itself. In those traditional creation myths, the god fashioned a creature after his own image. Equally, modern woman is fashioned after the male imagination, what men want women to look like or think that *they* would like to look like if they were women. Moreover, that fabricated pretty face (with no apologies to *Max Factor*) is also a male self-defense against their imagined monstrosities—actual females.

Some men are seduced by their own fantasy and become drag queens, transvestites or transsexuals. Others prefer vicarious enjoyment and become designers, make-up men, hair-dressers, etc.—all far more expert on feminine appearance than any mere woman. These are the men who, like Christian Dior, burn to "save" women "from nature."

That hope of salvation is dangled out for nearly all. A long-running ad for Merle Norman cosmetics (the place for what they call the "Custom Face") shows and tells us that "Last Year, 1,400,000 women discovered that they were more beautiful than they thought they were." More beautiful means less monstrous, less real, more culturally contained, more politically corrected, sanitized. It also means that each individual *identity* (i.e., uniqueness) was subsumed into a class or sex *identity* (i.e., interchangeability, sameness).

The didactic mode of this ad (also the "How do you look from behind?" one) is the before/after shot, one of the most common conventions in fashion imagery. The implication is that beauty is both a put-on and a choice, as is femininity. To paraphrase de Beauvoir, beauty is not born, but made; it *becomes* you, *fashions* you. Even the imagery of the I.Q. test question can be seen this way. It too appears as something of a magic mirror of two female possibilities, a before and after of *one* self. Each respondent must ask herself not only, "Which is prettier?" but also which do I identify with, which will *I* be? Will I be pretty—accepted, loved, desired? Or, will I be ugly—ridiculed, feared and despised? Most, of course, opt for the occupation of beauty since, faced with the enormous social negation, the taboo, of female "ugliness," women have learned to dread it along with themselves.

Although beauty is held up as every woman's dream, it is actually a male fantasy and a veritable female nightmare. The myth of feminine beauty reduces women to a faceless class, marked by a mask of artifice and trained for a lifelong preoccupation with appearance, not substance. Feminine beauty is no dreamy escape route to power or adventure (as in the 1960s Maidenform bra ads—"I dreamed I took the bull by the horns in my Maidenform bra," or "I dreamed I went to Paris ... etc.). Rather, it is an invitation to immanence, a permanent I.D. in a Twilight Zone populated by pretty pictures, sex symbols, slaves to fashion, Barbie dolls, Stepford Wives and assorted fembots.* In that world, there is only one consolation. An ad for Rutledge nightgowns poses that scenario. Five (apparently living) women are grouped in a store window; a man roams among them arranging the gowns. The copy reads: "If you happen to wake up one morning in the window of your favorite store, don't worry, you'll look terrific." In the words of Edward Behr, this is indeed a "final manipulation" for such women can no longer transgress; indeed this can no longer even move.

Notes

[1]Georges Bataille, *Death and Sensuality: A Study of Eroticism and the Taboo* (New York: Walker and Co., 1962), p. 145.

[2]Paul Galloway, "Artist Makes Reporter a Woman," *The Albuquerque Tribune*, 3 June 1983, p. B-1.

[3]Valerie Solanas, *The SCUM Manifesto*, in Robin Morgan, ed., *Sisterhood is Powerful* (New York: Vintage Books, 1970), pp. 514-9.

[4]Gaye Tuchman, Arlene K. Daniels and James Benet, eds., *Hearth and Home: Images of Women in the Mass Media* (New York: Oxford, 1978), pp. 7-8.

[5]Edna Woolman Chase, *Always in Vogue* (New York: Doubleday, 1954).

[6]Susan Sontag, "Fascinating Fascism," in *Under the Sign of Saturn* (New York: Farrar, Straus & Giroux, 1980), pp. 72-105.

Fembot is a word coined on the show *The Bionic Woman* to name some female robots created by a mad scientist. These fembots also wore the faces of our heroine's best friends.

[7]This line is cited in Una Stannard, "The Mask of Beauty" in *Woman in Sexist Society*, ed. Vivian Gornick and Barbara K. Moran (New York: Basic Books; rpt. Signet, 1972, pp. 187-203.

[8]Bela Balasz, *Theory of the Film* (New York: Dover, 1952, 1970), p. 284.

[9]George L. Mosse, *Nazi Culture* (New York: Grossett and Dunlop, 1966), p. 20.

[10]Charles Herbert Stember, *Sexual Racism* (New York: Harper & Row, 1976), p. 20.

[11]Lois Banner, *American Beauty* (New York: Knopf, 1983), p. 10.

[12]From *A Vindication of the Rights of Woman*, cited in Germaine Greer, *The Female Eunuch* (New York: McGraw-Hill, 1971), p. 47.

[13]Helene Roberts, "Submission, Masochism and Narcissism: Three Aspects of Women's Role as Reflected in Dress," in *Women's Lives: Perspectives on Progress and Change*, Ed. Virginia Lee Lissier and Joyce Wolstredt (Newark: Univ. of Delaware Press, 1977), pp. 27-65.

[14]Marabel Morgan, *The Total Woman* (New York: Pocket Books, 1975), p. 96.

[15]Simone de Beauvoir, *The Second Sex*, trans. H.M. Parshley (New York: Knopf, 1971).

[16]Jane Ellen Harrison, *Mythology* (London: Longmans Green, 1924), pp. 50-51. Harrison also includes the quotes from Hesiod.

[17]Mary Daly, *Gyn/Ecology: The Metaethics of Radical Feminism* (Boston: Beacon, 1978).

[18]Roberts, pp. 53-60.

[19]I refer here to the new disease, *anorexia nervosa*, a psychological phenomenon of self-starvation that strikes young, white, affluent girls and is now said to affect one in every hundred girls. Twenty percent die from this disease. See also Jane E.Caputi, "One Size Does *Not* Fit all: Being Beautiful, Thin and Female in America," in John Nachbar and Christopher Geist, eds., *The Popular Culture Reader,* 3rd ed. (Bowling Green, OH: Popular Press, 1983), pp. 186-204.

[20]"Plastic Surgery Boom," *Newsweek*, 24 Jan.1977.

[21]Andrea Dworkin, *Pornography: Men Possessing Women* (New York: Perigree Books, 1981), pp. 116-7.

[22]*Glamour* was originally used to designate a malicious and magical power of so-called witches. Other words which now refer to fashion and beauty but originally meant witchcraft include: *bewitching, enchanting, charming* and *fascinating*. See Jane E. Caputi, "The Glamour of Grammar," *Chrysalis*, no. 4, Winter 1977, pp. 35-43.

[23]Judith Thurman, "Never Too Thin to Feel Fat," *Ms.*, Sept. 1977, p. 82.

[24]R. Donovan, "That friend of your wife's called Dior," *Colliers*, 10 June 1955, pp. 34-9.

[25]Andrea Dworkin, *Woman Hating* (New York: Dutton, 1974), p. 42.

[26]"The Girls of Summer," *Playboy*, August 1981, pp. 104-9. Here girl-watching is described as an "unconscious obsessive ritual" as well as a "natural response" for men confronted with so much lush, female beauty. Compare this with the analysis of Pam McCallister, "Wolf Whistles and Warnings," *Heresies* 6, Summer 1978, pp. 37-9. McAllister sees girl-watching as public harassment aimed at reducing individual women to interchangeable sex-objects as well as linking attractiveness with victimization.

[27]Indeed, any heroines that are offered to women are often from the world of fashion, film and beauty and have no credentials other than a face that their culture desires. *Vogue*, June 1978, for example, offered its readers "four American heroines." These are four top fashion models. Significantly, three of them—Roseanne Vela, Patti Hansen and Rene Russo—are look-alike blondes and are grouped together on one page. The fourth, Beverly Johnson, who was described by the *New York Times* as looking like "a white woman dipped in brown paint," is set alone on another page. See also Ted Morgan, "I'm the Biggest Model, Period," *New York Times Magazine*, 17 Aug. 1975, p. 12.

[28]John Berger, *Ways of Seeing* (London: The BBC and Penguin Books, 1972), pp. 46-7.

[29]Susan Sontag, *On Photography* (New York: Straus, Giroux, 1977), p. 14.

[30]Susan Griffin, *Pornography and Silence: Culture's Revolt Against Nature* (New York: Harper & Row, 1981).

[31]"Fashion's Kinky Look," *Newsweek*, 4 Oct. 1976, pp. 98-9.

[32]Edward Behr, intro. to Helmut Newton, *Sleepless Nights* (New York: Congreve, 1978).

[33]"A Living Mannequin Startling Shoppers," *New York Times,* 13 Dec. 1977.

[34]"They Find Right Face—Then Create a Mannequin to Resemble It," *New York Times*, 28 Nov. 1977, p. 38.

[35]Richard Meryman, "Marilyn Lets Her Hair Down About Being Famous," *Life*, 3 Aug. 1962, p.36.

[36]Bert Stern, "The Last Sitting," *Vogue*, Sept. 1982, p. 583.

[37]de Beauvoir, p. 261.

[38]de Beauvoir, p. xvi.

[39]James Laver, *Taste and Fashion* (London: Harrap, 1938), p. 98.

[40]David Thompson, "The Director as Raging Bull," *Film Comment*, Jan.-Feb. 1978, pp. 9-15.

[41]James Tiptree, Jr., "The Women Men Don't See," in R. Silverberg and M. Greenberg, eds.,

The Arbor House Treasury of Modern Science Fiction (New York: Arbor House, 1980).

[42]Dworkin, *Woman Hating*, pp. 47-8.

[43]Pete Axthelm, et al., "The Sick World of Son of Sam," *Newsweek*, 22 Aug. 1977, p. 19.

[44]McCallister, pp. 47-9.

[45]Stephen G. Michaud and Hugh Aynesworth, *The Only Living Witness* (New York: Simon & Schuster, 1983), p. 130.

[46]Stern, p. 581.

Shame as Taboo in American Culture
Gershen Kaufman & Lev Raphael

Shame is a central dimension of human experience which remains under cultural taboo in American society. It is the most isolating and alienating of affects. To feel shame is to feel *seen* in a painfully diminished sense whether all eyes are upon us, or only our own. Shame suddenly and unexpectedly exposes the self inside of us, generating the torment of self-consciousness. It is the feeling of exposure along with constricting self-consciousness that characterizes the essential nature of the affect termed shame. "Contained in the experience of shame is the piercing awareness of ourselves as fundamentally deficient in some vital way as a human being. To live with shame is to experience the very essence or heart of the self as wanting" (Kaufman, 1980, p. 9). Shame is without doubt a sickness of the soul. While it is a profound inner torment, shame can be generated in a number of key cultural settings: the family, peer group, school and work. These settings are the instruments of culture, through which meanings, values and taboos are transmitted.

"Just as sexuality was tabooed in Freud's time, shame is still under taboo today. The paradox ... is that there is shame about shame. It is much easier to admit one is happy or sad than one feels ashamed. In part this is because of the close association between shame and inferiority. One is ashamed to announce shame as one is ashamed to announce the fact of one's inferiority. It is a self-validating affect (or so believed) insofar as one believes one should try to conceal feelings of shame. This is particularly amplified in a culture which values achievement and success" (Tomkins, 1980, p. XIV).

Shame needs to be examined not only as a central human experience but also as an often hidden or misunderstood cultural dynamic. A phenomenological approach enables the inner experience of shame to become grounded in culture.

In a society where the *success ethic* predominates, we are repeatedly stimulated to seek our advantage *over* others through competition. We are taught from an early age to view achievement as the measure of our intrinsic worth or adequacy. We are also taught to strive after success and to measure it precisely through our accomplishments. Hence, external performance becomes the measure of self-esteem, of basic satisfaction with self. However, striving for success can breed anxiety in the form of fear of failure as Karen Horney and Erich Fromm also have observed. Success breeds anxiety because whether we succeed at an undertaking is never entirely within our control. When success by any external standard (i.e., career advancement, social prestige, material wealth) becomes the measure of self-validation, then competition for these goals is inevitably fostered, generating hostility and fear. Failure to attain these goals produces loss of self-esteem and feelings of inferiority—this is shame.

Cultural injunctions such as achievement and success become *dynamic motives* guiding behavior and shaping personality. Being *independent and self-sufficient* is another powerful cultural injunction influencing our behavior. Much as the success ethic is embodied in the predominant portrait of the "self-made man" who becomes an executive, leading professional or millionaire, the pioneer, the woodsman and the cowboy are all *mythic American figures* (we still see them in cigarette ads) that exemplify the triumph of these values. They are solitary men who need no one to make their way in the world. The lessons of self-reliance and independence have been widely transmitted through folktales, literature, radio and television and films. We are not all heroes, but we can be heroic in our isolation. To stand proudly alone, never depending on anyone for assistance, is to partake of that cultural glamor, especially for men. The man who *does* need, who *does* feel, the man who admits vulnerability or fear falls pitifully short of those heroic standards. He is shamed for being human.

The need to belong to some group or cause larger than ourselves is universal. "Few strivings are as compelling as is our need to identify with someone, to feel a part of something, to belong somewhere. Whether it is in relation to one significant other, or the family, or one's own peer group, we experience some vital need to belong. And it is precisely the identification need which most assuredly confers that special sense of belonging. So powerful is that striving that we might feel obliged to do most anything in order to secure our place" (Kaufman, 1980, p. 33). Being *popular* and *conforming* become not only particular translations of that universal need, but more importantly, they are the pathways to belonging. Hence, being popular is exceedingly prized in our culture. Physical attractiveness, intelligence, talent, money, charm, social standing, sociability, agreeableness, skill, helpfulness, aggressiveness are examples of attributes or characteristics that will gain individuals acceptance and popularity in different groups. Participating in groups naturally increases the pressure to conform to group mores. Not conforming, not being popular or accepted, not participating or even valuing popularity itself potentially make one a cultural outcast. A society that prizes successful belonging and affiliation shames those who either fail to be popular or who are less social by nature. The social solitary is decidedly less valued than the social joiner. If team work or group activities are said to prepare young people for the responsibilities of adulthood, those who are either deemed unpopular or who do not join groups may experience their *difference* as indicted and shamed.

The need to belong, which becomes expressed through the cultural injunction to conform and be popular is further complicated by the fact that self-validation remains externally based. Just as the measure of self-worth is external and successful performance, particularly as judged by others, becomes the standard, our interpersonal value is based on the reflected appraisals of others. Rather than being founded in the self, one's inherent worth and adequacy as a human being are placed in the hands of others, beyond internal control. This inevitably increases the susceptibility to shame.

The impact of culture on personality is mediated through shame. It is the experience of shame which is so profoundly alienating and isolating, marking us as unworthy or deficient. Shame divides us from ourselves and one another. We feel cut off, unspeakably and irreparably defective. What is shamed consistently must be hidden from view. Hence, shame is the source of our cultural taboos.

Cultural motives that are imbedded in a particular culture create *values* and *taboos*. If we are widely enjoined to compete for success, then personal achievement in the eyes of others becomes a value highly esteemed, while personal failure becomes equally tabooed. Any failing, especially public, diminishes one in the eyes of others and certainly in one's own eyes. A competitive culture makes competitors of us all and those who fail to succeed will inevitably experience their failing as an injury to self-esteem. How can a failure continue feeling worthwhile in a culture which prizes success and holds no alternative models for garnering self-worth except through achievement? Simply being average must be felt as a burden or curse in a culture which respects only its heroes and stars.

The cultural injunction to be independent and self-sufficient firmly establishes self-reliance as a dominant value. Being strong, able to handle one's own struggles alone, and depending on no one become our clarion calls. In such a climate, *needing* itself becomes not a source of strength but a clear sign of inadequacy: to need is to be weak. Human vulnerability itself becomes almost abhorrent in a culture which implicitly defines maturity as emotional isolation, and strength as solitude. Open expressions of need and feeling—like crying, touching—are inevitably tabooed in such a culture.

When belonging to a group of whatever kind is a paramount value, then rejection is the ugliest imaginable fate. Basing one's worth as an individual on popularity, however defined, reduces one to a position of powerlessness. One's sense of human value can rise and fall as unpredictably as stock prices. In a culture which esteems popularity and conformity, individuality is neither recognized nor valued; being a loner, perceived social outcast or simply being different become marks of grave deficiency—and as such, are tabooed.

The basic way in which shame is generated involves a breaking of the interpersonal bridge between people who have become significant to one another. Relationships evolve through one person actively reaching out to another and establishing emotional ties, much as we might go about taming a strange animal. Such a process entails the establishing of a bond. A bond ever so gradually emerges out of reciprocal interest in one another along with shared experiences of trust. Trusting essentially means that we have come to expect and rely upon a certain mutuality of response. When two individuals communicated understanding, respect and valuing one another's personhood, needs and feelings included, an emotional bond begins to grow. It is that bond which makes possible experiences of openness and vulnerability. "The bond which ties two individuals together forms an *interpersonal bridge* between them. The bridge in turn becomes a vehicle to facilitate mutual understanding, growth, and change. These vital processes are disrupted whenever that bridge becomes severed" (Kaufman, 1980, p. 14).

The interpersonal bridge which spans the gulf between strangers convinces each that the relationship is wanted by the other. Each feels essentially wanted as a separate person in his or her own right. Through reciprocal experiences of one person trusting and having the other person prove trustworthy, a sense of certainty about the relationship evolves. In this manner, individuals relinquish their strangeness, establish emotional ties and become significant to one another. Whenever someone's caring, respector valuing begins to matter to us, the possibility for generating shame emerges. Breaking that vital interpersonal bridge is the critical event which induces shame.

Because gaining acceptance by peers is of fundamental importance, the peer group itself has the power to induce shame. Being laughed at, ridiculed or excluded by one's peers, especially in adolescence, is a poignant source of shame. Even younger children are repeatedly ridiculed for crying before their peers. "Cry-baby" is for a child, especially a boy, what the Scarlet A was for Hester Prynne in Hawthorne's novel: a public humiliation. Boys learn very quickly that being seen crying will cause derision or contempt. Crying itself must be hidden from public view and a natural part of the self may henceforth be experienced as shameful. A child is particularly vulnerable to such humiliation in the peer group because the respect and approval of those friends is deemed essential.

The natural human need for touching is another vital aspect of self which unfortunately becomes associated with shame. Touching is *not* inherently sexual, although the two become confused in our culture. The skin is one of our sensory organs (Montagu, 1972); hence, touching is pleasurable, much as stimulation of any *sensory* organ is, but that pleasure must be distinuished from sexuality per se. Touching can communicate a range of meanings: human contact, warmth, affection, tenderness, sympathy and comfort. Furthermore, there are significant moments of emotional distress in life when the experience of touching and holding is essential to restoring inner security. At these times touching communicates not so much affection as protection and security, the basis for trust. This is as true for adults as it is for children, but in a culture which prizes independence and self-sufficiency, needing another in so basic a way as through touching becomes acutely shameful. The association of touching with shame is created in the family when boys suddenly are greeted with handshakes instead of a hug by their fathers, when daughters are suddenly "too old" to continue sitting on their fathers' laps. It is also created in adolescence through peer group ridicule and name-calling.

Touching a member of the same sex is labeled "queer" while touching someone of the opposite sex is equally perceived as sexual. Males in particular experience intense injunctions against touching one another, unless it is disguised such as at the bar or on the gridiron. Thus a primary human need becomes either directly shamed or at best, confused with sexuality. Many men and women believe they must engage in sex in order to hold one another. When all voices in the culture tell us that the only reasons for wanting to feel especially close to another human being are sexual, eventually we will listen.

A child has no greater need than to identify with the loved or needed parent who is central in his world. Modeling of parental behavior is one key vehicle for identification. The wish to be like anyone deeply valued, admired or needed will later expand to encompass older siblings, peers, teachers in school and mentors at work. Learning how to become a person originates through identification. Much later we individuate by differentiating our unique self. We internalize, literally take inside, principally through identification (Kaufman, 1980). Through our relationships with significant others—parents, teachers and peers—we learn specific ways of thinking and feeling about ourselves. Verbal messages communicated by those others will likely become internalized as core affect=beliefs which then shape our evolving identity. Not only do we internalize what is said about us but we also internalize the specific ways in which we are treated by significant others. In this manner, interaction patterns in the family or even in the peer group become internalized and form the basis of our inner relationship with ourselves.

Additionally, the affect, need and drive systems (as conceptualized by Kaufman, 1980) are three motivational arenas in which shame can generate and eventually control whatever has become directly associated with shame. For example, if a child encounters sufficient experiences in which the expression of fear is met with ridicule and shaming, he will learn that there is something fundamentally wrong with him whenever he is afraid. Who among us has not felt the certain shame of cowardice before our peers? Feeling afraid has now become shameful and situations which trigger fear will also trigger shame. In this way, the expression of fear itself has become bound by shame. Thus, a particular affect can come to activate shame spontaneously without shame itself being directly induced. Analogously, the expression of *any* affect (fear, hurt, anger, etc.), need (for relationship, touching, identification, affirmation, etc.), or drive (sex, hunger, etc.) can become constricted by shame, thereby creating a distorted self.

When we feel acutely threatened we seek ways to protect against such threats. It is the internalization of shame which activates the especially acute need for defending. Defending strategies are adaptive; they are learned because they are the best means available for survival. The aim of such strategies is to protect the self against further shame while strategies of transfer are only aroused following an experience of shame. The aim of transfer strategies is to cause someone else to feel shame in order to reduce one's own shame. This interpersonal transfer of shame typically proceeds along the lines of the familiar pecking order or dominance hierarchy which emerges in most social groups. A dominance hierarchy based on either actual or perceived power emerges in the family, peer, school and work settings and shame will transfer from the stronger to the weaker. These critical, developmental settings are important instruments of culture in which shame is universally encountered.

In contrast to transfer strategies, defending strategies are acquired principally in an attempt to cope with externally based sources of shame. The most prominent strategies in relation to shame include rage, contempt, strivings for power or perfection, transfer of blame and internal withdrawal. *Rage* both insulates the self against exposure and actively keeps others away. In *contempt* we have the seeds of judgmental, fault-finding, critical or condescending attitudes; in so far as others are looked down upon, found lacking or seen as lesser or inferior beings, a once-wounded self becomes more securely insulated against further shame. While rage keeps others away and contempt elevates the self above others, the *striving for power* is a direct attempt to compensate for the sense of inner deficiency inherent to shame. The power strategy aims at maximizing control over others; through gaining power one becomes less vulnerable to shame. *Striving for perfection* is a different attempt to compensate for the inner deficiency of shame. It is a striving to erase every blemish of the self, coupled with an inordinate pressure to excel in an ever-widening circle of activities. The *transfer of blame* is a direct attempt to transfer responsibility for a failing or mishap which has triggered shame. In a blame-oriented environment, attention is focused not upon how to repair whatever mishap has occurred, but rather on fixing the blame somewhere, usually away from the self. *Internal withdrawal* is a final strategy of defense in which the self withdraws deeper inside itself to escape the agony of exposure inherent in shame or the loss of the possibility of reunion with whoever aroused that shame. These strategies become means of defending oneself in the interpersonal realm and thereby adapting to it.

We live in a culture infested with the transfer of blame for inevitable mistakes which unleash shame. Whenever something goes wrong, considerable attention is focused on discovering who is to blame. Someone must be found responsible for the mishap, so that everyone else associated with the event can feel innocent. We see this process occurring in the family and work setting, where natural culture shapes personality and, in so doing, binds culture with self.

What is the point of this discourse? Why must we examine the role of shame in our culture as a shaper of identity? Because not only has shame itself been misunderstood and mislabeled as an affect, but its prevalence in our culture has been all but ignored. Examining the role of shame can give us a deeper understanding of the American cultural personality, one which, perhaps more than any other in history, is shaping the world in its image. Highlighting shame's dynamic impact in our culture can very possibly alter the future so that the future citizen of the world *does* care about others, *can* be vulnerable, *can* need, and equally *honors* our essential human differences.

References

Fromm, E. *The sane society.* New York: Holt, Rinehart and Winston, 1955.

Horney, K. *The neurotic personality of our time.* New York: W. W. Norton, 1937.

Kaufman, G. *Shame: The power of caring.* Cambridge: Schenkman, 1980.

Montagu, A. *Touching: The human significance of the skin.* New York: Harper and Row, 1972.

Tomkins, S. S. Introduction to *Shame: The power of caring.* Cambridge: Schenkman, 1980.

accidents are greeted with blame, and even in government where failures of policy or initiative produce scapegoats rather than honest acknowledgment of responsibility. It is a rare parent or leader who can own such responsibility and freely admit to being imperfect.

The seeds of perfectionism are sown whenever love, acceptance and pride in self become contingent on our performance in the world. External achievement and accomplishment become the only culturally sanctioned measures of validation of self. Perfecting the self in an ever-widening circle of activities is an attempt to erase every blemish of the self, to compensate for a sense of inner deficiency, of shame. Our educational system directly or inadvertently stimulates the striving for perfection because it fails to teach its students how to develop an inner source of satisfaction with self. Perfectionism itself is doomed to failure: always "it could have been better." To feel shame is to feel inherently *not good enough* as a person. No matter how well we have actually done, we could have done "better." Only when we develop an *internal sense of how much is good enough* are we ever free from perfectionism.

We learn to treat ourselves precisely the way we either experienced or observed significant others to do. Hence, we learn to shame ourselves, hold ourselves in contempt, blame ourselves, hate ourselves and terrorize ourselves. We are especially likely to disown any natural part of the self that has been repeatedly shamed and consistently enough cast away by a parent, whether intentionally or inadvertently. Individuals literally are taught to disown those parts of the self which were disowned by significant others. Needs, feelings and drives are especially vulnerable to disowning, which, in turn, creates a distortion of the self. Disowning can be directed at the entire range of feelings or only at specific ones. Likewise, a specific need, or else the entire experience of *needing* itself, can be disowned. Thus, certain individuals become lacking either in awareness or expression of basic affect; they have no access to their feelings. Other individuals present a righteously self-sufficient stance to the world, seemingly contemptuous of those weaker ones who depend on others or express needs. In either case, a vital part of the self has become shamed, actively silenced and eventually disowned. Disowning of self evolves in an attempt to cope with the perceived locus of the shame which has grown so intolerable through internalization.

Furthermore, disowning of self creates a split within the self which gradually widens over the years, eventually fully isolating that disowned part of the self. The acceptable parts remain conscious while the disowned part withdraws deeper inside the self. Disowning robs the self not only of integrity but of inner security as well.

The final step in the developmental sequence is one's essential identity becoming based on shame so completely that an individual experiences himself as an inherent failure as a human being. Even simple mistakes may activate agonizing self-torture. When disowned parts of the self make themselves felt the self is likely to inflict unrelenting suffering upon the self. The internal shame process has now become painful and punishing beyond what the simple feeling of shame might produce. "The internalization of shame has produced an identity, a way of relating to oneself, which absorbs, maintains, and spreads shame ever further" (Kaufman, 1980, p. 121).

In contemporary culture there are three particular aspects of the self which become associated with shame and eventually disowned. Cultural pressures to become independent and self-sufficient teach us to hide our natural human needs and feel ashamed for having them in the first place. These are fundamental needs for emotional connection with others. Both our need for relationship and need for human touching, to mention but two, become bound by shame and, hence, taboo. In our culture needing itself is a clear sign of deficiency or inadequacy and an essential part of the self thus becomes distorted.

The equally widespread cultural pressure to be popular and to conform crushes individual differences. We feel ashamed of our differences instead of learning to value them. We may feel impelled to even disown those things about us which make us unique in the unfortunate pursuit of social acceptance.

Finally, in an environment stressing achievement and success at all costs, competition becomes the widely encouraged mode of survival because competitors cannot afford to care too deeply about one another. Inevitably, our capacities for caring and vulnerability become diminished in such a climate. Through striving for success, we inadvertently disown our capacity to care about one another. Human caring is strangled in a competitive environment.

Conclusion:
Impact of Cultural Disowning on Personality
The process by which shame is induced and internalized in the various cultural settings described has profound impact on the self. It is no exaggeration to say that identity is molded by shame and all too frequently distorted. Shame is the instrument through which

The Bloody Chamber:
Terror Films, Fairy Tales and Taboo

Harold Schechter

"I had planned to depart as soon as I'd seen enough to write a clever pan, but we stayed to the bitter and bloody end—committed participants in the quintessentially American ritual of the drive-in and the junk movie. Like a religious rite, this nightly national ceremony focuses on life and death, by offering the celebrants a succession of flesh films and meat movies. The mood is wild and Dionysian; hidden in their autos, the participants drift into dreamlike, ecstatic trances as forbidden mysteries are revealed and taboos violated on screen."

Lew Brighton, "Saturn in Retrograde"

Making filmgoers jump—out of their seats, if possible—is, of course, one of the primary ambitions of most horror movie directors (though few are prepared to go to the same lengths as the legendary William Castle, who, for his 1959 schlock classic *The Tingler* came up with the clever idea of installing electric joy-buzzers in the seats). Of all the startling moments in recent American terror films (as S.S. Prawer calls them),[1] perhaps the one that comes closest to fully realizing this worthy goal—i.e., that of getting the audience to respond in roughly the same way as the frog in Galvani's experiment—is the climax of Brian De Palma's *Carrie*, when the dead heroine's arm suddenly erupts from the grave. To a certain extent, there's no mystery about what makes this scene so jolting. The sequence is the cinematic equivalent of a Jack-in-the-box, a mechanism constructed solely for the purpose of giving unsuspecting onlookers a start. De Palma beguiles us with lush, romantic music and a picture-pretty image: Carrie's only friend, flowers in hand, approaches the grave in lyrical, gauzy slow motion. Then, when we're least expecting it, up pops the boogy-man.

Still it's not only the skillful (even sadistic) way the scene is put together that accounts for its impact. After all, there are many other moments in horror films that function the same way—in essence by reassuring the viewer that the worst is over and then, when his defenses are down, sneaking up on him in a fright mask and yelling, "Boo!" But most of these scenes, even when they do manage to give viewers a turn (I'm thinking, for example, of the "trick" climax—

67

clearly ripped-off from De Palma—of Sean Cunningham's *Friday the 13th*), deliver easy, utterly evanescent shocks. In contrast, the ending of *Carrie*, which takes the form of a particularly vivid and harrowing nightmare, leaves us feeling almost as shaken as the dreamer. It would seem that, quite apart from the scene's effectiveness at catching us off-guard, there is something fundamentally unsettling about the image itself: the cursed and tormented girl, buried but refusing to rest in peace.

To find out what makes this image so disturbing, we might begin by asking where it comes from, since it has no parallel in the Stephen King novel on which the movie is based. King's book does have its own "shocker" ending, but it is of the slightly timeworn "here-we-go-again" variety: the ominous "epilogue" which makes it clear that the horror, far from being over, has only just begun. (Ira Levin uses the identical device at the close of *The Boys from Brazil*, and Grade-Z, 1950s science-fiction films contain any number of variations, my personal favorite being the blood-curdling technique of flashing the words "The End?" on the screen as the final image fades to black.)

One possible source of the ending of *Carrie* is the somewhat similar nightmare that climaxes the film version of James Dickey's *Deliverance* (Pauline Kael was, I believe, the first to make this connection). We see a water-level view of the river at night; slowly, a man's arm—presumably that of the slain hillbilly—breaks the surface and rises menacingly from the depths. The film cuts suddenly to a shot of Ed Gentry (the character played by Jon Voight) awakening in terror, and we understand that he has been in the grip of bad dreams.

But though there are obvious parallels between this (genuinely chilling) sequence and the conclusion of *Carrie*, there are important differences, too, in terms of the setting, the sex of the corpse, and—most significantly—the psychological meaning of the nightmare. In the case of *Deliverance*, the dream is clearly a function of the protagonist's guilt; Gentry, a decent and civilized soul, is haunted by the memory of the man he has brutally, if justifiably, killed. In *Carrie*, the situation is entirely different. For a variety of reasons—the way Carrie is perceived as accursed ("Carrie White is burning for her sins," reads a sign at her grave) because of her terrible, telekinetic powers; the awful death she meets at the hands of her fanatical mother, who increasingly comes to regard the girl as wicked, sin-hardened, and irreclaimable, deserving of death and damnation—for these and related reasons, the fantasy image De Palma uses to cap his movie suggests a darker, more disquieting complex of meanings.

Interestingly (and unexpectedly), a parallel image—much closer to *Carrie* in every respect than the ending of *Deliverance*—does exist, not in another piece of pop-horror but in the *Nursery and Household Tales* of the Brothers Grimm. The image appears in a fairy tale called "The Willful Child," which is short enough to be quoted in its entirety (indeed, the tale consists of little more *than* this particular image):

> Once upon a time there was a child who was willful, and would not do what her mother wished. For this reason God had no pleasure in her, and let her become ill, and no doctor could do her any good, and in a short time she lay on her death-bed. When she had been lowered into her grave, and the earth was spread over her, all at once her arm came out again, and stretched upwards, and when they had put it in and spread fresh earth over it, it was all to no purpose, for the arm always came out again. Then the mother herself was obliged to go to the grave, and strike the arm with a rod, and when she had done that, it was drawn in, and then at last the child had rest beneath the ground.[2]

The similarities between *Carrie* and this grisly little cautionary tale are notable. Though De Palma's movie, following King, possesses a sentimentality wholly missing from the Grimm story (Carrie is portrayed as pathetic, persecuted and misunderstood), both works center on the figure of a young girl who, having incurred the displeasure of God by disobeying her mother, is punished by death for her iniquity. As for the image of the arm protruding from the ground, the illustration which accompanies this tale in the Pantheon edition of Grimm's—a line drawing of a grave with the dead girl's hand jutting out of it—might almost be a storyboard sketch from the climactic sequence of *Carrie*.

What are we to make of this striking correspondence? It seems highly unlikely that "The Willful Child"—in many respects one of the slightest and certainly one of the most obscure tales in the Grimm Brothers' collection—served as either source or inspiration for De Palma. A much more plausible explanation, and one which goes a long way toward accounting for *Carrie*'s power not only to provide us with a fleeting, funhouse thrill but to touch some sort of deep-psychic nerve, is that the dream-sequence and the *märchen* derive from a common source: from that "symbol-inventing" level of the mind,[3] that reservoir of primordial images, which is the matrix of all folk-dream and myth—the place (to lift a line from Emily Dickinson) "where the Meanings are."[4] That De Palma and the unknown storyteller, diving into that reservoir, should come up with the same compelling image is not surprising, since both artists are engaged in creating essentially the same type of fiction, one intended to elicit an intense combination of wonder and fear.

What we have in the contemporary terror film *Carrie*, then, is a work which, for all its gloss, sophistication and unabashed commercialism, is a close analogue of a traditional folk tale. Looking at other recent works of pop-horror in light of this fact, we find similar correspondences. *Friday the 13th*, for example—about a group of youngsters who venture into a gloomy forest and encounter a murderous Terrible Mother—is essentially a splatter movie retelling of "Hansel and Gretel." *The Howling*—a contemporary werewolf movie which, thanks partly to a sly and witty screenplay by John Sayles and partly to some bloodcurdling special effects, manages to work as both social satire and seriously scary fright film—has connections to both "The Three Little Pigs" and "Little Red Riding Hood." Indeed, the movie itself draws attention to these links: in one scene, we catch glimpses of a TV screen showing Disney's famous "Silly Symphonies" version of "The Three Little Pigs." In a similar way, Stephen King, in his recent horror novel *Cujo*, lets us know from the start exactly what kind of story we're dealing with: The opening words of the book, printed by themselves on the first page, are "Once upon a time."

King is even more explicit about the connection between fairy tales and his brand of horror in his chatty book of pop criticism, *Danse Macabre*.[5] Analyzing the kinds of collective fears that terror films give expression to, he identifies two main categories of horror: a type that is "sociopolitical in nature," symbolizing the political, economic and cultural anxieties of a particular time and place (his examples include *Invasion of the Body Snatchers, The Amityville Horror* and *The Stepford Wives*); and a second, "considerably deeper," more universal variety which he labels "mythic fairy-tale horror." "This second sort of horror film," he writes, "has more in common with the Brothers Grimm than with the op-ed page in a tabloid paper. It is the B-picture as fairy tale"—and to illustrate his point, he offers a brief quiz in which he recasts the plots of twenty well-known horror films in the form of capsule fairy tales and challenges the reader to identify their titles. (Example: "Once upon a time some bad people tampered with the oxygen lines in one operating room of a major hospital and a lot of people went to sleep for a long, long time—just like Snow White. Only these people never woke up." Answer: *Coma*.)[6]

According to King, movies of the "mythic fairy-tale" variety achieve their power by confronting us with the forbidden: "This sort of picture doesn't want to score political points but to scare the hell out of us by crossing certain taboo lines."[7] To look once more at *Carrie*, however—what we see there, and this is true for the film as a whole—not just for its final dream-sequence, is an even more intriguing phenomenon: A pop entertainment which does not simply project nightmares, dabble in dangerous fantasy, but which contains precise parallels to particular and widespread primitive taboos, specifically ones dealing with menstruation and the dead. The association which exits from the start of the movie between Carrie's awesome, destructive power and the onset of her monthly periods reflects that archaic response to menstruation neatly summed up in Howard Nemerov's poem "Lore":

> Man walks, I learn in fear of woman,
> Possession of the constant moon;
> Because the moon has strength to summon
> Her blood to the full and ebb again,
> And gives her strength beyond her own.
>
> A girl, then, Graves writes in his book,
> Can fade the purple out of cloth
> And tarnish mirrors with her look,
> And by the power of her thought
> Make one branch grow and another rot.
>
> *   *   *
>
> So great the power of her moon
> That, as the Talmud said,
> If she should walk between two men
> And no appropriate prayer is read,
> The one of them will drop down dead.[8]

Similarly the attitude toward the dead which underlies the motif of the hand-that-rises-from-the-grave in both the horror film and the fairy tale parallels that primitive dread of corpses—the archaic "supposition" that even "a dearly loved relative at the moment of his death changes into a demon from whom his survivors can expect nothing but hostility"[9]—that Freud discusses in his classic psychoanalytic study, *Totem and Taboo*. Reviewing various anthropological theories concerning "the taboo upon the dead," Freud cites the work of one Rudolph Kleinpaul, who writes of the belief, common "among the civilized races" of the ancient world, "that the dead, filled with a lust for murder, sought to drag the living in their train."[10] This fantasy, of course, is central to the closing scene of De Palma's film and is portrayed even more explicitly in the newspapers ads for another, more recent pop-horror picture, whose very title conveys the essence of those primitive fears and associated prohibitions examined by Freud. The movie is called *The Evil Dead*, and the ads for it—clearly inspired by *Carrie*—show a corpse's arm thrust out of the earth, its hand clutching the throat of a screaming woman, who is being drawn slowly down into the grave.[11]

Beneath the more superficial aspects of *Carrie*, then—beyond the things we can say about De Palma's jazzy style and obsessive themes, about the insights the film affords into adolescent sexual anxieties and our society's attitude toward women—lies a cluster of images that does not reflect the filmmakers's artistic intent, personal unconscious or cultural conditioning but that emanates from a deeper and far more ancient source, from that immemorial dreaming self that is common to us all: indeed, that is the dark and fertile subsoil out of which our individual identities spring. Such imagery tantalizes us and tempts us toward rational explication. But this is a temptation which should, I believe, be strenuously resisted, since it stems in essence from the deep insecurity which our contemporary waking minds feel in the presence of the mythic.

This kind of discomfort is by no means a universal human trait. As Joseph Campbell points out, the motifs of myth and folk tale are "phrases from an image-language, expressive of metaphysical, psychological, and sociological truth. And in the primitive, oriental, archaic, and medieval societies this vocabulary was pondered and more or less understood. Only in the wake of the Enlightenment has it suddenly lost its meaning and been pronounced insane."[12]

Reviving our ability to understand this language, curing what Australian critic David Tacey calls our "imaginal illiteracy," requires, first, that we find ways of recognizing the myths embedded in our fictions, and, second, that we fight against the impulse—indeed, compulsion—to rationalize myth away in terms that offer the conscious mind the comforting illusion that it has gotten to the bottom of mythic meaning. (After all, does it really "explain" the symbol of a magical, singing toad, possessor of the finest carpet, most precious ring, and loveliest maiden in the world, to say, as Bruno Bettelheim does in *The Uses of Enchantment*, that "frogs symbolize the id"?)[13]

The second of these goals is, in many ways, the more difficult, since, to achieve it, we must overcome our deeply ingrained distrust and denigration of intuition (a form of knowledge typically derided

in our culture as "female," the ultimate patriarchal put-down) and
our correspondingly exaggerated elevation of intellect as the only
legitimate means of uncovering truth. Simultaneously, it requires
that we cultivate an ability to (as Campbell says) "ponder" and open
ourselves up to the emotional "meaning" of the image: to let the
symbol speak for itself.

As for the first prerequisite—seeing the myth to begin with—the
most effective method is the one Jungians call "amplification,"
which consists in essence of drawing out the meaning of a symbol by
looking at it in light of analogous myths. The term strikes me as
particularly apt, since it suggests an aural metaphor—i.e., a
correspondence between the method and a mode of nonrational
apprehension, of perception and understanding, every bit as valid
and precise as logic. The process can be likened to being on a busy
street and suddenly finding ourselves stirred or unsettled by what
we come to recognize as an alien yet strangely familiar melody
which we can dimly discern behind the distracting clamor of the city
noises. The full meaning of this melody can only be experienced in
one way: by getting as close as we possibly can to the source and
then listening intently to what the music has to say.

2.

Be bold, be bold, but not too bold,
Lest that your heart's blood should run cold."
                              from the story "Mr. Fox," in
J.J. Jacobs' English Fairy-Tales (1898)

To speak in terms of music, even metaphorically, seems vastly
inappropriate when the subject is Tobe Hooper's *The Texas
Chainsaw Massacre*, a movie in which the dominant sounds are
tortured shrieks, terrified moans, bestial grunts, lunatic laughter
and the incessant, inescapable roar of the titular weapon. The film
has become a virtual byword for cinematic sadism gone wild, a
prototype of that uniquely contemporary genre of horror pictures
which is known by its fond admirers as the splatter movie and
which, in the words of writer John McCarty, strives "not to scare . . .
audiences, necessarily, nor to drive them to the edge of their seats in
suspense, but to *mortify* them with scenes of explicit gore. In splatter
movies, mutilation is . . . the message."[14]

Interestingly, however, *The Texas Chainsaw Massacre*
contains very little "explicit gore," not only in relation to such
cheerfully demented splatter epics as *Bloodthirsty Butchers*, *I Eat
Your Skin* and *2000 Maniacs*, but, indeed, even when compared to

the average, contemporary, Hollywood action/adventure flick: *48 Hours,* say, or *First Blood*. Though a good deal of dismemberment takes place in Hooper's film, none is ever shown, and there is only one (extremely brief) shot of a chainsaw actually cutting into human flesh, when a fleeing damsel-in-distress flings a monkeywrench at the head of her pursuer, a squealing, subhuman hulk called Leatherface, who topples to the ground, dropping the blade of his buzzing weapon across his thigh. Considering the kinds of atrocities routinely portrayed in splatter movies— disembowelment, decapitation, castration, amputation (to name just a few of the more run-of-the-mill outrages)—it's no wonder that Stephen King says of *Chainsaw*'s director that "Hooper ... in his own queerly apt ways, works with taste and conscience."[15]

But it isn't, of course, Hooper's taste or conscience, any more than the film's (minimal) gore, that has made *The Texas Chainsaw Massacre* a cult movie classic, or that makes sitting through it a kind of *rite de passage*, a test of the horror fan's true mettle and commitment. If the movie strikes a particularly deep and resonant chord, it does so, I submit, because, like *Carrie*, it draws its power, not from its immediate modernday source, but from that timeless place far below the level of consciousness which is the universal wellspring of symbol and myth.

The original ads for *Chainsaw* titillate customers with the venerable freakshow promise that the monstrous display being offered for their entertainment is totally authentic: "What happened is true," the ad reads. "Now the motion picture that's just as real." And in fact, there *is* a real-life basis for the film: the case of the notorious murderer-necrophile Ed Gein, whose grisly crimes also served as the inspiration for Robert Bloch's *Psycho*.

In November 1957, Frank Worden, owner of the local hardware store in the tiny Wisconsin town of Plainfield, returned from a daylong deer-hunting trip to find his mother, Berenice—who had been tending the store in his absence—missing. Various clues led the police to Gein, generally regarded as a harmless, rather affable oddball, who picked up extra money doing handyman jobs for his neighbors and otherwise kept pretty much to himself on the 160-acre farm he'd lived on alone since the death of his beloved mother, ten years before. There, in a dingy woodshed attached to the house, the police found Mrs. Worden's headless body, butchered and hung by its heels from a pulley in the ceiling. Inside the house, they found even more ghastly remains: a bone-littered floor; a bowl full of noses; a refrigerator stocked with human viscera—hearts, lungs, livers— all neatly wrapped in brown butcher's paper; a frying pan holding a human heart (later identified as Berenice Worden's); a shoebox with a collection of female genitalia inside it; a pair of lips dangling from the pullstring of a window shade; a chair upholstered in human skin; soupbowls made from the sawed-off crowns of human skulls; the faces of nine women, carefully dried, stuffed with paper, and mounted, like hunting trophies, on a wall; a skin-vest, complete with breasts, which had been fashioned from the tanned upper half of a middle-aged woman's torso and which Ed liked to dress up in at night, pretending he was his mother.

Ed's ghoulish crimes—which began with graverobbing and evolved into murder after he'd exhausted the available supply of female corpses in local cemeteries—garnered him nationwide headlines, an eight-page spread in *Life* Magazine and a form of pop immortality, since there is little doubt that, in the fictional guise of Norman Bates, he will continue to haunt the dreams of filmgoers for a long time to come. (Unlike Norman, however, who was recently released from the madhouse to star in *Pshcho II*, Gein remains securely locked away in the Wisconsin State Hospital for the Criminally Insane.) And the true story of his "bizarre and brutal" crimes, as *The Texas Chainsaw Massacre* is described in the ads, promises to play forever on the midnight movie circuit.

In spite of the claims made in the ad copy, however, the fact is that the connections between Hooper's movie and the Gein case are really very tenuous. *Chainsaw* deals with the misadventures of five vacationing teenagers who (as Lew Brighton observes in a vivid, engaging essay on the film) violate the cardinal Texas taboo of trespassing on someone else's property,[16] thereby falling afoul of an all-male clan of psychotic former slaughterhouse workers. The patriarch of the group is a virtually mummified old grandpappy, who shows few if any vital signs until he's called upon to suck blood from the sliced finger of a captive nymphet.

The remaining crazies are three (apparent) brothers: a sniveling, lank-haired creep, who wears an animal-skin purse around his neck in which he carries his prized Polaroid snapshots of a butchered steer; a slightly more respectable-looking, though equally deranged, big brother type, proprietor of a combination gas station/roadside human-barbeque stand; and the overgrown baby of the bunch, the monstrous chainsaw-slinging Leatherface, who wears a mask of dried, human skin, communicates in pig grunts and spends his free time impaling visitors on meat hooks and converting them into assorted prime cuts.

The only ways in which this consummate teenage-slice 'n' dice picture—"the *Gone with the Wind* of meat movies," Brighton calls it[17]—resembles the Gein horrors are in its treatment of the victims as so many sides of beef; its attendant cannibal-fixation (Gein, in his neighborly way, periodically provided his acquaintances with packages of fresh "venison," though he later testified in court that he had never hunted deer); the human-skin deathmask that gives Leatherface his nickname; and the utterly demented decor found inside the seemingly innocent, white clapboard house that Leatherface and his kinfolk inhabit. Like the rooms in Gein's home (all, that is, except his dead mother's bedroom, which Ed neatly sealed off, preserving it as a shrine to the memory of that God-fearing woman, who taught him to regard all other members of her sex as vessels of sin), the interior of the *Chainsaw* death-house is a chaos of skulls, bones, bodyparts (in one scene we catch glimpses of an armchair with real human arms), furniture upholstered in human skin, and a wall-to-wall carpet of nameless filth. One of Hooper's real achievements in the movie is creating a visual atmosphere so palpably sickening that the stench of the charnel house seems to waft off the screen.

The power of Hooper's movie, then, clearly has very little to do with its ostensible, true-life source. The Gein story casts the same morbid spell as the case histories recorded by Krafft-Ebbing—Ed could easily have stepped out of the pages of *Psychopathia Sexualis*—but to locate the source of *Chainsaw*'s fascination we have to look somewhere else.

To a certain extent Hooper's film functions as the kind of sociopolitical allegory that Stephen King identifies as one of the two main categories of cinematic horror. Released in 1974 and made by a young man whose previous feature, an extremely obscure picture called *Eggshells*, focused on the anti-war movement, *Chainsaw* can be viewed as a Vietnam-era vision of America's killer side. *Chainsaw*'s cannibal clan—three brothers and their venerated patriarch (once "the fastest cattle-slaughterer in the land")[17] are a kind of nightmare version of the Cartwright family from "Bonanza": Ben, Little Joe, Adam and Hoss, those archetypically decent Americans, exposed as a pack of cretinous butchers and their little house on the prairie as nothing more than an abattoir with a porch swing.

Still, while *The Texas Chainsaw Massacre* offers us insight into the effect of the war on the collective imagination of young Americans during the Vietnam years, we can't, obviously, explain the movie's popularity in 1982—when, as Jim Hoberman and Jonathan Rosenbaum report in their book, *Midnight Movies*, *Chainsaw* "became the best-selling home-video cassette" in the country[18]—by pointing to the way the film expressed widespread cultural anxieties a decade earlier. To find a clue to *Chainsaw*'s continuing appeal, we have to look back: beyond the sociopolitical situation that prevailed at the time it was made and that it (inevitably) reflects, beyond the sensational crimes of the late 1950s that supplied some of its superficial details—back, indeed, to the same age-old source that our analysis of the ending of *Carrie* ultimately led us to. For at the core of *The Texas Chainsaw Massacre*, and accounting, I believe, for a great deal of its impact, is an archetypal motif found in scores of folk stories throughout the world and powerfully embodied, like the analogue to De Palma's film which we uncovered, in one of the tales recorded by Jacob and Wilhelm Grimm.

That motif is known to folklorists as the Forbidden (or Bloody) Chamber. In a long essay on the subject in the 1885 issue of *The Folk-Lore Journal*, British scholar Edwin Sidney Hartland presents a large number of variants assembled from around the world, introducing them with a quote from a colleague that summarizes the motif in typically prim Victorian terms: " 'It is a peculiarity of Fairyland,' says Mr. Clouston in a note to his useful edition of *The Book of Sinbad,* 'that there are certain rooms which the fortunate mortal who has entered the enchanted palace is expressly forbidden to enter, or doors which he must on no account open, or cabinets which he must not unlock, if he would continue in his present state of felicity'."[19]

Of the different categories of Tabooed Chamber tales identified by Hartland, the best known is the "Bluebeard" type, represented in the Grimm Brothers' collection by the powerfully unsettling story "Fitcher's Bird." Here, a young woman unlocks the one door that her wizard husband, before leaving on a brief journey, forbade her to enter in his absence: "But what did she see when she went in? A great bloody basin stood in the middle of the room, and therein lay human beings, dead and hewn to pieces, and hard by was a block of wood, and a bleeding axe lay upon it." When her husband returns and discovers her disobedience, he wastes no time in taking his revenge: " 'Since you have gone into the room against my will,' said he, 'you shall go back into it against your own. Your life is ended.' He threw her down, dragged her along by her hair, cut her head off on the block, and hewed her to pieces so that her blood ran on the ground. Then he threw her into the basin with the rest."[20]

This fantasy, of course, is central to *The Texas Chainsaw Massacre*: indeed, it is the very essence of this movie, in which the victims venture into a place they have been warned is off-limits

("You don't want to go foolin' around other folks' property," advises
the kindly gas station owner, who later turns out to be one of the
cannibal killers), and are instantly translated from their "present
state of felicity" into a state somewhat resembling that of the
offerings in the fresh meat section of the local supermarket. Pam,
the first of the female victims in the movie, tries to escape after
discovering the horrors contained in the house, only to be seized by
the monster and, like the luckless young woman in "Fitcher's Bird,"
dragged back into the death chamber.

There are other similarities between details of Hooper's movie
and those of various folk stories that Hartland discusses. In certain
tales of the Forbidden Chamber variety, for example, the antagonist
is not a single villain but an "ogre [who] is the head of a band of
assassins"[21]—a situation very much like the one portrayed in
Chainsaw, where the chief executioner of the demented clan is the
hideous Leatherface. In another variant, the protagonist—in this
case a woman (though, as Hartland points out, the victims are
frequently males)[22] is led to disaster by a "hollowing groaning"
issuing from somewhere in the castle. "The heroine, hearing the
groaning and tracing it to the Forbidden Chamber, is overcome by
curiosity and opens the door."[23] There is a close analogy to this in
Hooper's film, in the killing of the first victim, Kirk, who, hearing
strange animal noises coming from a mysterious room, walks over
to investigate and is instantly slain by Leatherface, who leaps out
and smashes the boy's skull with a sledge hammer. The victim
collapses—dead, though still convulsing—across the doorsill:
another image paralleled in one of the variants noted by Hartland,
in which the victim "opens the door [of the Forbidden Chamber] and
falls dead on the threshold."[24] Cannibalism is implied in many of
the tales collected by Hartland, and in the Grimm Brothers story
"The Robber Bridegroom," another "Bluebeard analogue (though
one that does not contain the image of the Forbidden Chamber), this
theme is treated very explicitly. Here, a beautiful maiden is
betrothed to a sinister stranger, who turns out to be the leader of a
gang of cannibals. Spying on the "godless crew" from behind a
"great hogshead," the heroine sees them drag home "another young
girl." They were drunk, and paid no heed to her screams and
lamentations. They gave her wine to drink, three glasses full, one
glass of white wine, one glass of red, and a glass of yellow, and with
this her heart burst in twain. Thereupon they tore off her delicate
raiment, laid her on a table, cut her beautiful body in pieces, and
strewed salt thereon."[25]

Toward the end of *Chainsaw*, the massacre's only survivor, a
pretty blonde teenager named Sally, also witnesses a cannibal feast,

when she is forced by her captors to sit at the table while they dine on what are evidently the remains of her friends. Finally, there is the common motif of the protagonist's ultimate escape, which Hartland refers to as "the flight of the heroine." *Chainsaw*, too, ends with this image, when Sally, battered, bloodied, and in hysterics, manages nevertheless to break out of the deathhouse and elude her berserk, chainsaw-wielding pursuer.

Psychologists of both Freudian and Jungian persuasions have tried their hands at explicating the meaning of the Forbidden Chamber myth. The results have been less than satisfactory, though they do have the virtue of neatly illustrating the limitations of the respective methodologies. Bettelheim, for instance, does his best to rationalize the fundamentally horrific story of "Fitcher's Bird" into yet another safely domesticated, easily understandable, morally edifying fable, a tale designed to inculcate a "higher ... humanity" by warning: "Women, don't give in to your sexual curiosity; men, don't permit yourself to be carried away by your anger at being sexually betrayed."[27] Unfortunately, it is hard to fit an image as ghastly as that of the "corpse chamber" (to use another of Hartland's vivid phrases) into such an uplifting reading, so Bettelheim is compelled not simply to underplay its significance (virtually to the point of ignoring it) but to misrepresent it as well, referring to it as a "room full of dead people," when, to be exact, it is a room full of hacked and dismembered human bodies (including those of the heroine's own sisters) and certainly the most nighmarish and haunting detail in the story, indeed perhaps in the whole of Grimm.

Analytical psychology fares no better than Freudian psychoanalysis. Marie-Louise von Franz, one of the old-guard Zurich luminaries and a specialist in fairy tales, reduces "Bluebeard" to an intrapsychic allegorical drama featuring the usual cast of Jungian personifications, so that the figure of the wife-butcher/cannibal-monster/necrophile turns out to be the "ferocious aspects of the animus in his most diabolical form" in a tale whose (supposed) unconscious intent is "to show how a woman can deal with this inner figure."[28]

Though Hartland himself announces his intention to "arrive at a rational explanation of the origin, evolution and meaning" of the motif, his article does not really go much beyond collecting examples. Still, he does offer a suggestive clue to the meaning when he observes that "the myth of the Forbidden Chamber is one of a large class which finds its central thought in a taboo."[29] Indeed, like the earlier Grimm story we looked at, the tale of "Fitcher's Bird" seems to embody a very precise and widespread primitive taboo, one having to do, not with menstruation or the dead, but with human sacrifice, and even more specifically with the kind of human sacrifice in which the victim's corpse is ritually cannibalized. Well-documented in anthropological literature,[30] this type of taboo is graphically described near the end of Herman Melville's *Typee*, in a passage with interesting parallels to the fairy tale motif of the Forbidden Chamber. Exploring the "Taboo Grove" on the day following a "hideous rite" which he has not been permitted to witness, the narrator, Tommo, notices "a curiously carved vessel of wood, of considerable size, with a cover placed over it":

> ... prompted by a curiosity I could not repress, in passing it I raised one end of the cover; at the same moment the chiefs, perceiving my design, loudly ejaculated, "Taboo! taboo!" But the slight glimpse sufficed; my eyes fell upon the disordered members of a human skeleton, the bones still fresh with moisture, and with particles of flesh clinging to them here and there![31]

In spite of the outcries, then, of right-minded critics like Gene Siskel and Roger Ebert, who denounce splatter films in general as a symptom of a profound cultural neurosis, it is clear that *The Texas Chainsaw Massacre* is no aberration but a cinematic variant of a story far older than the cinema itself—and, indeed, not even one of the grislier variants. (There's nothing in Hooper's movie to compare, for example, to the scene in "Bloudie Jack of Shrewsberrie"—one of Richard Harris Barham's *Ingoldsby Legends* (1860)—in which the heroine discovers a locked cabinet containing the amputated "wedding fingers" and severed "great-toes" of the villain's previous brides.)[32] Since myths can only appear clothed in the cultural trappings of a particular time and place, the superficial details of the story have changed. The deranged aristocrat (or wizard) in his enchanted castle is now a family of rustic blue-collar crazies living in a farmhouse in cattle-country, U.S.A., and the instrument of destruction has evolved from an elegant medieval weapon, a "gleaming axe," into a revved-up, gas-powered McCulloch. But the archetypal essence of the story remains the same.

In a very real sense, the appeal of Hooper's movie—the fascination it exerts—is beyond rational comprehension. But that is just the point. If we are to grasp the meaning of *The Texas Chainsaw Massacre* at all, we have to suppress our rationalizing tendencies and recognize the movie for what it is: a fairy tale, a "form of entertainment" that communicates in the primordial "picture-language of myth."[33] Approaching a work like *Chainsaw* in this way is, for most of us, an extremely difficult task, since it means unlocking a perceptual door which, like the heroes of "Bluebeard," "Fitcher's Bird" and countless other tales of this type, we have been warned against entering—in our case by a culture which, having lost its sense of the value and meaning of myth, offers us no key.

Notes

[1]S.S. Prawer, *Caligari's Children: The Film as Tale of Terror* (New York: Oxford Univ. Press, 1980), p. 6 et passim.

[2]*The Complete Grimms' Fairy Tales* (New York: Pantheon Books, 1977, pp. 534-35.

[3]Joseph Campbell, "Folkloristic Commentary" in *The Complete Grimms' Fairy Tales*, p. 860.

[4]Emily Dickinson, "There's a certain Slant of light" (J. 258).

[5]Stephen King, *Danse Macabre* (New York: Everest House, 1981). King is not only the preeminent contemporary practitioner of terror-fiction, "the master of modern horror," as the advertising blurbs say; he is also one of its shrewdest theoreticians, though *Danse Macabre*, for all its very real intelligence, is a seriously off-putting work. What makes it, finally, so annoying is partly King's prolixity but even more so his tone. King takes a great deal of pride in his humility, making a great show of being no different (give or take several million dollars) from the ordinary devotee of E.C. Comics, *Famous Monsters of Filmland* and the movies of George Romero. But while his "plain-fiction-for-plain-folks" persona works to his advantage as a novelist, it results in an unpleasantly—indeed obnoxiously—hypocritical brand of criticism, in which he resolves the conflict between his anti-elitist sentiments and the inherently elitist nature of his undertaking by ridiculing his intellectual sources. Throughout the book, King strains to ingratiate himself with his hypothetical audience by sneering at anything the average subscriber to *Spiderman* comics might consider a load of bull (as King would put it)—Freud, for example. At the same time, his insights clearly come directly out of his own academic training. The results are often unattractive—there's a pervasive sense that King is currying favor with the philistines—and at other times fairly amusing, as when he interprets the Jekyll and Hyde story as a "pagan conflict between man's Apollonian potential and Dionysian desires" and then defines the Dionysian as the "get-down-and-boogie side of human nature" (83).

[6]*Danse Macabre*, pp 132-33, 176ff.

[7]Ibid., p. 133.

[8]Howard Nemerov, "Lore," in *Mirrors & Windows: Poems* (Chicago: Univ. of Chicago Press, 1958), p. 74.

Neverov's poem is based on, and alludes to, a passage in Robert Graves' *The White Goddess* (New York: Farrar, Straus, and Giroux, 1966), p. 166, n. 1.

[9]Sigmund Freud, *Totem and Taboo* (New York: Norton, 1950), p. 58.

[10]Ibid., pp. 58-59.

[11]The connection between this advertisement and the ending of *Carrie* has been noted by *New York Times* film critic Vincent Canby, who calls the ad for *The Evil Dead* a "direct lift from the climactic moment" of De Palma's film. See *The New York Times*, 24 April 1983, Section 2, p. 17.

[12]Joseph Campbell, "Folkloristic Commentary," pp. 861-2.

[13]Bruno Bettelheim, *The Uses of Enchantment* (New York: Knopf, 1976), p. 101.

[14]John McCarty, *Splatter Movies* (Albany, N.Y.: FantaCo Enterprises, 1981), p. 8.

[15]*Danse Macabre*, p. 132.

[16]Lew Brighton, "Saturn in Retrograde, or the Texas Jump Cut," in *Graphic Violence on the Screen*, ed. Thomas R. Atkins (New York: Monarch Press, 1975), p. 73.

[17]Ibid., p. 76.

[18]J. Hoberman and Jonathan Rosenbaum, *Midnight Movies* (New York: Harper & Row, 1983), p. 289.

[19]Edwin Sidney Hartland, "The Forbidden Chamber," *The Folk-Lore Journal*, vol. III (1885), p. 289.

[20]*The Complete Grimms' Fairy Tales*, p. 217.

[21]Hartland, p. 209. Cf. the Grimm Brothers' story "The Robber Bridegroom," discussed elsewhere in this section.

[22]Hartland, p. 193.

[23]Ibid., p. 210.

[24]Ibid., p. 207.

[25]*The Complete Grimms' Fairy Tales*, pp. 200-204.

[26]Hartland, p. 202.

[27]Bettelheim, p. 302.

[28]Marie-Louise von Franz, *An Introduction to the Interpretation of Fairy Tales* (New York: Spring Publications, 1970), Chapter VII, p. 43.

[29]Hartland, p. 193.

[30]See, for example, Captain James Cook's account of a Tahitian sacrifice, "the earliest scientifically recorded anthropological document" of this taboo. Reprinted in Joseph Campbell, *The Mythic Image* (Princeton: Princeton Univ. Press/Bollingen Series C, 1974), pp. 430 ff.

[31]Herman Melville, *Typee* (Evanston and Chicago: Northwestern Univ. Press and The Newberry Library, 1968), p. 238.

[32]Richard Harris Barham, *The Ingoldsby Legends* (London: Everyman's Library, 1960), p. 205.

[33]Joseph Campbell, "Folkloristic Commentary," pp. 862 and 860.

NOTE: Research for this article was supported in part by grant number 662223 from the PSC-CUNY Research Award Program of the City University of New York.

Murder and Other Hazardous Occupations: Taboo and Detective Fiction

Gary Hoppenstand

When asked if he thought crime to be terribly sordid, John Mortimer's fictional English barrister, Horace Rumpole, perhaps put it best when he replied (in a somewhat philosophical mood at the annual Scales of Justice ball): "Abolish crime and we should all vanish. All the barristers and solicitors and dock officers and the dear old matron down the Old Bailey who gives aspirins away with sentences of life imprisonment."[1] Crime *does* offer a certain legal definition for society, death a certain physical definition for life. Both, as Rumpole so often informs us in his memoirs, keep him well fed on steak-and-kidney pud and cooking claret at Pommeroy's Wine Bar in Fleet Street. Crime also maintains a healthy industry for the book publisher and television producer, which is interesting since local shootings at the neighborhood carryout or the excavated trashpile of some misunderstood (but rather successful) mass murderer keep the newspaper page well-heeled in black ink and the evening newscast nicely stocked with "eye-witness" video. With such a saturation of real blood confronting us over the breakfast table via the morning paper, why would seemingly sane people invest three or four dollars in a novel which demonstrates the fine art of a judiciously placed dagger? For an answer, let's see what several of the perpetrators of the fantasy first-degree murder say.

Dorothy L. Sayers offers for our first course of the solution of the mystery genre definition, recipe by Aristotle, the notion that fictional mayhem provides "a sort of catharsis or purging of . . . fear and self-questioning."[2] Part of this catharsis, Sayers says, stems from our ability as readers to stylize the violence of invented crime, removing it even further from reality and thus intellectualizing it, so that the "unknown and unknowable" (frontier domain of both the horror and crime story) are framed by the formula of the puzzle. Puzzles are meant to be solved, and Sayers' analogy suggests that the literary mystery is also meant to be solved; so as where the domestic bashing of the wife's head by the more than slightly inebriated husband at the dinner table (because coffee was served rather than the expected lite beer) presents society with an unresolvable act of violence (twenty years in the slammer for voluntary manslaughter with no access to lite beer), the mystery story introduces a culturally stabilizing resolution for criminal violence. Convincingly preoccupied with the rules of the mystery puzzle, S.S. Van Dine, for our second course of definition, nicely details his pedestrian scenario (which no one could remain faithful to except, naturally, Van Dine) for the composition of detective fiction; his most palatable ingredient being an obvious re-statement of the formula's generic term:

The detective novel must have a detective in it; and a detective is not a detective unless he detects. His function is to gather clues that will eventually lead to the person who did the dirty work in the first chapter; and if the detective does not reach his conclusions through an analysis of those clues, he has no more solved his problem than the schoolboy who gets his answer out of the back of the arithmetic.[3]

In detective fiction there abides a personification of the rational mind, a master game player, a character who can invite a reader's empathy while at the same time marshaling a society's cultural perceptions of right, moral and good around his presence. The detective is much more than a literary agent of the cheap thrill, of the pleasant intellectual diversion that entertains, amuses and passes time, and the detective story more than a vehicle of psychological and emotional catharsis. For the final course of our mystery genre definition, served appropriately under the detective fiction *entree*, the role of the detective as moral gatekeeper and the function of detective ficion as cultural educator shall be examined.

Detective fiction closely resembles another game, in addition to the aforementioned puzzle variety, that being the party favorite, "Pin the Tail On the Donkey." In this game a sampling of the participating characters reveals an outrageous cast of literary performers: a newspaper voyeur who washes society's "dirty linen" overlooked by the police while rarely quitting the confines of his comfortable armchair; a financially bankrupt, morally righteous gumshoe who saves young damsels in distress (without benefit of flashing white charger) only to bed or be bedded by them; a razor-jawed government bureaucrat who bedevils a circus sideshow assortment of social deviants; and a city-street vigilante who metaphorically dons the cap of judge, jury and executioner as he repairs societal woes with a barrage of steaming hot lead from blazing .45 automatics directed at the local chapter of the Criminal

Element International. The players of "Pin the Tail on the Detective Story Donkey," the authors of the above cast, know the general direction of their objective, know the purpose of their objective, but they nonetheless stab with blindfolded fury at the creature's rear end. Though the products of their writing reveal an interesting grouping around the donkey's posterior, the makeup or cultural elements of the donkey's posterior remain constant.

This game serves as a metaphor for a cultural dialectic that operates in every form of popular literature and furthermore in every form of cultural expression, a cultural dialectic which illustrates a type of polarized tension between the ever-changing and the ever-constant, between the social perception and the archetype subsisting within our life experience. Social perception, on the one hand, functions according to the Social Construction of Reality model as described by Peter Berger and Thomas Luckmann. Their model suggests that a legitimating process buttresses the formation of "symbolic universes." Individuals locate themselves within these symbolic universes, which have constructed their own social histories and life biographies, and adopt institutional roles which become modes of participation.[4] However, Berger and Luckmann's Social Construction of Reality presumes a free-floating historical and social drift, which, though partially valid, fails to account for universal constants, such phenomena as birth and death, right and wrong, good and evil. Universal constants are indeed modified by the singular culture, funeral practices vary from society to society as do practices of social prescription and proscription, but the fiber of universal constants remains essentially unchanged. Every social system maintains a moral structure. Components of a society's moral structure which remain constant, Joseph Campbell has termed the archetype. According to Campbell: "archetypes ... are precisely those that have inspired, through the annals of human culture, the basic images of ritual, mythology, and vision."[5] Referring to the party game, "Pin the Tail on the Detective Story Donkey," the various efforts of individual detective fiction writers center on particular universal constants or cultural archetypes, and despite the vast range of sub-formulas within the parent formula, the basic subject matter of all detective fiction details the same picture. Detective fiction is *not* concerned with what is accepted or acceptable in society. It *is* concerned with what is legally and morally forbidden; the donkey's posterior in this game embodies the realm of social taboo.

A.R. Radcliffe-Brown states that taboo is part of a social

maintenance system in which rituals are employed to define 1) what is culturally acceptable, and 2) the consequences of planned or potential infractions.[6] The central concept manifest in all forms of detective fiction is "Justice." The hero's generic appellation implies the process of detection, the detection of crime, the detection of criminals ... and the detection of social taboos. The detective searches for information and discovers not only the means, method and motive of the criminal, but the relationship between aberrant individual and society. Detective fiction stages a morality play. The subject of the play revolves around an individual's violation of taboo and society's reaction (implemented by the detective hero) to that violation. The detective, then, as one of the principals of the play, assumes the function of a Justice figure, a type of doctor of crime who eliminates the individual aberration and restores the validity of the taboo structure within the culture.

The relationship between taboo and taboo-breaking in detective fiction is intimate and dynamic. After all, fictional formula is little more than a literary stylization of non-fiction ritual, and thus what is defined in ritual as taboo (i.e. a system of prohibitions observed as custom)[7] transcends the ritual and lodges itself into the myth-worldview of a pluralistic, popular reading audience. The translation from ritual to formula is akin to the abstraction of act into thought, but nonetheless it is a translation pregnant with meaning and import. Fiction does little to obscure the power of taboo. Since popular formulas deal with archetypal concerns within a culture, such as birth and death, they are constructed with the same sort of apprehension of future uncertainties that give rise to rituals and other social controlling systems. The supernatural, or those cosmic forces that are perceived by members of a culture as being beyond their personal control, dictate the invention of ritual. A strict adherence to ritual can perhaps placate the cosmic, and an avoidance of taboo can perhaps protect the culturally valued. One of the roles that detective fiction serves for its readership is that of a program of personal and social control of future uncertainties. It is a backward looking program which searches for social and personal security from the past to apply to the future.

Detective fiction like most other forms of popular fiction drew its genesis from the steam-roller presses of a newly industrialized Europe and America. The serial magazines of the 1840s and 1850s, the dime novels of the 1880s, the pulp magazines of the 1920s, the mass market paperbacks of the 1940s and 1950s, each component of print mass media etched upon the various detective formulas the imprint of a capitalistic, stratified, highly moral and rigidly championed urban society. But unlike the Marxist position which argues media manipulation via idea reification and hegemony, print media are an affected product in addition to being an affecting product. Capitalism, the very concept that the Marxists attack in the production and distribution of media, functions as a cultural dog leash which restrains the movement of a developing entertainment formula. Hence, the media are essentially conservative in nature. The media distribute a product manufactured to be sold for a profit. There is capital investment in the product, and subsequent grave interest on the producer's part that the investment realizes a healthy return. The various mass media do nothing to offend their audience since that audience's purchasing power determines whether a particular magazine or paperback book will return a profit.

Entertainment media are thus generally backward-looking, searching for past commercial success, cannibalizing themselves of that success, hoping that the blood of bygone triumph will vitalize present effort. Media producers will sell their audience anything that audience desires, and if they could manipulate the consumer, then every book would be a bestseller and every movie and TV show a success. All media, in fact, undergo a "leap-frogging" in their commercial development. They depend on historically proven techniques until, either by accident or plan, a novel formula is discovered which is quickly imitated and sustained (until a new discovery occurs). This pattern of discovery/imitation/discovery/ imitation manifests itself in the development of detective fiction, and emerges as a point of philosophical debate that historically would lead to the creation of the Gothic horror story.

The Gothic horror story constructed the foundations upon which the very creation of the detective story was engineered. Phyllis A. Whitney suggests that this formula drew its inspiration from an 18th century author:

Horace Walpole probably started it all when he built his monstrosity of a pseudo-Gothic castle at Strawberry Hill, adding numerous rooms to the original cottage, as well as a round tower, a cloister, and a gallery, and filling it all with period pieces and oddities that he regarded as suitable to the mood. Then having created his charming folderol, he became obsessed by it and put it into his most famous novel, *The Castle of Otranto* (1765). The novel became so popular that it was followed by many imitators. Among the better known contributors to the genre were Mary Shelley (Frankenstein, 1818) and Lord Byron's physician Polidori (Vampyre), who added their own touches of monster and vampire.[8]

Horace Walpole did indeed synthesize one of the first "bestsellers" in Europe with his short novel *The Castle of Otranto*. It was essentially a commercial effort geared toward the popular press of its time and marketed with the burgeoning middle class in mind. Walpole blended elements of folklore, supernaturalism, mystery, political intrigue, vengeance, sadism and repressed sexuality together and specifically tied these motifs to an atmospheric setting of stormy nights, stormy passions, crumbling castles and requited family curses. This brew was a wild and animated concoction which swiftly followed upon the heels of a boringly rational age of Western culture.

From the death of Descartes in 1650 through the death of Hume in 1776, there established itself in European thought an Age of Enlightenment in which the mechanistic Newtonian model became an overriding metaphor, and in which scientific experimentation founded on empiricism became the basis for philosophical self-confidence.[9] This paradigm eventually became intellectually stifling and soon gave way to the Romantic movement, and the Gothic novel. The literary universe of the Gothic threw the mechanism of social control to the four winds as novel after lurid novel was published featuring moaning ghosts drifting through the dark corridors of hidden torture-chambers enforcing Gypsy maledictions. The Gothic remained quite popular through the conclusion of the 18th century and the beginning of the 19th. It provided for its readership an untamed vicarious excursion into the reservoir of social taboo. Incest, murder, torture and rape crowded the pages of massive three-volume Gothic novels, and the only requirement made of their authors was that for each item of broken taboo early in the story there would be even more shockingly broken taboos later. Needless to say, there ceased to exist in the Gothic that sense of societal Justice, that sense of cultural vindication of the morally pure that was to later reassert itself in detective fiction. And, of course, the Gothic was profoundly anti-heroic.

Edgar Allan Poe successfully transplanted the Gothic from Europe to America, and developed a reputation on such stories as "Ligeia" and "The Fall of the House of Usher." In "Usher" one rediscovers many of the motifs first established by Walpole: a crumbling mansion infused with a melancholic sense of the supernatural. Whether "Usher" is interpreted as a tale of insanity or the supernatural, the basic confrontation between Man and the Universe nevertheless concludes in like fashion. Man is totally vulnerable and victim to the forces of the Universe. His will and intellect, those qualities so important to the Age of Enlightenment, are meaningless when exposed to various natural or supernatural elements beyond his personal control. The raging storm in the Gothic, as an agent of Fate, destroys the hero and villain alike, and the only chance for physical or mental survival is escape. Thus, the final passage of Poe's "Usher" defines Man's sense of helplessness when challenged with the Cosmic:

> From that chamber, and from that mansion, I fled aghast. The storm was still abroad in all its wrath as I found myself crossing the old causeway. Suddenly there shot along the path a wild light, and I turned to see whence a gleam so unusual could have issued; for the vast house and its shadows were alone behind me. The radiance was that of the full, setting, and blood-red moon which now shone vividly through that once barely-discernible fissure of which I have spoken as extending from the roof of the building, in a zig-zag direction, to the base. While I gazed, this fissure widened—there came a fierce breath of the whirlwind—the entire orb of the satellite burst at once upon my sight—my brain reeled as I saw the mighty walls rushing asunder—there was a long tumultuous shouting sound like the voice of a thousand waters—and the deep and dark tarn at my feet closed sullenly and silently over the fragments of the "House of Usher."[10]

Any violation of taboo in the Gothic, as with Manfred's betrayal of his wife's loyalty in *The Castle of Otranto* or as with Roderick Usher's possible incestuous relationship with his sister Madeline in "The Fall of the House of Usher," results in the *total* destruction of the protagonist's sense of being or importance. There is little chance for forgiveness and almost certain chance for havoc.

Poe is not just remembered for his excursions into the Gothic formula, however, and with the publication of his story "Murders in the Rue Morgue" (*Graham's Magazine*, April 1841), he helped to reverse the stream of popular mystery fiction in both America and Europe. Though "Murders" possesses all the trappings of a Gothic shocker—including the expected crumbling mansion (the protagonist's home), grotesque murders and an even more grotesque murderer, Poe's contribution to the mystery story, a contribution that was to provide the first major leap-frog jump in the formula, was the invention of an uncommonly intelligent hero, a character who could set the wrongs of evil in a proper moral cast, and who could reinforce the security of social rituals in the face of criminal anarchy and violence. Poe's Monsieur C. Auguste Dupin thus became the first modern detective and the prototype for one of the four major detective formula archetypes, the classical detective.

These four detective archetypes, the classical detective, the hard-boiled detective, the police detective and the avenger-detective, serve, as we shall see, as cultural reflections of the socialization process. This socialization process is not manipulated by the media's power elite, as the Marxists claim, nor does it strictly manifest itself within the mass society model. Instead, the four archetypes reveal similarities among a pluralistic society, a society whose members adopt the world construction and world maintenance practice operant in the Social Construction of Reality, while yet adhering to universal constants as touchstones of common experience and common knowledge. A critical examination into these four archetypes can reveal the social prescriptions and social proscriptions evident within our culture; indeed, the existence of a "social attitude textbook" persists in all mass media products since these products fulfill audience needs and gratifications in highly ritualistic or formulaic ways.

The substance of plot in classical detective fiction consists of anti-social behavior. The fictional catalyst which motivates the act of detection revolves around three levels of taboo violation. At the most basic level,the role of the criminal serves as a social definition of what is acceptable and unacceptable behavior. He *is* a criminal because his individual accomplishments scratch taboo areas. He is a murderer, a thief, a liar and the detailing of his actions defines society's objections to and limits of taboo violation. For example, it is culturally acceptable in classical detective fiction to kill an individual in self-defense. However, if one plots the killing of a person for purposes of revenge, financial gain or sexual gratification, a culturally accepted act becomes unacceptable and falls into the realm of taboo. Thus is defined the difference between hero and villain, between taboo enforcer and taboo breaker. At the next level, the objects of interest in classical detective fiction, icons of wealth and power, function as symbols of fulfillment of the myth of material success. Money, jewelry, stocks, art treasures, these things are immensely desirable for members of a large middle-class readership, unless, of course, they are acquired by acts of unacceptable violence or theft. Unless taboos are observed in the acquisition of such wealth, the formula reminds us, then swift and powerful sanctions soon follow. Finally, the classical detective himself establishes an illustrative example of how intellectual control can dominate anarchism. If the criminal represents a type of social hoodlum, an aggressively amoral character who over-indulges his more primitive urges, then the classical detective, as a creature of emotionless reason, suggests in an allegorical manner how the unswerving ritual of observation, detection and discovery can solve seemingly irrational violations of taboo. Ultimately the classical detective argues the most radical separation of emotion and reason in taboo maintenance, and the culmination of social Justice rests upon the hero's successful manipulation of mental resources and defiance of rampant emotional individualism

As the early years of the Great Depression began to gauge its economic impact on American society, the classical detective held less relevance for a popular readership, and thus a new archetype, first begun in the dime novel some two decades earlier, emerged in the popular press and radio to captivate the nation's fancy by effectively solving criminal problems with vigilante violence. This new detective, the avenger-detective, catered to the societal desire for simplified solutions to complex problems. With the publication of the April 1931 issue of the *Shadow Magazine*, the first of the Depression-era vigilante pulp magazines, the parameters of detective fiction taboo and taboo violation altered significantly from their classical predecessor.

Though the relationship between criminal and society—and icon and society—remained basically the same, the degree to which these motifs affected standing taboo systems intensified. The threat of the criminal to society assumed epic proportions in avenger-detective pulp magazines. Super-criminals threaten the lives and fortunes of great numbers of people, not just certain selected individuals, and law enforcement agencies themselves, seen merely as incompetent in classical detective fiction, crumble against the villains of the avenger-detective. Thus, the fabric of crime in these stories is woven of Apocalyptic thread. Walter Gibson, one of the creators of The Shadow, and writing under the "house name" of Maxwell Grant, the major author of The Shadow's adventures, describes the relationship of The Shadow and his adversaries:

As his [The Shadow's] forays expanded, The Shadow came into conflict with formidable antagonists, whose own cryptic identities became the titles for the stories in which most of them met their deserved doom, notably, *The Silent Seven, The Black Master, The Crime Cult,* and *Six Men of Evil.* These involved spy rings, murder cults, mad scientists, and haunted houses .... At times, The Shadow's exploits became topical: when New York police were baffled by a real-life terrorist who signed himself "Three X," The Shadow met and conquered his fictional counterpart in the form of "Double Z" .... Most important, however, were the supervillains who developed during The Shadow's saga .... Always, when The Shadow defeated some monstrous scheme, he would be spurred on to tackle something bigger; while, conversely, master criminals, learning that one of their ilk had been eliminated, would logically profit by that loss and devise something more powerful to thwart The Shadow.[11]

The vigilante hero of these stories resorts to radical methods to deal with radical social dangers. The avenger-detective is less skilled in observation and detection and more skilled in violence. Rarely in classical detective fiction does the hero utilize violence to apprehend criminals. The avenger-detective, on the other hand, *always* employs his blazing automatics or his fists to kill, rather than to apprehend, the crook. At no other time in American history did the traditions of capitalism come under greater duress than during the Depression. Social taboos that a decade earlier had possessed great power in controlling economic and cultural forces no longer seemed to have any effect in directing personal and governmental actions. Frustrated at the inability of society's leaders to solve the morass of Depression problems, Americans turned to the pulp magazines for a formulaic examination of their troubles. And to protect taboo systems that had routinely proven effective, the vigilante pulps contributed a detective hero who was up to the task of defending home, mom and apple pie by any means possible.

The hard-boiled detective, who was another product of the pulp magazines, contradicted the formulas established in the classical and avenger-detective archetypes. Finding its genesis in the pages of the pulp magazine, *Black Mask*, which, under the editorial supervision of "Cap" Joseph Shaw in the 1920s, produced such popular hardboiled writers as Dashiel Hammett, Raymond Chandler, Erle Stanley Gardner and Carroll John Daly, this new formula reversed the role of the detective within society. In defining his rationale as editor of *Black Mask,* Shaw says:

In physics, an explosion sends out sound waves. But if there are no ears within their range, there is no sound. If you read of a thousand aborigines wiped out by earthquake or flood, you are abstractly interested, but you are not distrubed. But let a member of your own family be even remotely threatened and you are at once intensely concerned, emotionally aroused. This is true in real life. Why shouldn't it hold true in fiction, which must create the illusion of reality?[12]

To help create this "illusion of reality," hard-boiled writers developed ambivalent heroes. Carroll John Daly, the creator of the archetype and one of *Black Mask*'s most popular writers, has his detective hero, Race Williams, describe himself in *The Hidden Hand* as being misunderstood: "People—especially the police—don't understand me. And what we don't understand we don't appreciate. The police look upon me as being so close to the criminal that you can't tell the difference."[13] Rather than being portrayed as a symbol of Justice for urban society, the hard-boiled detective serves as an emblem of personal honor, a knight operating within a social structure of civic corruption, decadence and dishonesty. No longer were city streets worth defending. They were dark, dangerous places, the abode of murderers and thieves, organized by political grafters who operated at every level of government. New York, Chicago, Los Angeles, the names of these cities became euphemisms for evil in the hard-boiled story. Of the four archetypes, the setting of the hard-boiled story resembles closest the turbulent formula of the Gothic: a literary universe where traditional cultural rituals fail to protect individuals and institutions from malevolent cosmic forces. The difference between the two formulas rests with the role of the protagonist. In the Gothic, no single person can withstand the forces of nature (or *super*nature), and thus any human enterprise contrary to the will of Fate is doomed. On the other hand, in the hard-boiled detective story the detective hero *can* face monolithic urban evil because of his intensely defended code of personal honor. Raymond Chandler states:

But down these mean streets a man must go who is not himself mean, who is neither tarnished nor afraid. The detective in this kind of story must be such a man. He is the hero, he is everything. He must be a complete man and a common man and yet an unusual man. He must be, to use a rather weathered phrase, a man of honor, by instinct, by inevitability, without thought of it, and certainly without saying it. He must be the best man in his world and a good enough man in any world.[14]

In all detective fiction, the hero stands as the primary defender of taboo, but the hard-boiled detective defends traditional taboo systems in the face of a hostile and deadly environment. Often he is beaten by agents of society, but he is like an egg: he becomes tougher the more he's "boiled." His health serves as a peculiar sacrifice for the sins of the city as he is battered from chapter to chapter in his heroic quest for Truth. The detective in the hard-boiled story, rather than being the criminal—as the criminal-as-radical-individual is portrayed in the other archetypes—is instead the last bastion of honor in an amoral world that has lost all sense of moral meaning.

The final detective fiction archetype, the police detective story, re-establishes the conventional role of the urban setting. Most scholars of detective fiction agree that Chester Gould's comic strip, *Dick Tracy*, was the first modern police detective story. In describing the history and social function of the strip, Garyn Roberts states:

In October of 1931, the newspaper audience learned very quickly of Dick Tracy's characteristics and purpose. In the first daily episode of *Dick Tracy* the hero was the helpless witness of a hold-up, during which his girlfriend, Tess Trueheart, was kidnapped, and her father shot dead. Emil Trueheart (Tess' father), the owner of a delicatessen, was just beginning, after a lifetime of work, to enjoy a little financial comfort. Tracy had come over one evening for supper with the family of his sweetheart. A pair of gangsters enter the residence of the Truehearts and shoot Emil. When Tracy attacks the gangsters, he is jumped and gunwhipped. He awakes to find Emil dead and Tess kidnapped. Tracy states, "Over the body of your father, Tess, I swear I'll find you and avenge this thing—I swear it." . . . . A hero is born whose cause is evident and justified, and who is destined to grow with the American public for more than fifty years.[15]

Unlike the other three archetypes where the police are viewed as incompetent, useless or corrupt, this last detective fiction archetype marries the detective hero to official law enforcement agencies. Perhaps the actual horrors of the Second World War muted the impact of the hard-boiled setting of the 1920s and 1930s. Perhaps audiences were becoming more sophisticated in their readings of detective fiction, believing more in professional crime solvers than in their amateur counterparts. Roberts suggests that with *Dick Tracy*: "the hero joined the police force rather than becoming a ruthless avenger . . . . He is and was a believable, yet ideal citizen."[16] After the book publication of Lawrence Treat's novel, *V As In Victim* (1945), the police detective story eventually found widespread popularity in paperback and hardcover books and in television. George Dove says of the book:

Treat's *V As In Victim*. . .introduced a new way of dealing with the police story. The cops bore the burden of detection, but they were not 'heroes,' nor did they display any suggestion of awe-inspiring powers of ratiocination. For the most part they worked in teams, using the methodology normally employed by policemen in real life.[17]

With the urban setting restored and with the criminal element again defined as socially deviant, the element of the police detective story that distinguishes it from the other three types of detective fiction is the hero's method of investigation. The classical detective safeguards cultural rituals with his skills of observation and ratiocination, the avenger-detective with his skills of violence, the hard-boiled detective with his code of personal honor. The police detective, as mentioned by Dove, often lacks any of the above abilities, but he nonetheless enforces taboo systems (in this instance, specifically defined as the law) from anti-social menaces. His persistence on the "case" usually spells success and suggests for his readership the notion that vigilance and dedication are enough to stem the tide of crime, and that fulfilling the duties of one's job well on a steady basis can produce positive personal and social results. The police detective is the bureaucratic bulwark of cultural taboo and is conceivably the most digestible of the four detective types for a modern corporate-minded America.

Social anthropologist and ethnologist Franz Steiner states that taboo is connected with, among other things, the social mechanisms of obedience which have ritual significance, and the specific and restrictive behavior in dangerous situations.[18] Detective fiction, as a reflection of the socialization process in our culture, functions as a formulaic textbook of how capitalistic mass media operate, and since detective fiction is primarily concerned with criminal acts and social retribution for those acts, the genre as a whole illustrates the range and respective importance of various taboos in our society. The social mechanisms of obedience in detective fiction detail the "evilness" of individual disregard (or societal disregard, as in the hard-boiled detective story) of ritual and taboo. Violations of these mechanisms lead to powerful sanctions enforced by the detective hero.

Of all popular fiction formulas, the detective story is *most* concerned with social proscriptions of behavior, and *that* not only keeps Horace Rumpole happily reveling in steak-and-kidney pud, it keeps John Mortimer and society quite pleased as well.

Notes

[1]John Mortimer, *The First Rumple Omnibus* (London: Penguin Books, 1983), p. 200.

[2]Dorothy L. Sayers, "The Omnibus of Crime," in *The Art of the Mystery Story*, ed. Howard Haycraft (New York: Carroll & Graf Publishers, 1946, 1974), p. 72.

[3]S.S. Van Dine, "Twenty Rules for Writing Detective Stories," in *The Art of the Mystery Story*, ed. Howard Haycraft, p. 190.

[4]Peter L. Berger and Thomas Luckmann, *The Social Construction of Reality* (Garden City: Doubleday, 1966), pp. 88-90.

[5]Joseph Campbell, *The Hero With A Thousand Faces* (Princeton: Princeton Univ. Press, 1949), p. 18.

[6]A.R. Radcliffe-Brown, "Taboo," in *Reader In Comparative Religion: An Anthropological Approach* ed. William A. Lessa and Evon Z. Vogt (New York: Harper & Row, 1979), pp. 46-56.

[7]Hutton Webster, *Taboo: A Sociological Study* (Stanford: Stanford Univ. Press, 1942), p. 13.

[8]Phyllis A. Whitney, "Gothic Mysteries," in *The Mystery Story*, ed. John Ball (San Diego: Univ. of California, 1976), pp. 223-224.

[9]T.Z. Lavine, *From Socrates to Sartre: The Philosophic Quest* (New York: Bantam Books, 1984), p. x.

[10]Edgar Allan Poe, "The Fall of the House of Usher," in *The Annotated Tales of Edgar Allan Poe*, ed. Stephen Peithman (Garden City: Doubleday, 1982), p. 77.

[11]Maxwell Grant (Walter Gibson), "The Shadow," in *The Great Detectives*, ed. Otto Penzler (London: Penguin, 1978), pp. 210-215.

[12]Joseph T. Shaw, "Introduction," in *The Hard-Boiled Omnibus*, ed. Joseph T. Shaw (New York: Simon & Schuster, 1946), pp. vi-vii.

[13]Carroll John Daly, *The Hidden Hand* (New York: Edward J. CLode, 1929), p. 9.

[14]Raymond Chandler, "The Simple Art of Murder," in *The Art of the Mystery Story*, ed. Howard Haycraft (New York: Carroll & Graf, 1946, 1974), p. 237.

[15]Garyn G. Roberts, "The Many Faces of Dick Tracy," Bowling Green State University,

Thesis, 1983, pp. 37-38.
   [16]*Ibid.*, p. 39.
   [17]George N. Dove, *The Police Procedural* (Bowling Green, Ohio: Popular Press, 1982), p. 10.
   [18]Franz Steiner, *Taboo* (New York: Philosophical Library, 1956), pp. 20-21.

A Tankard of Sporting Taboos

David Quentin Voigt

Just suppose that whilst turning your radio dial you happened
to pick up a sportscast, narrated in impeccable sportsaguese,
describing a world championship farting contest, pitting Lord
Window-Smear of England against challenger Paul Boomer of
Australia! Would the explosive sounds from this judged display and
the solemn awarding of points for "fleeps" and "triple
thundergusts" gross you out? Stuff and nonsense, you say, and
you'd be right, for the above action is the subject of a fictionalized
party record entitled "The Contest." But what if I told you that in
fact student groups at certain colleges stage farting contests as
clandestine sport, or that a kid named John, a three-time farting
champ at a western university, used his talents extra-curricularly to
help his bowling team. He did this by popping triumphant
thundergusts every time he scored a strike, which grossed out the
other team.[1] If this account also offends readers who also think it
has no place in a serious essay, then that places me under the spell of
an American taboo. Of course, that is what this is about: taboos as
they appear in the American sports world.

A Tangle of Taboos

Not least among the great social regulators that restrict man's
freedom of action are forbidden acts and thoughts that all cultures
impose. Labeled *taboos*, after Captain James Cook's 1771
Polynesian reports, social scientists use the term to describe
forbidden and excluded persons, acts, words, thoughts and things
that supposedly threaten a group's welfare and survival and are
therefore used to that group's advantage. Born of fears, taboos
thrive on popular fears that evil, pain, loss and death may result
from violations of taboos. Thus to probe such forbidden acts is to

explore the dark and scary side of a culture. Nor is it an easy task, since undertaking such probes puts the investigator in the suspect (and tabooed) position of delving into matters which conventional wisdom says should be left alone. Nevertheless, the quest for human understanding insists that such forays be made. After all, learning what to fear is everyman's lot and man's diverse cultures impose a bewildering variety of taboos. Indeed, there is no universal consensus on forbidden behavior; what is tabooed in one society may be approved behavior in another. Still, no human claypot trods this earth without lugging taboos passed on by his learning. By his fears ye shall know man is the promise that guides those who would venture to study man's tangled taboos.

In probing such behaviors, social scientists have learned that tabooed behavior usually includes injunctions like "Don't do, don't say, or don't think." Indeed, if all three injunctions enround an act, suicide in America for example, you can be sure that you are confronted by a most highly powered taboo. But any taboo violations incur punishment. As harshly imposed mandates, taboos function to preserve a group's design for living by stifling undesired change. Thus, taboos are often a conservative force; by damping potent longings and drives, they restrict enjoyment, movement and expression—presumably for the greater good of preserving a way of life.

As forces of conformity, taboos often carry supernatural sanctions, punishments visited by angry gods. This is characteristic of religious-dominated societies. Likewise magic-minded societies back taboos with potential force threats. And science-minded societies like our own feature science-based taboos. As evidence, look to TV commercials which carry ham-handed threats of dire consequences, including social failure, perpetual ugliness or smelliness, to be visited upon any wretch who fails to use "scientific" products shilled by commercials.

Omnipresent, taboos thrive in magical, religious or scientific settings. Because science-minded societies are more receptive to change, new taboos compete with older ones. Yet no society follows a single belief system to the exclusion of others. Thus, any individual American is likely to embrace a complex mixture of scientific, religious and magical beliefs and is henceforth vulnerable to taboos from any of these three fronts.

In his insightful book, *Taboo Topics*, editor Norman L. Farberow marshalls the works of several taboo trekkers to illustrate that last point. Among those sighted, suicide looms large as a third degree taboo in America (Don't do, say, or think it!), but somewhat less horror attends a taboo on personal religious revelations (e.g. announcing one's imminent delivery of an immaculate conception) which runs afoul of scientific credibility. Other taboos noted include homosexuality (which threatens approved sexual relationships and, if fargone, threatens the species' survival); personal sex revelation (such as asking one's partner, "How am I doing, Edna?") because this threatens one's self image; taboos on hypnotism, graphology and ESP, also discussed, smack of forbidden magical arts; and a taboo on discussing one's imminent death threatens our faith in medical science as well as stirring ancient horrors of mingling with a doomed person.[2] In the final analysis, of course, tabooing behavior does not mean individuals will eschew forbidden behavior; indeed, most of us are taboo violators, sometimes forthrightly, more often deviously, but always we know that if caught, we face the punishments that are attached.

Taboos like these rank high in American forbidden behavior hierarchies, but lesser ones like farting are also verboten. Indeed, so strong is the farting taboo, so socially disruptive is such behavior viewed, that students of human biology know little of its etiology and say less. Hence, until taboo trekkers persuade Americans that such earthy popping is normal, prudence suggests that sneaking, waving the odor about, and downplaying clandestine farting contests are necessary social skills.

Sports, A Mirror of Popular Fears

The ubiquitous presence of big sports in American life affords promising opportunities for tracking taboos; after all, such spectacles are highly visible institutions. Formalized sport schedules convoke recurring dramas that are staged in designated areas with players, officials and fans onstage as fair game for behavioral observations. Indeed, candid media coverage of such scenes is a rich source of information about embedded taboos.

Among the taboos bared by Farberow's ferrets, fear of homosexuality enthralls Americans. That this taboo has strengthened over the years is evidenced by problems baseball travel secretaries now face in assigning players to hotel rooms. Today more players request single rooms and more married players request that their wives be allowed to join them on road trips. At the same time those willing to abide roommates are finicky; their compatibility demands certainly vex secretaries.

This is a vast departure from the early years of this century when players were arbitrarily assigned roomies; usually it was done

on an alphabetical basis and not seldom two were assigned to share
a single bed! An abomination say you? Aye, but many old timers can
recall when two adult males in a sack was all right. However, pitcher
Rube Waddell's roomie demanded in writing that Waddell be barred
from eating animal crackers in bed! Such privations disappeared
when single beds were assigned, although newer ones cropped up.
For one, Babe Ruth's roomie protested his carnal calisthenics with
female bedmates, complaining that Ruth was the noisiest fucker in
America! However, as baseball's superstar of the '20s Ruth soon
demanded and got private accommodations, as did others. Today
many players enjoy privacy, a trend that mirrors the increasing
power of the homosexuality taboo. Paradoxically, the taboo gains
strength even as homosexuals, reportedly numbering 10% of the
adult male population, are benefitting from facilitating groups and
from greater tolerance and understanding. Mayhap, the macho
world of male athletes is inordinately subject to the taboo; if so,
recent exposes of homosexuality among female tennis stars
suggests its broader extension.

Certainly the awesome force of the American suicide taboo is
evidenced in horrified reactions to stories of athletes taking their
own lives. In baseball at least four such cases occurred among major
league players in this century, including Marty Bergen in 1900,
Chick Stahl in 1907, Willard Hershberger in 1940 and just recently
when an All-American college star, frustrated over his abortive
career, shot himself on the college diamond where he had won his
greatest plaudits. If the suicides of athletes appall more than those
of other Americans, perhaps it is because fans expect athletes to be
made of sterner stuff.

Likewise America's taboos on revealing personal sexual
feelings seemingly weighs heavier on athletes. This may be due to
persisting myths of the vaunted sexual prowess of athletes or myths
which hold that sexual indulgence saps strength and dulls athletic
performances. Combined with the belief that clandestine sex
behavior is destructive to social ordering, this adds up to a potent
taboo. Apparently football coaches and fighter trainers are more
enthralled by the myth of sex sapping male strength. Among true
believers, Coach Frank Kush of the old Baltimore Colts (who also
bars post-game drinking), cloisters his coitusless Colts in a hotel on
nights before games, refusing to allow any to venture out.

Of course violations of the taboo are frequent, especially in
baseball where for years players and reporters mutually engaged in
elaborate concealment of such practices. Indeed, if a player mouthed
off about such goings on he ran afoul of a strong taboo against such

revelations. Obviously such exposure was a threat to personal reputations and to marriages. Hence, Jim Bouton, Joe Pepitone, Bo Belinksy and other muckraking player-authors were anathematized for telling in print. Bouton, indeed, has yet to be invited to a Yankee Old-Timers game, but his impact has been to make gossip about player sex dalliance routine stuff. But if sportswriters now make news items of such shenanigans, they run the risk of being frozen out of interviews by players and sometimes even by whole teams.

That American taboos wax and wane in strength also applies to the taboo on personal religious experience revelation. As William James's great study of such admitted experiences showed, it was more acceptable at the turn of the century for one to apprehend himself to be in the presence of a divinity. However, advancing science and secularism soon tabooed admitting to such encounters. Thus, baseball players came to be mocked for refusing to play on Sundays; in the case of Branch Rickey, he was heckled by catcalls like, "He promised his old lady!" Likewise, open praying or religious ritual performances were mocked. This is less the case now as religious revivals and born again experiences permit more open expression. Still, if open appeals, such as Manager Lasorda's exhortations to the Dodger sky god are more acceptable now, there are limits. As born-again pitchers and quarterbacks seek to blame God's will for their failings, they incur the wrath of managers and teammates. Apparently the taboo on involving god in athletic performances persists, and wisely so. After all, sabbath day games are the biggest crowd draws, yet when is the last time you heard a fundamentalist knocking such spectacles as Sabbath desecrations? Prudent sportsmen are smart enough to avoid such discussions; also, many players seem to follow writer Peter Gent's observation of not asking God for victory, lest God get pissed off!

Cycles of waxing and waning strengths also seem to apply to taboos on magical practices. Like religious beliefs, faith in magical efficacy has come back in America, perhaps due to science's failure to supply enough credible answers to life's problems. Athletes, indeed, always have leaned on magical rites and fetishes. What makes our generation of baseball players different from those of a half century ago is that moderns are less inclined to conceal their magical interests. Evidently the taboo on openly displaying magical practices is weaker now than when owner Phil Wrigley hired a witch to hex rival teams. Prudently Wrigley kept it a secret; had he not he might have been laughed out of baseball like the psychologist hired by the Browns in the early 1950s.

By the 1960s, however, the taboo on magical beliefs relaxed to the point where players soon indulged openly in witchcraft, hypnotism, astrology and bio-rhythms. Given the fact that no science has been able to banish the uncertainties of baseball makes this understandable enough. Be that as it may, players still lean on science, but instances of magical rites still blend with pragmatic scientific gimmicks like doping bats and balls to gain an edge. Like the ancient Chinese who grasped at any gods just in case it might help, who can fault ballplayers for wallowing in magic, religion and science?

Tabooed People and Forbidden Behavior in Sports

In addition to sharing taboos with ordinary Americans, athletes face extraordinary taboos stemming from the unique lifeways of the various sports. For each sport is a subculture, possessing its own rules, territory, language, standards of excellent performance, and behavioral expectations. Given the plenitude of sporting scenes in America, it is hopeless to try to ferret out the unique taboos of each. Hence, parsimony mandates a general approach to sporting taboos; to this end the topics of tabooed people and tabooed behavior in sports is briefly explored.

Tabooed people pose threats to a group's welfare and existence. Invariably stigmatized, such persons are considered evil, their presence polluting. In the macho world of American sports, male regulators have long tabooed women. Of course, this is true of the culture at large where male dominance is maintained by such structures as exclusive male clubs and even household "dens."

In major league baseball the notion of a woman playing on a team appears to be unspeakable and unthinkable. Till now the widespread exclusion of women from hardball play has kept women from aspiring to such careers. And despite equalitarian gains on other sexist fronts, the taboo on women in pro ball holds firm; after one woman briefly played minor league ball in the 1950s, there were no others. Hence, when Mrs. Kim Witt appeared among 407 players at a 1982 Minnesota Twins tryout camp, sportswriters did a double take. But after circulating her photo and noting that she was the first woman to try out with the Twins, the article noted with relief that she was rejected.

Also rejected have been female aspirants seeking to integrate all-male pro football and basketball teams. True, a female placement holder played briefly on a minor league football team and a couple of female hoopsters tried out for NBA teams, but no dent was made in the taboo. Similarly one searches in vain for any females among pro sport's officials and referees, although a few have umpired in baseball's minors. Moreover, female sportswriters still encounter sexist slights in attempting to crack the male world of sportswriters. And if a few have owned big league baseball teams, except in the case of Mrs. Effie Manley, a prominent owner of the defunct Negro National (baseball) League, all were obliged to maintain low profiles.

For many years black players were stigmatized as tabooed persons by white pro teams. In major league baseball Commissioner Landis defended segregation policies until his death in 1944. And once admitted, blacks suffered discriminatory slights, such as being excluded from "centrist positions" in batteries or infields, forced to room with other blacks, judged by higher performance standards than whites, and paid less. Worse, blacks still battle the "tipping point" myth, the paranoid notion that too many black faces in a lineup results in diminished attendance. Surely that persisting myth perpetuates the supposed polluting powers of black people. The same taboo afflicts Hispanic players, even though Hispanic and black players have dominated baseball offenses over the past 20 years.

Of course white players situationally find themselves branded tabooed persons. In times past ethnic origins stigmatized players, subjecting them to ugly epithets, and persuading some to anglicize their surnames. But powerful ethnic defense groups, refusing to yield to pressures of Anglo-conformity, have lessened this taboo. Today's baseball bench jockeys are more circumspect about mouthing ethnic epithets, especially the few who ran afoul of big Ted Kluszewski's powerful fist—"My Polish joke stopper." Nor would a present day newspaper dare to print such insulting words as a *Life* magazine writer did in a 1939 piece on Joe DiMaggio:

> [Joe] speaks English without an accent and is otherwise well adapted to most U.S. mores. Instead of olive oil ... he keeps his hair sleek with water. He never reeks of garlic ... [but like] Heavyweight champion Joe Louis, DiMaggio is lazy, shy and inarticulate.[3]

So much for Mr. Coffee! In other ways, the highly visible, fiercely competitive world of major league baseball situationally taboos persons. For a baserunning blunder in a 1908 game, Fred Merkle became known as "Bonehead" Fred. For delivering the pitch that killed Cleveland's Ray Chapman, Yankee pitcher Carl Mays wore the mark of Cain, while another hurler, John Mails,

carried the nickname of "Duster." For consorting with gamblers
and allegedly throwing games, Hal Chase was branded a crook, but
this was slight punishment compared with the onus of "Black Sox"
affixed to eight players for throwing the 1919 World Series. They
were barred from organized baseball for life. And lesser acts also
taboo individuals. For playing a midget, owner Bill Veeck was
anathematized by his colleagues, and a hastily invoked rule
reminded midgets that they had no place in organized baseball.
More recently Mike Marshall, Bill Lee, Curt Flood and Andy
Messersmith were branded taboo persons by irate owners. Flood
was stigmatized for challenging the reserve clause in court and
Messersmith got the same treatment for winning re-entry rights for
players by successfully challenging his contract in an arbitration
case. As for Marshall, he was branded for asserting his own rules of
training, while Lee, a self-acknowledged "flake," caught it for acts
of lese majesty such as publicly ridiculing Commissioner Bowie
Kuhn and publicly berating club officials. Unquestionably the fear
of being branded a flamboyant flake cows many players, but
injuries, ineffectiveness, slumps, defiance of discipline, salary
demands, excessive religious zeal, and excessive wenching,
drinking and eating can also make tabooed persons of players. Nor
are officials invulnerable; for supporting the cause of unionism,
umps (like player representatives) become tabooed persons, and for
scabbing on striking umps, some active umps are now shunned as
scabs by their unionized colleagues. Fittingly, owners also become
tabooed persons, as Veeck, Charley Finley and George Steinbrenner
would attest. Veeck caught it for writing books depicting some of his
colleagues as boobs; Finley's erratic actions have been the subject of
two books. And today Steinbrenner stands alone as the premier
tabooed owner. For selling Reggie Jackson, Steinbrenner endured
loud choruses of "Georgie Sucks" from outraged fans at Yankee
Stadium.

That X-rated refrain urges us on into the tangled thicket of
tabooed behaviors in sports. As speech and language are essential
measures of one's humanity, so is knowing what words are
forbidden. In general polite American discourse taboos cursing,
swearing and obscenities; cursewords and swearwords are tabooed
because they affront accepted divinities while obscenities violate
taboos on body and sexual functions. Nevertheless, we are a robust
cursing, swearing and foul-mouthed people. Certainly this has been
the case since the late 1960s, although the collapse of the Filthy
Speech Movement as a facilitating structure attests to the lingering
power of such verbal taboos.

Be that as it may, in major pro sports, athletes have reversed the
taboo. Among pro players it is tabooed behavior not to use salty
words. Thus, an informant who employed words like "heck," "darn"
and "shucks" admidst all the curses and obscenities that purpled

the air was ridiculed by his mates. As a player once observed, "All athletes speak two languages—English and profanity," but he might have added that one better use the latter lest he be treated as a "wimp," "Jesus freak" or "goody two shoes."

Proficiency in profanity has long characterized baseball players. As Judge Landis observed during a hotly contested World Series match in the 1930s, "I learned from those young men such variations of the language even I didn't know existed." Half-heartedly Landis tried to curb foul language, but bench jockeys persisted. Still, there were limits; during the bitterly fought 1922 World Series, Babe Ruth invaded the Giants' locker room after a game and complained, "I don't mind being called a prick or a cocksucker or things like that .... But lay off the personal stuff." By that Ruth meant being called by the hated epithet, "Nigger lips." Such racist epithets reached crescendo proportions when Jackie Robinson and other black pioneers integrated the majors. Once settled in, however, black players gave as good as they got; as one player informant, recalling the 1950s, told me, the epithet "mother fucker" was a magic word, capable of bringing instant expulsion if heard by umpires. Likewise, gestures like thumbing one's nose (as Casey Stengel did to the Yankee bench during a World Series), giving the finger (as Gary Templeton recently gave to a St. Louis crowd), scratching crotches (a TV cameraman's nightmare), or spitting at crowds (as Ted Williams did to Boston fans) are heavily tabooed.

Constrained by the American taboo on such verbal behavior, yet forced to listen to such words has schizoid reporters using ellipses and bleeps in newspaper accounts, although books and magazines often quote the actual words. Not so with a physical education teacher I know. Whilst calling his class roll, he came across a Vietnamese student with the surname of Phuc; horrified by its pronunciation, he announced that henceforth he would address the student as "Puck," as in hockey puck! Of course sportscasters are the most muzzled of all. For example, Anglo-American norms bridle at the thought of kids named Jesus or Christ. Not so Hispanic parents who readily supply such names; thus, sportscasters slavishly pronounce shortstop Ivan de Jesus' name as E-von Day Hay-sus. Apparently the fear of offending deities is as strong as in the days of my youth when I learned that it was better to use the expression Jesus H. Christ. That, of course, is evasive, but in the matter of verbal evasions I have since followed W.C. Fields' lead. Fields once offered this advice to an unwanted caller: "Give him an evasive answer. Tell him to go fuck himself."

Among verbal taboo violators, bench jockeys risk rousing the ire of opponents. Indeed, in sports like tournament golf silence is the rule and such jockeying is unheard of. Likewise in tennis, although

John McEnroe is a notorious defier. Still, cursing or threatening umps **and** line judges is verboten and mocking an opponent is an awesome breach of decorum.

Still another behavioral taboo strikes at any disrespect during the playing of the National Anthem at sports spectacles. Woebetide the player who talks or picks his nose during this ritual. Even worse repercussions greeted Jose Feliciano's jazzed up version of the anthem while an NBA owner who tried to scuttle the ritual was anathematized.

High on the list of behavioral taboos in sports is cheating. Yet so much importance attaches to winning at all levels of play that cheating is widespread. Not surprisingly facilitating structures foster cheating, as illustrated by the recruiting scandals that perennially involve big time college and university coaches. Indeed, continuing allegations of illegal payments to football and basketball players in colleges recently led the American Council on Education to suggest "that one way out of the 'crisis' . . . would be for the major schools to pay athletes openly and not require them to be students."[4]

If recruiting violations are so widespread as to undercut the taboo, the same might be said of a taboo against bribing athletes to shave points in games. Back in 1951 this taboo was strong enough to anathematize three college basketball stars, and as recently as the early 1960s some pro football players were suspended for betting on games. Even today betting on sports is illegal in every state but Nevada. However, in 1981 the trial of a college basketball player accused of point-shaving stirred few shock waves; nor did a coach's conviction for defrauding the state of New Mexico by falsifying vouchers and using the money as a recruiting slush fund. As the judge in that case observed, "How fair is it to incarcerate . . . a coach who was basically doing what almost everybody in the community wanted him to do? Namely win basketball games at any cost."[5]

Still taboos on cheating refuse to down. During the 1982 baseball season a disgruntled catcher accused a Hispanic infielder of helping rival Hispanic players steal bases. It raised a mild stir, but in this case the accuser was ridiculed for being on unsound ground.[6] Nevertheless, such is the power of the taboo that cheaters suffer. Recipients of bribe money reportedly suffer pangs of conscience, and baseball players caught with doped bats or spitballs in hand, for all their bravado, feel guilty. So did a field hockey player who related the following incident. Tired of playing hockey, on a cold November day her teammates decided to throw the game and end the season. They did, but the coach chewed them out royally and excluded two conspirators from the next year's team.

Indeed, such is the force of the cheating taboo that one bucks it at one's peril. In baseball, memories of the Black Sox scandal and other scandals still exert a powerful constraining force on would-be cheaters. And lest one think that the cheating onus has disappeared from lesser pastimes, like friendly poker games, let him harken to Phil Harris' lyrics from " The Darkdown Poker Club":

> Now seated right there in that there clan, there chanced to be a one-eyed man ... old Bill kept watching him from the corner of his eye. Now old one eye was dealing then, and cost our Bill maybe five or ten, so Bill rose, looked all around with a sigh. Said he, lordy me it's an awful shame, but someone's cheating in this here game ... and if I catch him cheating just once again, I'm gonna take this big old fist and close that other eye!

Now that kind of backing still helps to support taboos on cheating!

Meanwhile other behavioral taboos are arbitrarily imposed on players and are potent enough to end careers. The natural human fate of growing old is the bugaboo of all athletes. To escape the onus of becoming 30 or 40, baseball players traditionally have lied about their age. This is harder to do now, so Pete Rose, who turned 41 in 1982, dyes his hair, affects a boyish hair style, hustles endlessly, and defiantly denies any waning powers:

> For those who think I'm old, I was the first 40-year old in the history of baseball to lead the league in hits in 1981. It doesn't matter how old you are, it's how old you play. That's what people don't understand. You can be 50 if you play like you're 30 .... Or you can be 30 and play like you're 60.[7]

Brave words those, but the fact remains that only seven 40-year olds played in the majors in 1982, and only Rose played every day. For many athletes, when the clock strikes 30, the aging taboo is potent enough to send them packing.

That sports are to be regarded as serious activity for all principals involved is evidenced by taboos against frivolity. For playing midget Eddie Gaedel, and for using zany giveaway gimmicks to lure fans, owner Veeck ran afoul of this taboo. Likewise, University of Texas basketball coach Abe Lemons' sprightly quips, like one proposing to end cheating in recruiting by rotating coaches, or another telling how he recruits at the Rio Grande River, choosing just the quick swimmers among the

Mexican wetbacks—those able to outdistance border patrol bullets! Sadly, when Lemons' team blew a promising season in 1981, he was fired.

Among pro athletes, bizarre behavior is an indulgence to be paid for. In baseball, fear of being labeled a "flake" or a "nut" keeps most in line. But Boston outfielder Jim Piersall's antics, such as appearing in the batter's box *sans* bat, running bases backwards, climbing backstops, hurling bats on the field, all made him a universal nut. Yet Piersall's antics were symptoms of a serious nervous disorder that eventually required long treatment. The root cause was held to be fear of failure. Because of a strong taboo against players showing their fears, Piersall's zaniness apparently was a displacement outlet that preceded a nervous breakdown. Doubtlessly many players still conceal surging fears, but only recently have clubs provided psychological services for players. Ironically, many players refuse to avail themselves of these (indeed, like American workers) for fear of being stigmatized. Seemingly, to be under psychiatric care is a taboo.

Any list of fears that beset pro athletes must include the fear of showing fear, fear of success, fear of injury, fear of being cut or traded, fear of failure on the playing field. That pro football players suffer heavily because of abundant talent waiting as replacements was recently revealed by a retired star. Pitifully vulnerable to peremptory dismissals, NFL players find themselves slavishly abiding taboos laid on by owners and coaches, including taboos on being overweight, on lack of speed, on lack of strength as measured by mechanical tests, on failing to show team spirit (such as refusing to play when hurt), on being seen as disloyal. The latter taboo has NFL players fearing to strike for better pay and job conditions lest they be sacked and blacklisted. And fear of harsh coaching judgments of one's game performance makes a fearful ritual of players gathering to watch weekly game films: "Every player is graded a plus or minus for every play. Some ... lose their jobs before the film ends." Of course, any wretch caught holding when his own running backs make a big gain, or caught jumping offside at a crucial moment, or fumbling during a drive, instantly becomes a tabooed person for his misdeeds. Indeed, the ability of coaches to cultivate a paranoid atmosphere and use fear to motivate player-behavior "is part of the mystique of football."[8]

As if coach-inspired fears were not enough, football players devise some of their own. Among some reported were taboos on saying that an upcoming game will be an easy one, allowing oneself to be carried off the field, crying or fouling the pre-game locker room air by crapping odors or farts.[9] True, some taboos reinforce a team's unity, like those calling for instant vengeance against rival players, as in hockey when a goalie (considered a mother figure) is run into by an opponent,[10] in football when the same happens to a punter or kicker, in baseball when an opposing pitcher hits a teammate with a pitch. A unique baseball taboo, that of forbidding any talk of a teammate pitcher's no-hitter in progress, certainly stirs unity. However, some taboos work to fragment team unity. One particularly vicious taboo involving scholastic basketball teams forbids any but starters to shed their warmup suits in pre-game drills. It would be unthinkable for a scrub to do the same; in this case the effect of this taboo is to create caste divisions between starters and scrubs. And in such an atmosphere *Schadenfrude* lurks.

Don't Let Your Schadenfrude Show!

This brief and tentative foray into American sporting taboos is fittingly concluded on the note of *Schadenfrude*. The word refers to one taking inordinate delight over the misfortunes and failings of others. Certainly this is a favorite indoor pastime of most Americans, and if we are to believe the words of the late German humorist Wilhelm Busch, "Schadenfrude is the best kind of frude!"

True enough, but a taboo on this behavior demands that one refrain from any overt expression of such joy; instead, one must mask joy behind hypocritical condolences and insincere sympathetic grimaces. While all competitive sports are rife with examples of players' practicing Schadenfrude, some by their very nature afford richer opportunities for such phoniness than others. Team bowling for one. Because there is no defense in bowling, when a member of a rival team misses a spare, or when a pin refuses to fall after a near-perfect hit, phoney expressions of sympathy conceal delight. And in many team sports players take Schadenfrudic delight at their own mates' failings. In basketball, where nowadays five men are likely to go the entire game, scrubs on the bench delight in seeing fouls accumulated by starters, or injuries strike them down; for such calamities maximize a scrub's chances of getting into the game.

Yet the taboo on Schadenfrude is strong; one must not let his Schadenfrude show, lest he be punished by social ostracism. One who paid that penalty was batting in a summer baseball game when his bid for a single bounced off the third baseman's face, enabling the batter to reach first base. While a sympathetic crowd gathered round the bleeding, prostrate infielder, the wretch on first base shouted joyously, "Was it a hit?"

For that graceless query, the boor was ridiculed and mocked. Hopefully he learned a lesson about the power of taboos to show the way to approved behavior. In and out of sports taboos serve to keep us in line socially, to housebreak us for main street, to remind us of overweening obligations to human groups upon which our very humanity depends. While lauding the wise and hoary words from the Epic of Gilgamesh which boldly declaim, "What men do is nothing, so fear is never justified," it is, nevertheless, the fears instilled by taboos that assure our social survival.

Notes

[1]David Q. Voigt, "The Fear of Farting," *Hustler*, July, 1977.
[2]Norman L. Farberow, ed., *Taboo Topics* (New York: Atherton Press, 1966), *passim*. William Graham Sumner, *Folkways* (New York: Mentor Books, 1960), pp. 477-514.
[3]Quoted in *New York Times*, May 15, 1978.
[4]*New York Times*, June 9, 1982.
[5]*Time*, Nov. 30, 1981.
[6]*New York Times*, June 25, 1982.
[7]*Reading Eagle*, April 7, 1982.
[8]Jean S. Fugett, Jr., "The Fear Factor in Pro Football's Contract Talks," *New York Times*, Sept. 5, 1982.
[9]Reported by Jack W. Berryman, Univ. of Washington, Seattle, Washington.
[10]Reported by Phil Berger, Member of the Society for American Baseball Research.
[11]Reported by Greg Holst, Albright College punter.

The examples from major league baseball are from the author's research notes, obtained from his work on three volumes of baseball history, entitled *American Baseball*, published by Pennsylvania State University Press, University Park, PA.

Breaking the Taboo of Sex and Adolescence: Children, Sex and the Media[1]

David Sonenschein

> For at least 10 or 15 years now, various newspapers and magazines have been promoting young girls between 9 and 17 as sex symbols or sexually tantalizing allure and veiled tinge of eroticism [sic], but in reality they are just children .... The public must feel *all* little girls are promiscuous .... Our adolescents have to be protected no matter what the cost .... Isn't it about time we adults put a stop to these crimes that promote an unnatural alluring reality? [letter to San Bernardino, California, *Sun*, Nov. 29, 1981]

This "unnatural reality" struck quite a number of people, and that phrase reflects the confusion, anger and fear felt by popular media producers and consumers alike. The relationship of children to sexuality—either externally as coming from adults, or, more controversially, their own internal sexual feelings—became important to the popular culture because of entertainment productions and advertisements, and through the selective designation of events, issues and viewpoints by the news media. Individual and organized reactions to these forces completed the makeup of a drama that is still evolving its cultural imagery.

The histories of children and sex are extensive and involve varying intensities of concern. Many of them are now fairly accessible, with perhaps the best documented crisis being that of the long and costly agony over masturbation which ranged from the early 18th century well into the middle of the 20th (Comfort 1967; Wrobel 1982). But from about 1975 into the present, journalists and professionals portray the subject of sex and children in near-apocalyptic terms as something very new and suddenly emerging, as having already spread throughout the culture (thanks to the mass media), and signalling the end of civilization. Surveys are made of media content, experts consulted or condemned, and key events and personalities designated as "beginnings" or "breakthroughs," after which one can see "floodgates opening" to inundate society. Indictments are written and blame directed by feminists to the oppressive patriarchy or by conservatives to the women's movement and moral permissiveness. Because of the centrality of the media, both sides attack "Hollywood" and "Madison Avenue." The reaction to kids and sex in the media has as its points that children are being fetishized, eroticized and corrupted by an external sexuality (Wolcott 1977; Connelly 1980; Rush 1980; O'Brien 1981; Winn 1981), and that the effect of this is to destroy the concept of childhood, damage the children and to subvert the sensibilities of society (Elkind 1981; Janus 1981; Postman 1982).

It will be fruitful to survey issues and images of children and sex and the reactions drawn forth indicating a cultural taboo. Many more representations of chidren's sexuality can be found but they have either gone unnoticed or have been accepted without much comment.

Ads, Models and Fashion

The most significant anchor for all reactions is to be found in the image of Brooke Shields. Both in film and advertisements, her presentations have crystalized widely shared and deeply felt concerns, and she has served as a focus for all the related anxieties that go along with sex in our society.

Shields was featured by fashion photographer Richard Avedon in a series of seven television ads for Calvin Klein jeans in 1980. Each ad had a distinctive set of postures and tag lines, the most famous being, "You want to know what comes between me and my Calvins? Nothing!" from the ad called "Feminist II" (Simpson 1981). The combination of implied intimacy from the tag lines and camera focus on her genitals and legs, along with her age (15), produced "a flood of viewer complaints about its suggestiveness" (Dougherty 1980). Two of the ads were banned and others shown only after nine in the evening by some stations. Other jeans companies used preteen models in similar ways. In a Jordache commercial, a 10-year-old girl "leans seductively toward a boy," and Bon-Jour jeans used a French-made commercial with children but cut some of the footage for American showings: "If I ran the full commercial, I'd be stoned," said a Bon-Jour Vice President (Salmans 1980). One journalist summarized the scene as "featuring 10-year-olds bumping narrow hips in discotheques, engaging in sexually suggestive dialogue and generally behaving in an unchildlike manner" (Salmans 1980).

Many merchandisers use preteen models in marketing their

products to preteen consumers. In 1980-81 five companies began a major push to sell cosmetics to 8 and 10-year-olds; one company had been selling them to 3-year-olds since 1975. A very negative reaction came from Action for Children's Television, but manufacturers stressed they were selling toys for play rather than makeup for training. Such items are officially classified by the industry as "toys"; a makeup kit called "Fresh 'n' Fancy" was one of the top selling toys of 1980 (Schiro 1981).

What was disturbing was not that very young children were being routed into American beauty rituals—they always have been from the standpoint of promoting beauty-as-health (Hope 1980), particularly in shampoo ads. People were disturbed because female children, previously taboo as asexual beings, were now being made a part of the iconography of feminity-as-sexual attractiveness. Earlier, Key (1976 , p. 55) cited a telephone company ad in which a 12-year-old girl was shown "in a sexually provocative posture"; he said citizen complaints caused the ad to be withdrawn. Florence Rush (1980, p. 125) was disturbed by an ad which carried the slogan, "Innocence is sexier than you think," along with a photo of a child or child-like model.

While there have always been child or "junior" models, they have been posed as traditional children within a realm of postures, costumes and cosmetics that ostensibly denied sexuality while it constructed the "presexual" attractiveness of Cute. If young teens were made to appear as adults, there were few if any overt expressions of sex, such as 15-year-old Carmen Dell'Orefice's 1947 *Vogue* cover (VerMeulen 1981).

Though some saw "the Sixties" as the beginnings of "Lolitaism,"[2] in fashion and entertainment (Bender 1967), many critics saw the late 1970s as "a new phenomenon—the coming of the make-believe adults" (Juffe & Haden-Guest 1980). The convergence of traditionally separate and equally sacred icons, the sexual woman and the innocent child, sharpened the "ambivalence about the relationship between the status of children and adults" (Bird 1980).[3] Some of this tension is relieved by humor, a natural response to incongruity. Wegman (1982) placed a pair of jeans on his now deceased dog and titled the photograph, "Brooke 1980."

Partially because of the short-lived children's liberation movement of the early 1970s, but more because of the severe critiques of educational and social relationships that have been carried well into the late 1970s, this feeling of unease spread to most adult-child relations. The ambivalence about sexuality came from images that simultaneously affirmed and denied children's

By permission of Johnny Hart and Field Enterprises, Inc.

sensuality. It was best expressed by Francesco Scavullo, a fashion photographer responsible for many of those very images: "their sex appeal is not sex at all [sic] ... they're nymphs and they have innocence too! And if it's decadent innocence, it's just that much more exciting!" (VerMeulen 1981).

Although there was a reluctance by some merchandisers to using preteens because of the sexual taboo, and some magazine editors doubted the "marketing efficiency" of eroticizing children (Juffe & Haden-Guest 1980), the "make-believe adults" continued to appear in ads throughout the period. Alarmed, reporters surveyed the girls active as models who were being featured with sensual attributes and their ages were given at the time of their professional fame: Bambi Black (15), Dina Meyer (12), Lena Reid (14), Kristine Alfonso (15) and Ingrid Chopping (14); the more well-known were Kristine Oulman (12), Cathleen Ess (13), Lisanne Faulk (14) and Tamara Jones (10). Those who were 16 were dismissed as "veterans" (Juffe & Haden-Guest 1980; Calixto 1980; White 1981; Winn 1981). So unnerving was the number of articles on transformed girls that a smaller number of counter-articles appeared on models who had retained their authentic (innocent) childhood (Steiger 1980; Anon., 1981a; Pratt 1982).[4] But, "despite a few yelps on the fashion scene," the industry and its media continued selling innocence "with a little cloud of scandal around it" (Skow 1981a).

Scandal was the word given to the efforts of publicist Tom Masters and the parents of Tina Payne who underwrote a series of five full page ads in show business trade papers during early November 1979. The ads carried a tag line meant to contrast with the visual image of Payne in which she appears much older and more sexual than one would expect from a 10-year-old. One photo showed her unclothed from the waist up, taken from the side with her hands covering her chest. Payne's mother was subsequently cited by Los Angeles City officials for "taking indecent photographs of a minor." The ads were said to be "pinup-style propaganda" (Jones 1980) or "controversial girlie pinup pictures" (Anon., 1981b). Young Payne herself, however, shrugged off criticism by reflecting, "well, nothing's showing, so it's really not a bad picture" (Eichel 1979; Brennan 1980). But the eroticism in these promotions implied to one critic that "this little girl might be fun to screw" (Kaye 1979). Kaye felt the willingness to use sexual tactics to enter the American Dream of Fame and Wealth meant that children are accepting of the monetary value of sex.

The whole idea of sensual photographs of children was the basic unease over the ads and movies. Nearly every such depiction has drawn forth labels of child pornography. Erotic photo studies of children as a form of popular art have a long history, ranging from Victorian times[5] to contemporary photographers. The most well-known presently is David Hamilton who has published seven books of sensual photos of young teen girls. All the books are still in print (and in paperback) and selling well; he has directed a similar movie, *Bilitis*. The success of his books (e.g., 1971; 1980) has perhaps inspired (some would say permitted) similar works by others (such as Angelo Cozzi [1977] or Marie Cosindas) although they have not limited their work to children.

One of the most noted instances of difficulty caused by such work was the case of photographer and teacher Jacqueline Livingston. She was fired from Cornell University because of publicity over her famous series of her son which included various nude and masturbatory poses. She then attempted to sell the prints by subscription, but her ads were refused by *Art in America, Ms., Playgirl,* and *Chrysalis* (a feminist art journal). She was subsequently investigated by New York authorities for "child abuse," and the *Village Voice*, in detailing her story and publishing the photos, was accused by the Director of the American Society for the Prevention of Cruelty to Children for printing "kiddie porn" (H. Smith 1979a; 1979b).

In the background still runs the image of Brooke Shields. Her first nude series was done when she was 10. The photographer, Gary Gross, said in the text to the pictures, "a littl girl often projects an identifiable sensuality" (1976, p. 36). She appeared "sensually posed" in controversial photos when she was 12 (*Esquire,* April 1977) and 13 (*Life,* Oct. 1978). A mass of articles have appeared, all trying to find the "real" Brooke Shields in an affirmation of the assumed dichotomy between sexuality and childhood (Skow 1981b). A series of anti-smoking ads from late 1981, in which she appears with cigarettes in her ears, was withdrawn because of Shields' "erotic image" (Daniels 1981). At that time, she and her mother were also involved in several highly publicized lawsuits to prevent the publication of her nude series. Her mother has become an accessory to her publicity with articles probing questions of maternal competence and parental permission (Goodman 1977; Leach 1981).

Fashion photographer Avedon accurately remarked that Shields "focuses the inarticulate rage people feel about the decline in contemporary morality and destruction of innocence in the world" (Peer 1981). This rage, however inarticulate, had been building for some time, and Shields was a focus for it even before her fashion modelling when in 1978 she played a preteen prostitute, at age 12, in the film *Pretty Baby*.

Film

Pretty Baby was preceded by *Taxi Driver* in 1976 in which Jodie Foster played a 12-year-old prostitute in a story context much grimmer than the almost romantic setting of *Pretty Baby*. There had been a great deal of pre-release publicity for *Pretty Baby*, but most of the reaction to it was put down as only "a mild outcry" (Skow 1979). Skow claimed the effect was to "clear the air so that the sexuality of the very young can be dealt with without the eye rolling formerly considered appropriate to the violation of a taboo." The two films, however, framed the 1977 sensationalistic height of public concern over child pornography, and for many, the two films not only represented but legitimized what they felt to be a definite trend.

As they did with fashion models, journalists inventoried young actresses who seemed to play roles with inappropriate sexuality, with ages again given: Diane Lane (13 in *A Little Romance*, a film about two young lovers); Mariel Hemingway (13 in *Lipstick*, a film involving rape), and "older" girls like Tatum O'Neal and Kristie McNichol (15 in *Little Darlings,* a story of a race between them to be the first to lose her virginity), as well as others with Shields and Foster.

Unchildlike behavior aroused the anxieties that usually surround sex, as did the films *Bad News Bears* and *Paper Moon* in which Tatum O'Neal does quite a bit of swearing at ages 12 and 9 respectively. The use of adult (and masculine) "obscene" language was meant to shock, to be sure, but it also played upon, consciously or not, the cultural assumptions that see an association between bad language and bad behavior, especially in the case of sex. It further played upon the traditional division between females as either "virgins" or "whores," an absolutism that allows only total innocence or total corruption. It is an assumption that makes possible the "evil child" genre of film and books. It was one of the most successful "evil child" films in fact that was a marker for the emergence of a "sexual child" genre. In *The Exorcist*, Linda Blair's preteen character is featured in a masturbation scene, a significant point of explicitness for children's sexuality in the film.

Some journalists gave the impression that kids were suddenly and without precedent being corrupted, but others excavated some of the lines leading to the current views. Most start with Mary Pickford who did her first film for D.W. Griffith when she was 16. Most agree her roles were "Victorian" in their purity, although Walker (1966) sees a sensuousness in her adolescent films, and Haskell says Pickford's child roles "were perhaps the first ... chapter of the American Lolita cult" (1974, p. 60). Griffith supposedly gathered a group of "nymphets" (Rosen 1973) for his films: Blanch Sweet (17), Lillian Gish (16), Dorothy Gish (14) and Mae Marsh (17). One of his most famous films is his most sexual. In *Broken Blossoms*, Lillian Gish at 23 played a 12-year-old who arouses the sexual interest of a Chinese man. Based on a classic of pedophile (and racist) fiction (Burke 1917), Rush (1980) condemns the film because it "evokes lust, murder, and suicide."[6]

The Lolita-line then runs directly from Pickford to Shirley Temple. Not exactly famous either for her sexual roles, she was seen as "one of the greatest vessels of virgin worship" (Haskell 1974, p. 123). One critic, however, thought Temple "may well be the most powerful sex symbol Hollywood has produced" (Goldstone 1980). That view had come up before. Graham Greene (1972) in his 1936 review of *Captain January* ascribed to her "a coquetry quite as mature as [Claudette] Colbert's and ... an oddly precocious body as voluptuous in gray flannel trousers as [Marlene] Dietrich's."

Critics of "Lolitaism" have neglected mention of *The Major and the Minor* in which Ginger Rogers plays a woman masquerading as a 12-year-old girl. In this disguise, she draws the romantic interest of the adult male hero. Billy Wilder claims he "had the first American movie about pedophilia" (Zolotow 1977, p. 107), but the film caused no real concern.

After WWII, "teen movies" became a more defined product, and the films could develop roles and actresses that shifted between "babyhood" and womanhood with varying degrees of sexuality. The bobby-soxer was the basis for the image of "saccharine, candy-brained, star-struck girl-children" (Rosen 1973, p. 241) in which *Gidget* and *Tammy* erased many of the differences between girls and women in a pejorative manner. The cultural view of women became structured by a complex of "virgin-pal-tomboy-child" characteristics (Malone 1977).

The other side of this complex contained the darker sexuality of the "whore-stranger-feline-adult" female. The image was present from the late 1950s onward, and it is the one that causes the most concern when applied to children. Carroll Baker's role in *Baby Doll* preceded the classic *Lolita*, played as a mid-teenager by Sue Lyon rather than the 12-year-old of the novel. There was reaction to these characters but there was also realization that they were adults playing child-like roles.

It was at this time that a variation on the child-woman character appeared in the image of Brigitte Bardot, publicized extensively as "the sex kitten." This version was something almost totally new to American audiences because it contained a much more positive and assertive young female sexuality than could be found among domestic creations. Roger Vadim's development of Bardot in *And God Created Woman* was, according to Simone de Beauvoir (1959), the reworking of the old "eternal feminine" icon into a new type of eroticism; the attraction was based on difference and distance rather than the familiar and accessible.

American film remained limited in possibilities and flat in character depth. Two main branches of the "dark sexuality" emerged when applied to the sexual potentials of children and young teens. One was the "evil child" imagery we have mentioned found in the occult and religion, or in horror/murder films such as *The Little Girl Who Lives Down the Lane*, all of which involve children's sexuality as dangerous or frightening. Rush claims (1980, p. 129) that the director of *Audrey Rose* purposely sought a "sensuous" 9-year-old to complete the role.[7]

The other branch of "dark sexuality" has been a full line of "troubled teen" movies. Wolcott (1977), for example, was concerned about the child character of Melanie Griffith in *The Drowning Pool* and *Night Moves*. Others include films with young teens tempted by drugs, sex and rock 'n' roll, the most recent example being *Christiane F*. The film is the greatest money-maker in German history (Freeman 1982), a part of a trend of young teen dropout movies. The story of a girl turning to prostitution at 13 to support her drug habit is actual biography, and the distributors brought the young woman to the United States for a promotional tour (Christiane F. 1982; Chute 1982). This country has produced its share of such films and actresses. Mackenzie Phillips, for example, has been cited for her "Lolita-like" roles and status as a "jaded teen," as in *Rafferty and the Gold Dust Twins*.

Two recent varieties of film have appeared that have generated some unease because they feature children's sexuality from a positive and supportive view. Some of them have had limited showings, such as the Danish film *You Are Not Alone*, which was forbidden by the Danish Board of Censors to be shown to kids under 12 in that country; that it featured homosexuality added to the alarm. Haskell (1976) has doubts about the "fiction-documentary," *A Child is a Wild Young Thing*, featuring an erotic relationship between a mother and her son. Similar doubts were felt by McBride (1977) about Dyan Cannon's *Number One* which dealt with children's sexuality as play rather than the anxious eroticism more familiar to adults. A number of others have been released, but critics have tried to be understanding, made easier perhaps because they have mostly been foreign films dealing with early sexuality such as *The Devil's Playground*, *L'Adolescent* or *Pixote*.

American films of that nature have had harsher receptions, such as *Little Darlings*, *Foxes* with Jodie Foster, and of course Brooke Shields in *Blue Lagoon*. There was an effort in this latter film to raise the age of sexual involvement into the mid and late teens, and in the publicity, care was taken to both advertise the nudity and to brag about the precautions taken to preserve the personal integrity of Shields: she wore flesh-colored pasties with her hair literally glued over her nipples, and 33-year-old Kathy Trout did her nude scene. Despite all this, she and her co-star (Christopher Atkins) were perceived as children with appropriate negative reactions (McMurran 1980).

The other recent variety has a few roots in previous films; these feature sexual relationships between children and adults, and they too tend to be more sympathetic than has been the case in the past.[8] Goldstein and Zornow (1980) deny a sexual element between a 10-year-old girl and a man in the older *Tiger Bay*, but they say there is definitely some kind of "attraction," one similar perhaps to the one in the relationship in *Circle of Two* with Tatum O'Neal as a 16-year-old involved with a 66-year-old man. Despite some doubts about the whole thing, Boyum (1982) thinks *The Nest* is an accurate depiction of a 13-year-old girl's relationship with a middle-aged man. Stone (1980) generally likes *In A Wild Moment* even though the characters go "outside the 'proper' parameters of desire." *Nea* features a girl's assertive and self-possessed sexuality by which she writes an erotic novel and has an affair with the man who publishes it. Ann Zacharias' 16-year-old character got attention from the "men's" magazines (she was referred to as a "nymphet" in *Playboy*), and reviewer Williams (1979) classed her as a "Lolita type."

A film that received much more attention was *Beau Pere* in which Ariel Besse plays a 14-year-old involved with an older ("29 ½") man. Rainer (1981) lumps the film along with *Lolita* and *Manhattan*, and he is very unsympathetic to director Bertrand Blier's "fixations." Ariel is a French schoolgirl and her mother, in a move similar to Brooke Shield's mother, tried to prevent the display of a French promotional poster showing Ariel bare-breasted (Eder 1982).

A minor side of child-adult films are those in which an older woman becomes sexually involved with a younger male. *Get Out Your Handkerchiefs* was called "one of the first films about an older woman who falls madly in love with a [13-year-old] man-child" (Farber 1979). The well-received film bears similarity to a situation in France in which a woman teacher took a 15-year-old lover (one of her students). She was heavily and repeatedly prosecuted by the state for "corrupting the morals of a minor," and was ultimately driven to suicide by the harassment. It became a popular cause in France, especially among feminists, and a film was made, released in this country as *To Die of Love*. In *Private Lessons*, a 14-year-old boy is given sex instructions by an older woman. The film was rated R which prevented many boys the same age as the film's hero from seeing the movie, although personal observations indicate the film was well attended by boys of that age.

That restriction was because the effect of sex in film on children is a long standing concern. Beginning in the early 1900s, children were the first class of people to be prohibited from seeing films thought to be "immoral" or "obscene" (McCarthy 1976). The anxieties were well maintained by the Legion of Decency, founded in 1934, and by a 1936 encyclical from Pope Pius XI which spoke of "the loss of innocence ... suffered in motion picture theaters" (DeGrazia & Newman 1982, p. 46). The early 1930s held intense interest in the effects of sex on children's morals (Goldberg & Goldberg 1935). The Payne Fund studies produced thirteen books (Charters 1933) reminiscent of the Commission on Obscenity and Pornography of the late 1960s. The researchers interviewed "delinquent teenage girls all of whom admitted truancy from school to see movies," and found, to the shock of a nation, that 48% felt like making love after seeing a "sex movie," and 40% actually did invite men to make love to them after seeing the films (Blumer & Hauser 1933), pp. 222, 232).

Television has long since replaced movies as a center of concern, largely because many feel the rating system to be somewhat effective as a filter, and because for many years the TV set was a kind of family altar and children had easy and immediate access to the programming. It was not until the late 1970s that sex on TV was to be investigated for it was not until then that sex became a real presence. Sprakfin & Silverman (1982) see the 1977 prime-time sitcom *Soap* as the start of "a new era of sex on television." They found "serious" references to sex increased from 2 per week in 1975 to 77 per week in 1978. One can now better understand the formation of such groups as Morality in Media and the Coalition for Better TV.

Many were concerned with the kinds of information children would obtain from TV's sexual allusions, especially given the sensationalism over a "taboo" subject. In a recent survey, parents were concerned that their children would become curious about sex and either ask "unanswerable" or "inappropriate" questions, or would experiment with sex (Sprafkin, Silverman & Rubenstein 1980). It is for these reasons the National Association of Broadcasters' Code still prohibits commercials for contraceptives. The possibility of imitative behavior is one of the greatest fears. The Los Angeles County Commission on Obscenity and Pornography was worried that a projected TV series, *Paper Dolls* (a spin-off from the TV movie), about two 16-year-old models might turn into a "junior jiggles" show and would make "countless" girls run away from home searching for TV and movie parts only to end up in child pornography (Anon., 1982a).

The most famous example of TV imitation involved the NBC made-for-TV film *Born Innocent*. Linda Blair played a 14-year-old prison inmate who is raped by other girl inmates using a wooden implement. It aired in 1974 on prime-time and because of Blair's recent appearance in *The Exorcist*, it was preceded by a good deal of publicity. Within a week, a preteen girl was similarly raped by several teenage girls, one of whom said she got the idea from watching *Born Innocent*. The event prompted the National Association of Broadcasters and the Federal Communications Commission to devise the "Family Viewing Hour" in 1975, an agreement not to broadcast sexual material up till 9 P.M., and to carry viewer warnings on "doubtful" material after that time (Cole 1981).

Fallen Angel, a TV movie about pedophilia and child pornography, was the second most watched film of the September 1980-August 1981 period according to *Variety*. Conceived in early 1979 by writer and co-producer Lew Hunter, the film received raves from viewers, journalists, police departments, academics, citizen groups and others. Although some referred to the visceral reactions viewers might have, such as "stomach-wrenching" or "makes your skin crawl" (C. Smith 1981), the film was hailed as a "landmark" and "the most extreme test thus far of the tolerance of viewers nation-wide to accept taboo subjects in their homes" (DuBrow 1981). In Arizona, there was considerable debate over its appropriate showing time, and it was pre-screened to "religious and community leaders" and prefaced with an editorial to "warn viewers" (Wilkinson 1981).

The network did not balk at the suggestion of a film on child pornography when Hunter was asked if he had anything "hot."[9] Production was careful to avoid "unnecessary elements"; when the film was shown to the network for final review, no changes were made. Asked if he would have added anything to the film, Hunter said, "I would like to have had a section where I could show the media sensuality [around us] ... because we have gotten into the Brooke Shields era where most of the models have that baby-doll look about them." Dana Hill, then 16, was selected to play a 13-year-old because she looked the part. Hunter said, however, "she had none of the Brooke Shields-Linda Blair kittenish quality" (S. Smith 1981). Another instance of TV imitation came in the wake of the film when one month later four girls reported a man who had allegedly "taken indecent liberties." Police said, "We believe the film was responsible for the [arrest]" (Anon., 1981c).

Radio and stage are other media recently involved in the taboos of children and sex. Comedian George Carlin was accused of corrupting the morals of the 13-year-old son of a Morality in Media member when the boy heard Carlin's famous "Seven Dirty Words" monologue (DeGrazia & Newman 1982, p. 48). Anything dealing with homosexuality may be taboo. John Zeh, host of a Cincinnati radio show for gays, was charged with "disseminating materials harmful to juveniles" when he broadcast a satire of sexual lubricants (Clark 1982).

Rebecca Saire played Juliet when she was 14, the same age as Shakeseare's heroine. However, she felt stifled by the director of the filmed play, broadcast over Public Television. "He stamped on my efforts to make the girl more sexually aware .... I wanted to play the child-woman and wasn't allowed," she said (Anon., 1979).

The best-known reaction against children's sexuality in the theatre came with Edward Albee's adaptation of *Lolita*. The play's producer, Jerry Sherlock, toured parts of the country "looking for an 11-year-old who really knows what's going on in the world" (Knoedelseder 1980); ads in the trade papers said "none over 13 need apply." Sherlock said "the role will involve ... plenty of overt sexuality," with some on-stage nudity and, according to an article by Richard Goldstein (1980), there would be "at least a hint of fellatio."

It was this article by Goldstein and the release of Florence Rush's book that year that brought a number of activists in the New York Women Against Pornography (WAP) to protest "the Lolita Syndrom" found throughout the media (Leidholdt 1981). The role of Lolita was finally given to 24-year-old Blanch Baker, and Albee observed that "there were no nymphets ... very few of [the girls] understood the sexual implications of the role" (Leidholdt 1981). WAP's news conference in early 1981 was widely publicized nation-wide (Klemesrud 1981); the opening night the play was picketed by them and this also was widely publicized. A member of WAP noted, "there is only one color fashion advertisement in the *Lolita* playbill. It is a Brooke Shields-Calvin Klein Jeans ad. How fitting" (Sporn 1981).

Books

Concern about books and their influence can be over the visuals, as with Holt's worry (1982) about Brooke Shields' picture autobiography (1982), or the praising of young teen models (Cameron 1979). But most of the attention has been directed at "junior" novels. While there is some disagreement over their origin and age range of readership, Freemont (1980) quotes a bookseller as saying that "true readers" among 12-year-olds are reading "adult" novels, including those with sexual content.

Perhaps Richardson's *Pamela* (1740) established the icon of the "innocent as hostage" (Savage 1978) and typified the emphasis still to be found on extreme youth, total inexperience, dangerous vulnerability and complete asexuality. The form we are most familiar with seems to have been solidified in the 1930s as formula writing aimed at specific audiences (Stanek 1973). Later significant points of violation of the sexual taboos came with Betty Smith's *A Tree Grows in Brooklyn* and Salinger's *Catcher in the Rye*. Even though the "Sixties" were blamed for a sexual revolution, little of that appeared in junior novels until the early 1970s when "an explosion of realism" (Harvey 1982) brought sex among the young to the mass of preteen readers.

The start of these explorations of heterosexual and homosexual experiences is usually given to Zindel's *My Darling, My Hamburger* and Donovan's *I'll Get There. It Better Be Worth the Trip.* They attracted a good deal of attention because they brought into the junior novel, even if only at the level of mere mention, such topics as body awareness and development, abortion and varieties of sexual feelings and experiences. Many kept the sex on a more emotional than physical plane, but a 200 year tradition of realism pushed sex into explicitness (Carlsen 1980). For many, it was too much too soon, and they laid the blame for this directly at the feet of Judy Blume.

At the height of concern over kids and sex, Maynard (1979) counted over six million copies of Blume's books in print. Her impact and popularity was because she wrote plainly and directly (and well) for young readers of the social, emotional and physical events with which they were involved. Her book *Then Again Maybe I Won't* (20 printings by late 1980) deals with a 13-year-old boy faced with a pal's shoplifting, involved in watching a girl neighbor undress, and experiencing wet dreams. *Are You There God? It's Me, Margaret* (30 printings by late 1980) caused greater concern because its 12-year-old heroine simultaneously doubts her religion and breast development and begins menstruation.

Her most explicit book aimed at late teens, *Forever*, features an 18-year-old who has her first intercourse and tries to sort out love and sex. Harvey (1982) says this book "blew the lid off," and throughout the 1970s explicit sex could be found in novels for readers who were classed as children by the culture. Even when Blume wrote an "adult" book, *Wifey*, her young readers followed her name rather than marketing boundaries and many young people shared the book's humorous sexual adventures.

Fremont (1980) quotes figures from *American Bookseller* showing that juvenile paperbacks rose in sales 850% from 1971 through 1977; many if not most were aimed at girls aged 11 to 14, "an extraordinarily susceptible audience," says Harvey (1982). In reviewing one of the earlier "explicit" novels, Frank (1973) says of Stirling's *You Would If You Loved Me* that "if [the reader] identifies with the girl in the story, she is led to a very high point of sexual stimulation." Worries of this sort over books and magazines (Sonenschein 1972) are a cultural tradition.

The most famous historical protector of the young against popular media sex was Anthony Comstock. His books (1883) and police tactics earned him the memorial term "Comstockery." More recently a book with a similar title appeared by the psychiatrist Fredic Wertham (1954). His protests over the association of sex and violence (which he called "sexism") in comics earned him a resurrection in the 1970s. He felt children needed to be protected from "harmful influences," and that "comic books stimulate children sexually . . . sexual arousal amounts to seduction" (p. 175).

Because this view of sex and children has been maintained by journalists and the psychological and social work professions, the concerns range beyond the mass media because many assume that sex in the media can be causally connected to child pornography, child prostitution, incest, abortion, child neglect and battering, divorce, runaways, drug and alcohol use, murder of children and even lack of school prayer. With this sense of social and moral collapse, fanned by sensationalistic coverage, especially in popular women's magazines (Signori 1980), it is no wonder that many books found themselves being banned and burnt.

The burnings have been spectacular, and were meant to be. This history has been a long one, the most recently memorable event being the burning of six tons of Wilhelm Reich's writings by the United States Government in 1956. The newer burnings can be said to have started in the early 1970s when the Drake, North Dakota, School Board burned Vonnegut's *Slaughterhouse Five* for being "profane." In mid-1982, Jerry Renner, Director of the Religious News Service, said that burnings had been "so commonplace in the last five years that we don't report them anymore unless there's some unusual twist" (Cass 1982).

A more common reaction has been the censoring of books. Jenkinson (1979) reports that during the 1977-78 school year, "more incidents of removing or censoring books occurred nationally than at any other time in the last 25 years."

The fear of sexual corruption by the media (now often called "psychological abuse" [Levin 1973] or "stress" [Miller 1982]) has always been the rationale for censorship and the protection of children. However, Davis (1979, p. x) says "censorship in the schools in the 1970s represents something new in degree and kind." Targets are not so much "dirty books" as has usually been the case, but now are "entire courses, teaching methods, entire programs, and educational philosophies" (Jenkinson 1979, p. 2). Criteria for banning have included "trash" (almost any contemporary junior novel), realistic dialogue, accounts of "harsh realities,"[10] homosexuality, sex education and suggestive titles.[11] One of the most famous cases occurred when the Long Island, New York, Island Trees School Board banned nine books in 1976 for being "anti-American, anti-Christian, anti-Semitic, and just plain filthy." After six years of court battles, the books were ordered returned to the shelves (Press 1982). Feeling that "nudity is wrong," the children's librarian in Caldwell Parish, Louisiana, painted diapers on the nude hero of Sendak's (1970) *In the Night Kitchen* (Harvey

1973). Palo Alto High School officials banned one of V.C. Andrews' famous books (1980) because of its young teen incest theme (Anon., 1981d). The Warsaw (Indiana) *Times-Union* excerpted *Go Ask Alice* (Anon., 1971a), and apologized for the "dirty, filthy, vulgar language," but said that people had to know what schoolchildren were being exposed to (Jenkinson 1979, pp. 12f).

The health book *Our Bodies, Ourselves* (Boston Collective 1976) was banned from a number of schools and public libraries. The Attorney General of Montana, banning the book following a complaint by Phyllis Shalfley's Eagle Forum, said it "commits the offense of endangering the welfare of children by assisting, promoting or encouraging a child to engage in sexual conduct" (Jenkinson 1979, pp. 36f). Several states have attempted similar legislation, the most recent being New York where a bill has been introduced to make it a crime of conspiracy "to promote, engage in, or cause the performance of sexual conduct" between someone over 18 and someone under 17. While expressly an anti-pedophile bill, if passed the law would also make it a crime to advocate in print *any* sex involving children (Nelson 1983). The impetus for this came from the unprecedented and unanimous Supreme Court ruling that "certain depictions of sexual activity involving children" are now outside the protections of the First Amendment—despite an admission of a possible "chilling" effect (Kaufman 1982).

Such in fact occurred with the well-known and much-banned sex education book *Show Me!* (McBride & Fleischhauer 1975). An earlier version (Goldstein, Haeberle & McBride 1971) received only mild reaction (Anon., 1971b), but St. Martins Press removed *Show Me!* from distribution in late 1982 because they and their booksellers became open to criminal charges in 20 states.

Many have felt something fundamental to have happened in the culture in the last ten years, but others have their doubts. No "new Liberalism" was seen in an early evaluation of junior novels. "What *is* there is the Old Morality disguised as New Sex ... those who are pregnant are sorry; those who might have been homosexual, go straight; [and] those who are promiscuous are guilty" (Wersba 1973). The ferocity of the reaction to mixing children and sex has had the effect of returning junior novels to more traditional views—ironically at a time when "adult" romance novels (often read by young girls) are becoming more sexually explicit (Thurston, n.d.). Harvey (1982) quotes the editor of Grosset & Dunlap's *Caprice* junior novel series: "there's no development of sexuality because the readers are too young and we don't want to alienate the adult community." Children have been returned to the realm of the innocent, and any sexual influences come only from the outside. Correspondingly, the reaction against "Lolitaism" of the late 1970s has turned in the early 1980s to an increasing prosecution of pedophilia, defined only as sexual abuse. Pedophiles (and pedophiles-as-pornographers) have replaced the homosexual as the culture's most insidious corrupter of youth.

Judith Krantz (1983), in trying to finish off the remaining reaction to children's sexuality in the media, says it was not the advertising industry or its photographers that "infuriated" people. It was the innate sensuality of Brooke Shields. The female body has been "desensualized" she says, and we will not see the likes of "Lolitaism" again. The taboos of the media have held: "no matter how [a model] is encouraged to pout and posture in a stylized manner, any truly erotic vibration is just as unwelcome as it ever was. Nothing has changed."

Notes

[1] I am indebted to Richard Bishop and David Lane Smith for research assistance, and to others who helped: Will and Linda Palantiri, Valida Davila, Steve Mullins and Dorchen Leidholdt. I have emphasized popular articles as references because they are as important as artifacts as the media they are writing about; many of them also contain illustrations of the ads and films discussed here.

[2] "Lolitaism," the sexual precociousness of preteen and young teen girls, comes from the name of the character in Nabakov's novel. His book distilled a traditional erotic interest into a cultural category and institution. The importance of the concept deserves a more detailed history and analysis of its varieties than can be done here.

[3] Without going into detail, several other images need to be mentioned because they constitute part of the environment that helped erode the fixity of the concept of childhood and they added to the sexual anxieties surrounding it. There were several news items in 1981-82 about 10 to 12-year-olds becoming pregnant. The most publicized involved a 12-year-old who sought a court-ordered abortion because the pregnancy was the result of an alleged rape. The abortion was denied, and the girl later was charged in court with the emotional neglect of her baby.

Another series in 1982 talked about females in general reaching puberty earlier, a decline in age at menarche consistent over the last 150 years. A variety of this story type featured cases of idiopathic precocious puberty, a syndrom where both genders may develop "sexual characteristics" as early as age 2 or 3.

Perhaps the most striking series was the wide publicity given to two boys and one girl in 1981-82 who had progeria, the premature aging disease. Photos of the boys were widely circulated adding to the emotional impact.

[4] A related area not included here is the similar dialectic of alarm and affirmation surrounding the worlds of child beauty contests.

[5] Ovenden & Melville (1972) cite Lewis Carroll, Oscar G. Rejlander (an influence on Carroll), Julia M. Cameron ("the finest woman photographer during the 19th century"), and others who did erotic studies of children. Photos of children having sex appeared in some bulk in the late 1800s, then decreased until nearly a century later when they reemerge in the early 1970s in a number of films, photos and magazines.

[6] In the absence of specification, there may be various estimates of the age (and presumably degree of eroticism) of a female heroine. Wagenknecht & Slide (1975, pp. 131f) say the girl in *Broken Blossoms* is really 15, and they feel there is more eroticism in the story (where she is 12) than in the film. Some of these estimates are a function of historically variable perceptions of children's sexual capabilities, i.e., whether they are seen to be innocent/unable or corrupt/able.

As for *Broken Blossoms*, part of the shock adding to the "eroticism" has been lost to us today. In 1919, the country was still muttering about the non-white immigrants who came in great numbers late in the 19th century. Anger against "The Yellow Peril" (which included a sexual fear) was fed significantly by one of the greatest of racist agitators, Samuel Gompers, himself an immigrant Jew (Hill 1973).

[7]Rush uses the word "sensuous" indicating it came from an interview with director Robert Wise (Shay 1977). In the interview, however, there is no use of the word, nor any indication that Wise intended the role to have an erotic dimension.

[8]Another "discourse" popular in the late 1970s contributing to the unease over the relative status relations of adults and children involved the question of cross-generational relationships; the subject was brought up in a number of magazine articles and books and in some films. Because this involved only adults with other adults (people in their 20s in sexual relationships with people in their 60s for example), it cannot be detailed here.

[9]Interview with Lew Hunter, July 1981. All subsequent unreferenced quotes are from this interview.

[10]Books about young teens and children involved with drugs and prostitution have become a genre in themselves (those cited, plus Lloyd 1976; Greller 1976), but students the same ages have been prevented from reading them as popular literature or social studies. Winn (1981) is disturbed that Arrick's (1978) book about a 14-year-old addict/prostitute is being read by 10 and 12-year-olds.

[11]Jenkinson (1979, p. 82) reports that *Making it With Mademoiselle* was to be banned from a school library until it was discovered that it was a sewing pattern book.

References

Andrews, Virginia C. *Pedals in the Wind.* New York: Pocket Books, 1980.

Anonymous. *Go Ask Alice.* Englewood Cliff, Prentice-Hall, 1971a.

Anonymous. "The Sex Book." *Newsweek,* May 17, 1971b.

Anonymous. "Lookout—A Guide to the Up and Coming." *People,* March 12, 1979.

Anonymous. "Child Model, 9, A Sensation with Everyone—Even Dad." *National Star,* Nov. 3, 1981a.

Anonymous. "Nymphet Tina Is Set For TV Plunge." *The Star,* March 24, 1981b.

Anonymous. " 'Fallen Angel' Spurs 4 Girls To Report Abuse To Police." Austin *American-Statesman,* March 10, 1981c.

Anonymous. "Palo Alto High Bans 'Incest' Book." San Francisco *Chronicle,* Dec. 23, 1981d.

Anonymous. "Obscenity Groups Keeps An Eye on 'Paper Dolls'." Austin *American-Statesman,* June 13, 1982a.

Arrick, Fran. *Steffie Can't Come Out To Play.* New York, Bradbury, 1978.

Beauvoir, Simone de. *Brigitte Bardot and the Lolita Syndrome.* London, Deutsch, Weidenfield & Nicholson, 1959.

Bender, Marylin. *The Beautiful People.* New York, Coward-McCann, 1967.

Bird, Frederick. "The Contemporary Ritual Milieu," in *Rituals and Ceremonies in Popular Culture,* ed. Ray B. Browne. Bowling Green, Oh., Popular Pres, 1980.

Blume, Judy. *Are You There God? It's Me, Margaret.* New York, Dell, 1970.

Blume, Judy. *Then Again Maybe I Won't.* New York, Dell, 1971.

Blume, Judy. *Forever.* New York, Bradbury, 1975.

Blume, Judy. *Wifey.* New York, Pocket Books, 1978.

Blumer, Herbert and Philip Hauser. *Movies, Delinquency and Crime.* New York, Macmillan, 1933.

Boston Women's Health Collective, *Our Bodies, Ourselves.* New York, Simon & Schuster, 1976.

Boyum, Joy. "Obsessions of a Strange Kind." *Wall Street Journal,* August 13, 1982.

Brennan, Peter. "Daring Advertising Blitz Turns Tiny Tot Tina Into a Hollywood Sensation ... At Age 10." *The Star,* Jan. 8, 1980.

Burke, Thomas. "The Chink and the Child," in *Limehouse Nights.* New York, McBride, 1917.

Calixto, Judy. " 'Pretty Baby' Craze Is Turning Preteen Girls into Sexy-Looking Wealthy Models." *The Star, Nov. 11, 1980.*

Cameron, Betsy. *Lisanne: A Young Model.* New York, Clarkson Porter, 1979.

Carlsen, G. Robert. *Books and the Teenage Reader.* New York, Harper & Row, 1980.

Cass, Julia. "Book Bonfires Rage in the South, West." Houston *Chronicle*, July 3, 1982.

Charters, W.W. *Motion Pictures and Youth: A Summary.* New York, Macmillan, 1933.

Christiane F. *Christiane F.: Autobiography of a Child of the Streets and Heroin Addict.* New York, Bantam, 1982 (German original 1978).

Chute, David. "A Harrowing Tale of Wasted Youth." Los Angeles *Herald-Examiner*, Feb. 26, 1982.

Clark, Jil. "Ohio Court Upholds Dismissal of Charges Against Gay Broadcaster." *Gay Community News.* Jan. 22, 1982.

Cole, Barry. "Introduction: Censorship and Control." in *Television Today: A Close-Up View.* New York, Oxford, 1981.

Comfort, Alex. *The Anxiety Makers.* New York, Delta, 1967.

Comstock, Anthony. *Traps for the Young.* New York, Funk & Wagnalls, 1883.

Connelly, Sherryl. "Eroticization Of Children: Facts of Life." San Francisco *Examiner/Chronicle*, May 25, 1980.

Cozzi, Angelo. *Innocence in the Mirror.* New York, Morrow, 1977.

Daniels, Graham. "Why Brooke Won't Give Up Battle to Ban Those Nude Photos." *Globe*, Dec. 1, 1981.

Davis, James E., ed. *Dealing with Censorship.* Urbana, National Council of Teachers of English, 1979.

DeGrazia, Edward and Roger Newman. *Banned Films: Movies, Censors and the First Amendment.* New York, Bowker, 1982.

Donovan, John. *I'll Get There. It Better Be Worth The Trip.* New York, Harper & Row, 1969.

Dougherty, P. "Sultry Jeans Ad Banned By WABC-TV, WCBS-TV." New York *Times*, Nov. 20, 1980.

DuBrow, Rick. " 'Angel'—A TV Landmark." Los Angles *Herald-Examiner*, Feb. 22, 1981.

Eder, Richard. "Kiddie Sex: When Art Becomes Exploitation." San Francisco *Chronicle*, Jan. 10, 1982.

Eichel, Larry. "A 10-Year-Old's Drive To Be A Star." San Francisco *Examiner-Chronicle*, Dec. 2, 1982.

Elkind, David. *The Hurried Child.* Reading, Addison-Wesley, 1981.

Farber, Stephen. "What Does a Woman Want?" *New West*, Feb. 12, 1979.

Freeman, Patricia. "The Real Christine F. Talks Of A Past With No Future." Los Angeles *Herald-Examiner*, Feb.26, 1982.

Fremont, Lora. " 'Nancy Drew and The Case of the Bisexual Gynecologist'." *Los Angeles*, August 1980.

Goldberg, Jacob and Rosamund Goldberg, *Girls on City Streets.* New York, American Social Hygiene Association, 1935.

Goldstein, Martin, Erwin Haeberle and Will McBride, *The Sex Book.* New York, Herder & Herder, 1971.

Goldstein, Richard. "Kids Do The Darndest Things." *Village Voice*, Sept. 24, 1980.

Goldstein, Ruth and Edith Zornow. *The Screen Image of Youth: Movies About Children and Adolescents.* Metuchen, Scarecrow, 1980.

Goldstone, Patricia. "Hollywood's 'Little Girls' ... and Sex." Los Angeles *Times*, March 9, 1980.

Goodman, Joan. "Pretty Baby." *New York*, Sept. 26, 1977.

Greene, Graham. *Graham Greene on Film.* New York, Dell, 1976.

Greller, Joyce. *Young Hookers.* New York, Dell, 1976.

Gross, Gary, et al., *Sugar and Spice.* Chicago, Playboy Press, 1976.

Hamilton, David. *Dreams of a Young Girl.* New York, Morrow, 1971.

Hamilton, David. *David Hamilton's Private Collection.* New York, Morrow, 1980.

Harvey, Brett. "Boy Crazy—How Far Can You Go In A Teen Romance?" *Village Voice*, Feb. 10-16, 1982.
Harvey, James. "Acting For The Children?" in *Issues in Children's Book Selection*, ed., L. Gerhardt. New York, Bowker, 1973.
Haskell, Molly. *From Reverence to Rape*. New York, Holt, Rinehart & Winston, 1974.
Haskell, Molly. "Kids Are Hot Again." *Village Voice*, Nov. 1, 1976.
Hill, Herbert. "Anti-Oriental Agitation and the Rise of Working Class Racism." *Society*, Feb. 1973.
Holt, Patricia. "Lolita As Role Model." San Francisco *Chronicle*, Dec. 27, 1982.
Hope, Christine. "American Beauty Rituals." in *Rituals and Ceremonies in Popular Culture*, ed. Ray Browne. Bowling Green, Oh., Popular Press, 1980.
Janus, Sam. *The Death of Innocence*. New York, Morrow, 1981.
Jenkinson, Edward. *Censors in the Classroom*. Carbondale, Southern Illinois Univ. Press, 1979.
Jones, Tamara. "Groomed for Stardom: A Child Actress' Story." Santa Ana *Register*, August 3, 1980.
Juffe, Mel and Anthony Haden-Guest. "Pretty Babies." *New York*, Sept. 29, 1980.
Kaufman, Henry. "Supreme Court's Unanimous Ax Falls on 'Child Pornography'." *Newsletter on Intellectual Freedom*, Sept. 1982.
Kaye, Elizabeth. "Year of the Child." *New West*, Dec. 17, 1979.
Key, Wilson. *Media Sexploitation*. Englewood Cliffs, Prentice-Hall, 1976.
Klemesrud, Judy." 'Lolita Syndrome' Prompts Women's Group To Action." Los Angeles *Herald-Examiner*, March 4, 1981.
Knoedelseder, William. "The Manhunt is on for 'Lolita'." Los Angeles *Times*, Sept. 12, 1980.
Krantz, Judith. "Are Models Sexier Today?" *Parade*, Jan. 2, 1983.
Leach, Robin. "Why I Let Brooke Pose in The Nude—By Her Mother." *Globe*, Oct. 27, 1981.
Leidholdt, Dorchen. "Women Against Pornography Protests 'The Lolita Syndrome': Anatomy of an Action." *WAP Newsreport*, Spring/Summer, 1981.
Levin, Alan. "Impressionable Minds—Forbidden Subjects," in *Issues in Children's Book Selection*, ed., L. Gerhardt. New York, Bowker, 1973.
Lloyd, Robin. *For Money or Love*. New York, Ballantine, 1976.
Malone, Michael. "Will America's Sweetheart Grow Up?" *Human Behavior*, Dec. 1977.
Maynard, Joyce. "Coming of Age With Judy Blume." New York *Times*, Dec. 3, 1978.
McBride, Joseph. "Childhood's Innocence Getting Lost? Teen Harlots, Perverts in Scripts." *Variety*, Feb. 9, 1977.
McBride, Will and Helga Fleishhauer-Hardt. *Show Me! A Picture Book of Sex for Children and Parents*. New York, St. Martins, 1975.
McCarthy, Kathleen, "Nickel Vice and Virtue: Movie Censorship in Chicago." *Journal of Popular Film* 5 (1976), pp. 37-55.
McMurran, Kristin. "Blue Lagoon's Brooke Shields and Chris Atkins Cruise Into Yet Another Furor Over Kiddie Porn." *People*, August 11, 1980.
Miller, Mary. *Childstress!* Garden City, Doubleday, 1982.
Nabakov, Vladimir. *Lolita*. Paris, Olympia Press, 1955.
Nelson, Bob. "Anti-NAMBLA Law Prompted by New Group." *Gay Community News*, Feb. 26, 1983.
O'Brien, Patricia. "Dope, Sex, Crime, What Happened to Childhood?" Chicago *Tribune*, March 8, 1981.
Ovenden, Graham and Robert Melville, *Victorian Children*. New York, St. Martins, 1972.
Peer, Elizabeth. "The Two Faces of Brooke." *Newsweek*, Feb. 9, 1981.
Postman, Neil. *The Disappearance of Childhood*. New York, Delacorte, 1982.
Pratt, Bob. "11-Year-Old Earns $70,000 A Year—But Without Her Makeup Model Is Just A Typical Kid." *National Enquirer*, Jan. 5, 1982.

Rainer, Peter. "A Teasing Tale Of Man Meets Girl." Los Angeles *Herald-Examiner*, Oct. 23, 1981.

Rosen, Marjorie. *Popcorn Venus*. New York, Coward, McCann & Geoghegan, 1973.

Rush, Florence. *The Best Kept Secret: Sexual Abuse of Children*. New York, McGraw-Hill, 1980.

Salinger, J.D. *The Catcher in the Rye*. Boston, Little, Brown, 1951.

Salamans, Sandra. "Those Precocious Jeans Ads." New York *Times*, Nov. 5, 1980.

Savage, Walter. "Lost Innocence in the American Comics," in *Society and Children's Literature*, ed. J. Fraser. Boston, Godine, 1978.

Schiro, Anne-Marie. "Cosmetics Customers Get Younger." San Jose *Mercury*, Feb. 27, 1981.

Sendak, Maurice. *In The Night Kitchen*. New York, Harper & Row, 1970.

Shay, Don. "Robert Wise on Audrey Rose." *Cinefantastique* 6 (1977), pp. 26ff.

Shields, Brooke. *The Brooke Book*. New York, Simon & Schuster, 1982.

Signorielli, Nancy. "Magazine Coverage." in *Child Abuse: An Agenda for Action*. ed. G. Gerbner, et al., New York, Oxford, 1980.

Simpson, Maria. " 'Does She or Doesn't She?' Revisited: The Calvin Klein Jeans Ads." *ETC* 38 (1981), pp. 39-400.

Skow, John. "Hollywood's Whiz Kids." *Time*, August 13, 1979.

Skow, John. "Modelling The 80s Look." *Time*, Feb. 9, 1981a.

Skow, John. "Stunner—or Nice Kid?" *Time*, Feb. 9, 1981b.

Smith, Betty. *A Tree Grows In Brooklyn*. New York, Harper & Row, 1947.

Smith, Cecil. " 'Angel' Examines Child Porn." Los Angeles *Times*, Feb. 24, 1981.

Smith, Howard. "Scenes." *Village Voice*. Oct. 8, 1979a.

Smith, Howard. "Scenes." *Village Voice*. Oct. 29, 1979b.

Smith, Stacy. " 'Fallen Angel'—Pedophile Sickness Out Of The Closet." Austin *American-Statesman*, Feb. 15, 1981.

Sonenschein, David, et al., "A Study of Mass Media Erotica: The Romance or Confession Magazine." in *Technical Reports* of the Commission on Obscenity and Pornography, Vol. 9, Washington, GPO, 1972.

Sporn, Jessica. "Taunting Female and Tormented Males: Edward Albee's Lolita." *WAP Newsreport*, Spring/Summer, 1981.

Sprafkin, Joyce and L. Silverman. "Sex on Prime Time," in *TV and Teens*, ed., M. Schwartz. Reading, Addison-Wesley, 1982.

Sprafkin, J., L. Silverman and E. Rubinstein. "Reactions to Sex on Television: An Exploratory Study." *Public Opinion Quarterly* 44 (1980), pp. 303-315.

Stanek, Lou. "The Maturation of the Junior Novel: From Gestation to the Pill," in *Issues in Children's Book Selection*. ed., L. Gerhardt. New York, Bowker, 1973.

Steiger, Lucretia. "Little Girls Are Little Girls Here." San Diego *Union*, Oct. 19, 1980.

Stirling, Nora. *You Would If You Loved Me*. New York, Avon, 1969.

Stone, Judy. "On Love and the Generation Gap." San Francisco *Chronicle*, August 13, 1980.

Thurston, Carol. "Popular Historical Romances: Agent for Social Change?" *Journal of Popular Culture*, in press.

VerMeulen, Michael. "Turning Kids Into Sex Symbols." *Parade*, March 8, 1981.

Wagenknecht, Edward and Anthony Slide. *The Films of D.W. Griffith*. New York, Crown, 1975.

Walker, Alexander. *The Celluloid Sacrifice*. New York, Hawthorn, 1966.

Wegman, William *Man's Best Friend*. New York, Abrams, 1982.

Wersba, Barbara. "Sexuality in Books for Children." in *Issues in Children's Book Selection*, ed. L. Gerhardt. New York, Bowker, 1973.

Wertham, Fredric. *Seduction of the Innocent*. New York, Rinehart, 1954.

White, Jane. "Only Eleven, But ... Oh, What A Woman's Look!" *Imperial Valley Press*, May 5, 1981.

Wilkinson, Bud. "KOOL Queries Community Leaders About CBS Movie on Kiddie Porn." *Arizona Republic*, Feb. 24, 1981.

Williams, George. "A 'Lolita' Writes." Sacramento *Bee*, Jan. 11, 1979.
Winn, Marie. "What Became of Childhood Innocence?" New York *Times Magazine*, Jan. 25, 1981.
Wolcott, James. "The Cult of the Little Girl." *Village Voice*, March 7, 1977.
Wrobel, Arthur. "Mark Twain Bates the Master: 'Some Thoughts on the Science of Onanism'." *Journal of Popular Culture* 15 (1982), pp. 53-59.
Zindel, Paul. *My Darling, My Hamburger*. New York, Harper & Row,1969.
Zolotow, Maurice. *Billy Wilder in Hollywood*. New York, Putnam, 1977.

Filmography

L'Adolescent. D: Jeanne Moreau (1982, France).
A Little Romance. D: George Roy Hill (1978, US).
And God Created Woman D: Roger Vadim (1956, France).
Audrey Rose. D: Robert Wise (1977, US).
Baby Doll. D: Elia Kazan (1956, US).
Bad News Bears. D: Michael Ritchie (1976, US).
Beau Pere. D: Bertrand Blier (1979, France: 1981 US release).
Bilitis. D: David Hamilton (1977, France).
Blue Lagoon. D: Randal Kleiser (1980, US).
Born Innocent. D: Donald Wrye (1974, US, NBC-TV).
Broken Blossoms. D: D.W. Griffith (1919, US).
Captain January. D: David Butler (1936, US).
A Child Is A Wild Young Thing. D: Peter Skinner [pseud.] (1976, US).
Christiane F. D: Ulrich Edel (1981, German; 1982 US release).
Circle of Two. D: Jules Dasin (1980, Canada).
The Devil's Playground. D: Fred Schepisi (1976, Australia).
The Drowning Pool. D: Stuart Rosenberg (1975, US).
The Exorcist. D: William Friedkin (1973, US).
Fallen Angel. D: Robert Lewis (1981, US, CBS-TV).
Foxes. D: Adrian Lyne (1980, US).
Get Out Your Handkerchiefs. D. Bertrand Blier (1979, France).
Gidget. D: Paul Wendkos (1959, US).
In A Wild Moment. D: Claude Berri (1980, France; also known as *One Wild Moment*).
Lipstick. D: Lamont Johnson (1976, US).
Little Darlings. D: Ronald Maxwell (1980, US).
The Little Girl Who Lives Down the Lane. D: Nicholas Gessner (1977, US).
Lolita. D: Stanley Kubrick (1962, Britain: 1963 US release).
The Major and the Minor. D: Billy Wilder (1942, US).
Manhattan. D: Woody Allen (1979, US).
Nea: A New Woman. D: Nelly Kaplan (1978, France).
The Nest. D: Jamie De Arminan (1982, Spain).
Night Moves. D: Arthur Penn (1975, US).
Number One. D: Dyan Cannon (1976, US, American Film Institute).
Paper Dolls. D: Edward Zwick (1982, US, ABC-TV).
Paper Moon. D: Peter Bogdanovich (1973, US).
Pixote. D: Hector Babenco (1981, US).
Pretty Baby. D: Louis Malle (1978, US).
Private Lessons. D: Alan Myerson (1981, US).
Rafferty And The Gold Dust Twins. D: Dick Richards (1975, US).
Tammy and the Bachelor. D: Josephy Pevney (1957, US).
Taxi Driver. D: Martin Scorsese (1976, US).
Tiger Bay. D: J. Lee Thompson (1959, Britain).
To Die Of Love. D: Andre Cayatte (1970, France).
You Are Not Alone. D: Lasse Nielsen (1978, Denmark).

Cheaters Sometimes Win:
Sexual Infidelity in Country Music

C.R. Chandler
H. Paul Chalfant
Craig P. Chalfant

Originating in the conservative, religiously fundamentalist South, commercial country music was a popular culture form long influenced by the taboos endemic to the region of its birth. Especially strong in early southern music was the taboo against any mention of sexual infidelity, particularly if the transgressor was a married woman. At the same time, country lyrics have often been described as presenting a much more realistic portrayal of everyday life than might be found in the words of most other types of popular music. The emergence of so-called cheatin' songs, in which sexual infidelity is explicitly depicted, indicates a movement away from the old euphemisms and taboos and toward an expression of the modern realities of adultery and divorce.

Country Cheatin' Songs

Country music developed among southern whites and, after northern entrepreneurs discovered its commercial value in the late 1920s, rapidly spread to nearly all regions of the United States as well as to many other nations.[1] It is impossible to provide exact quantitative data on the popularity of this type of music, although DiMaggio, et al.,[2] presented some information on its growing appeal following a temporary eclipse by rock and roll. As a substitute for "hard data" on this point, we invite the reader to turn on a radio and note the number of stations billing themselves as "country."

A fairly recent development in country music has been the increased popularity of so-called cheatin' songs, which modify the formerly nearly unbreakable taboo. These describe in fairly explicit terms instances of sexual unfaithfulness between either marital partners or lovers who have a serious commitment to each other. The infidelity is viewed as a betrayal which must, at least nominally, be performed clandestinely in order to keep the original, publicly recognized relationship intact. These characteristics of cheatin' lyrics distinguish them from songs about other types of romantic situations such as failure to attract a lover or the open termination of a relationship. And, unlike most earlier ballads of unfaithful lovers, cheaters are clearly depicted as engaging in sexual intercourse.

Earlier songwriters of all types of music have insinuated references to sex acts into their lyrics; but, in the western tradition, for quite some time now, such expressions had to be in the *double entendre* style. ("Bawdy ballads," usually sung at single sex gatherings, are exceptions). Early country music featured dark, tragic ballads of heartbreak and gory murders of unfaithful or uninterested women, but disloyalty might only be hinted at obscurely. The "Knoxville Girl,"[3] for instance, was brutally murdered solely, as far as one can tell, because she's "got dark and rollin' eyes." Words to some traditional fiddle breakdowns, such as "Run Mountain," contained lines like "me upstairs with another man's wife, better be gettin' away"; and Jimmie Rodgers, the "father of country music," employed the *double entendre* occasionally. But throughout the 1920s, country music, commercial or not, dwelt primarily upon love (with almost no explicit sexual content), home, family and church.[4]

Incongruously, given the alleged devotion of southerners to fundamentalist religious and other traditional values, which they had raised into icons, it was southern country music which, among white people at least, first began to reflect the realities of modern, urban life. Alan Lomax says southerners were the last Americans to experience the traumas of urban society. If so, they were the first white Americans to sing about those shocks in hard, realistic, though sometimes humorous, terms.

Malone noted that when rural folk started to visit and move into the city—including the "honky tonk"—country music was forced to change, and thus to modify some of the taboos that had been strictly observed for generations. "Songs about 'poor old mother at home' and 'the old country church' seemed somewhat out of place in the honky tonk environment."[5] Music as well as lyrics altered to fit the milieu. The taboos, as they always do, were modified to fit the altered environment and social needs.

But it was only after World War II that the sexual content of honky-tonk lyrics became sufficiently transparent to leave no doubt about their meaning even to the most naive of listeners.

One of the first real country cheatin' songs was Floyd Tillman's popular "Slippin' Around," recorded in the late 1940s. At that time, the lyrics could not be completely open about sexual union, but nobody who heard the record could possiby have any doubt as to what the couple who "slipped around" were up to.

The lyrics to "Slippin' Around" contained no guilt whatsoever about the doubly adulterous affair. Only in the last verse was a slight bow made to conventional taboos. Tillman hoped someday he and his lover would no longer have to slip around to be together. This song, along with others like Webb Pierce's recording of "Back Street Affair" and Hank Thompson's "Wild Side of Life" ("I didn't know God made honky-tonk angels"), launched cheatin' songs into American popular culture. But by then it was the early 1950s, and country cheatin' honky-tonk was about to suffer an even greater eclipse than other forms of country music from the onslaught of rock and roll and, later, the emergence of "country pop."

But there has been a comeback. Cheatin' songs, now sung by women as well as men, may be found on practically every *Billboard* "Hot Country Singles" list of the seventies and eighties. As one song title has it, "There's a Whole Lot of Cheatin' Goin' On," and it is in the lyrics of such music that we shall try to find tentative answers to some sociological concerns about current values, attitudes and emotions surrounding the taboo of infidelity and sex roles in general.

Men, Women and the Taboo of Cheatin'

Until very recently, women have seldom played leading roles in country music, and the field is still dominated by men. This, plus the fact that the music came out of an especially conservative region as far as traditional sex role taboos were concerned, has influenced the treatment of women in song lyrics. According to Horstman,[6] women were portrayed as either good or bad, and sexual taboos tended to bind them into the stereotype. The "good" woman was chaste before marriage and then submissive to her husband. She devoted herself entirely to husband and children. There was never any mention of her finding pleasure in sex; and, when she ventured out of her home, it was to attend church, not to go drinking, dancing and flirting in saloons.

Women singers could not until recently employ even the mildly risque material that a male artist, like Jimmie Rodgers, could get away with as far back as 1927.

Sexual love, a mainstay of the modern repertory, was taboo. Women, after all, were the repositories of Christian virtues; they were expected to behave "properly"—and this including singing "proper" material in "appropriate" places.[7]

The "wicked woman" did not "preserve her virtue," although her failure to do so could only be suggested in early lyrics. She could be treacherous, flirtatious, unfaithful and, of course, she would violate the taboo against not being a "good" wife and mother.

This extreme good vs. evil view of women in country lyrics may have been overemphasized by some writers, at least as far as the postwar period is concerned. In their content analysis of country songs, DiMaggio, et al. found indications that even "good" women were feared and resented to some extent by their lovers or husbands, especially when the latter were economically unstable and thus had little power.

Another alleged characteristic of women in country lyrics was their tendency to "fight for their man" when threatened by a rival, thus to observe the taboo against having a "broken" association. The weapon women used to keep their men was, according to the DiMaggio study, their sexuality. The most famous song exemplifying women's fighting attitude is Loretta Lynn's "You Ain't Woman Enough To Take My Man." And Moe Bandy, a prominent honky-tonk specialist, sings of how, when the devil and drink tempt him to cheat, he runs home to his woman "who loves the devil out of me."

According to the DiMaggio study, men in country lyrics did not address their rivals, but were simply shattered by betrayal. We have found no mention in the literature of men using their sexuality to keep "their women." Whether men, in country lyrics, really react so differently than women do when threatened by a rival is a question we will explore further.

Other findings by DiMaggio, et al., relevant to the present study include characterization of males as *not* taking a "love 'em and leave 'em" attitude toward women. Men also expressed remorse after allowing themselves, often because of drink, to succumb to the temptations of "honky-tonk" women, thus hurting, and perhaps losing, the women they have betrayed. No mention was made of similar behavior by women who were unfaithful.

Women were, however, described in the DiMaggio study as "feeling victimized," jilted and left responsible for children. Men were not referred to in this context, but it may be that they too can feel themselves victimized in certain ways.

It would appear, then, that early country music—prior to World War II—maintained extremely traditionalist, male-dominant taboos toward sex roles, but that this situation may have been changing during the period 1950-1970, and examination of these themes in music lyrics published in 1980-81 will reveal how they have been treated more recently.

Methods and Sources

The analysis of these themes is an interpretive one of the lyrics of a sample of country songs. It has been pointed out by several students of popular music that analysis of country lyrics is much less difficult than that of the lyrics of other music for three reasons: the thrust of the story told in the song is presented in unambiguous fashions; lyrics tend to present an individual situation in some detail; and, the words are given more emphasis than the music, with a "commercial lyric" being more important than a "commercial sound."[8]

The songs selected for analysis were taken from two periodicals, *Country Song Roundup* and *Country Hits*, which reprint the lyrics of what are considered "hit" country songs. The publication dates of the magazines were, for the former, December, 1980 through August, 1981, including a special issue, and, for the latter, Spring, 1980, through Winter, 1981, including one special edition. *Country Song Roundup* was the source of lyrics in the DiMaggio, et al., study, and when we drew our sample, had the same editor and publisher as *Country Hits*. Thus, our source was essentially the same as that used by DiMaggio, et al. However, we analyzed every lyric printed in the magazines instead of drawing songs randomly from every fifth issue over a twenty year period as was done in the earlier study. DiMaggio, et al., ended up with a random sampling of 40 country songs, whereas we examined all the several hundred lyrics published during the indicated period of time, identifying 75 of these as cheatin' songs to be included in our study.

In analyzing the songs, we rely much more heavily on an interpretation of the presence of certain themes in the songs, as judged by three independent readers, than on our listing of frequency counts. In other words, we will present our data more in the sense of a recounting of the lyrics than in numerical tables.

However, in judging the various lyrics we did carry out a content analysis for which we had several protocols in mind, namely eleven questions we asked regarding each lyric. These questions concerned frequency of unfaithful acts by sex and marital status, attitudes toward cheating, motivations and a number of other variables which should be apparent from our exposition.

Three coders independently attempted to answer these questions for each lyric, with disagreements being resolved by majority vote.

Frequency by Marital Status and Sex

Although marital status was not indicated in 25 of the songs, no clear case of unmarried lovers cheating on one another was identified. In consequence, we have treated all infidelities as involving marital partners and refer, in the remainder of our discussion, only to spouses and not unfaithful lovers. In 14 instances both cheaters were identified as married. Four songs were about husbands and wives both of whom were involved in outside affairs.

Male cheaters outnumbered females. In the 75 songs, there were 89 cheaters: 50 men and 39 women. Omitting cases of cheating in which both persons were married, 11 men and 6 women were described as engaging in frequent, short-term sexual episodes, while 12 men and 11 women cheaters were involved in longer-term affairs. In most cases, differences between short- and long-term episodes could not be distinguished.

It is important to note and keep in mind throughout the analysis and discussion that 54 of the 75 songs were recorded by male vocalists, 3 were duets by men and women, and only 18 were female solos. Perhaps of greater importance, only three women songwriters could be identified, and two of these were co-authored with men.

Attitudes Toward Cheating

While several views and feelings with regard to cheating might be found in the same lyric, most songs fell into one of a limited number of types depending on attitudes expressed toward surreptitious infidelity. For instance, about one-fifth of the songs might be termed *celebrations* of the joys of illicit love and sex. Little or, in most cases, no expressions of guilt or fear intruded upon the cheaters' happiness. These were simply love songs in which one or more of the lovers happened to be married to someone else. Two of the celebrations were more like male "hell-raising" than cheating songs, although infidelities were involved.

Most of these songs depicted male cheaters whose liaisons had so far gone undetected. Female cheaters were less likely than men to express simple joy untainted by fear, anger at their spouses, or rationalization; but their songs often were dominated by expressions of pleasure and gratification.

Guilt-tinged, remorseful *confessionals* made up another twenty percent of the songs. Again, all but three or four of these lyrics were sung by male cheaters. Several of the songs were both confessionals and lamentations, the cheaters expressing extreme sorrow at having yielded to temptations in such a way as to destroy, or place in jeopardy, their marriages.

As examples, George Jones sings about drinking himself to death as a result of losing his woman because he was "caught cheatin' twice" ("Still Doin' Time"). Roger Bowling sings of himself as a "Friday Night Fool" who has a good wife and teaches Sunday School but cannot resist risking everything to pick up "a lady with the Friday night blues." Fear of being detected is often expressed as in "Sometimes I Talk in My Sleep" and the more recent "Lovin' up a Storm." (These two were recorded by Randy Cornor and Razzy Bailey respectively.)

It was only in very rare cases that songs sung by women about women cheaters were openly expressive of guilt or remorse, and these feelings were usually rationalized. Of course, men rationalized their behavior quite frequently, but in the guilty confessional songs being considered here, self-blame was paramount and almost the only excuse men offered for their behavior was drunkenness. As will be seen, one reason women cheaters expressed guilt less often than men was that their infidelities were in several instances described as acts of retribution against cheating husbands.

In summary, male cheaters tend to celebrate the romantic, joyful aspects of their affairs unless they get caught. Then they express extreme remorse, guilt and regret. Women cheaters usually display more complex attitudes, seldom confining themselves to simply joy or sorrow.

In *accusatory* songs, attitudes of persons who had been betrayed were never completely positive. Men tended to agonize in a self-pitying, passive way. Women much more often responded with anger, confrontation and reprisal.

Occasionally the attitude toward infidelity was humorous or ironic with some humorous intent. The most obvious example of this may be found in Bill Anderson's recording of "Mr. Peepers." In the first half of the song, a woman is riding in her husband's funeral procession and thinking how disappointing he had been as a mate. "She was glad he was gone and would soon be forgot." The man had been so dull, shy and quiet that she referred to him as Mr. Peepers.

The second half of the song pulls what is meant to be a comical surprise on the widow (or listener). In the crowd surrounding the grave she sees

> Forty-four weeping stewardesses with
>   children kneeling down.
> They look just like the man they
>   were laying in the ground.

As the song continues, it becomes apparent that Mr. Peepers was one of the most notable philanderers of his time. The "other women" who have come to express their respect and gratitude to "Mr. Peepers" include twenty-three fashion models, seventeen Playboy bunnies, Mr. Peepers' so-called niece, "with a disco dancing trophy in the name of the deceased," a smiling nun, and neighbor's wife. ("They say she caused his heart to quit the night he lost his life.")

Instead of denouncing adultery, as would have been expected in the old country songs, and thus supporting the universal taboo, these lyrics exalt it, having thus shattered the taboo. However, this could be seen as merely a more contemporary expression of the traditional double standard taboo. The song was written and recorded by males and includes presumed justification of Mr. Peepers' marathon cheating. The wife derogated him, was disappointed in his (only apparent) lack of ability to acquire money, and never believed in him or "tried to understand." This supposedly justified Mr. Peepers' behavior in copulating with around one hundred other women, including a nun.

"She Can't Say That Anymore" is another unremorseful opus of irony with apparently humorous intent; and, once again, the butt of the humor is a woman. Purely humorous songs aimed at men by women were absent. The only lyrics approaching this type were dominated by irony, as in songs like "Teach Me to Cheat."

Besides humor and irony, accusatory songs often expressed anger. Condemnation of cheating in general could be found in lyrics presented as third person *editorials* or moralistic narratives, such as Bobby Borcher's "Cheap Perfume and Candlelight" which, incidentally, accuses a male adulterer of trying to prove his manhood with a "now and then girl" because he lacks the ability to perform on a more regular basis at home. Anti-cheating editorial songs which did not describe specific instances of infidelity were not included in the analysis. An example is "I Do My Swinging at Home," recorded by David Houston.

Motivations for Cheating

Sexual pleasure and love are manifest reasons for cheating: so obvious, in fact, that lyricists seldom state these motivations explicitly enough to satisfy a strict empiricist attempting content analysis. We believe, however, that when a man and woman who are married to others are described as "sneaking around," entering motel rooms and taking off wedding rings and garments in preparation for experiencing "a different kind of lovin'," we can safely assume that they intend to perform sexual acts of such quality as to raise serious objections from their publicly recognized mates. Many songs are not this explicit, but we would contend—and current dictionaries agree with us—that the very term *cheating* denotes illicit sexual intercourse. In addition, 21 songs described multiple "one night stands," often with a variety of partners. Sexual pleasure was at least one motivation in these instances. On the other hand, the 28 songs which described single affairs might indicate, and in several cases clearly stated, a quest for love and affection.

It is the failure of the publicly recognized partners to provide adequate love and sexual gratification that cheaters frequently proclaim to be the reason for their infidelities. Both males and females, equally, expressed resentment and regret that their spouses, who, of course, had to carry all the blame, had withdrawn love, sex or both, thus "forcing" their partners to seek satisfaction elsewhere.

In some instances it appeared that the cheater had a powerful sex drive which the spouse either could not or would not satisfy. This was true of the male cheater in "Hold Me," who seemed to have the view, often attributed to husbands, that wives must always accede to their requests for sex. The female cheater in "A Little at a Time" lamented the fact that her husband's "need for love" didn't "run as strong as mine/And so I gave your part away a little at a time." Other lines appear to specify the "need" as largely sexual.

But the joys of love and sex were not the only motivations for infidelity. Cheating was also seen as a form of excitement and adventure even outside the motel room. This was the case in, for example, the song "Steppin' Out." Even the phrase "steppin' out" connotes going to exciting places "on the town," in a somewhat swaggering, ego-gratifying fashion. Another married female cheater was described as having "neon mania." She frequented honky-tonks and did not restrict her activities to out-of-the-way motels. The lure of excitement as well as sexual gratification was specifically mentioned in a song recorded by Freddy Weller entitled "Ask any Old Cheater Who Knows." For the woman involved, "There's thrill in the danger/Of lovin' a stranger."

Women were also seen as taking pleasure in making themselves attractive and receiving the admiration of men. The woman burning from "One Night Fever" is pictured at the mirror making herself "so doggone pretty it's almost a crime," and for "steppin' out" the woman owns a new dress and has "a new way of walking and fixing her hair." Similar motives were apparent in the fantasies of another female in "Cheatin' is Still on My Mind."

Finally, a motivation of considerable importance, women were depicted on several occasions as cheating, or threatening to do so, in reprisal for their husband's infidelity. None of the men gave this as a reason for cheating.

Alcohol and Cheating

Consumption of alcohol, including "moonshine," has long been a theme of country music. Country lyrics express ambivalent attitudes toward alcohol consumption: one commonly expressed idea being that drinking is bad because "it leads to illicit sex".[9]

Many of the lyrics examined recounted the joys and sorrows of drinking—especially by carousing males—but were not cheating songs. Of the cheating songs, four blamed alcohol consumption for lowering inhibitions or removing all consciousness of one's actions and thus leading one into infidelity. The cheaters in these songs were men, as were the singers, who, in three lyrics, were following up their indiscretions by consuming even more alcohol, thus breaking two taboos, one in order to forget the breaking of the other, not an unusual practice; frequently the fear among conservative taboo-observers is that, following the domino theory, if you break one taboo you will break them all. No women were depicted as cheating solely because of drink or as trying to obliterate unpleasant memories through use of alcohol.

Both males and females were frequently portrayed as drinking moderately prior to or during romantic episodes. This, as in the song "Let's Forget That We're Married," may have facilitated lovemaking, but apparently had little or no influence upon the original decision to engage in sexual intercourse.

Even when alcohol consumption was not specifically mentioned, drinking behavior was implied, since the initial stages of cheating were often pictured as taking place in bars. This was specifically mentioned in 9 cases and could be assumed in several other lyrics which spoke of "steppin' out" and "neon mania." "Neon mania" objectifies another taboo, at least among strict moralists, since bright lights represent temptation and loose living and therefore should be forbidden and tabooed.

Conclusions

Despite its conservative origins, the tendency toward realism has almost completely broken down the taboos against references to sexual behavior, including infidelity, in commercial country music. Most of the songs are simply he-she love ballads but lyrics about sexual infidelity now comprise a significant genre in country music. Male cheaters out-number females, but the fact that over forty percent of the cheaters in our sample were women may indicate a trend toward more open recognition of infidelities by females. This marks a definite break with the past and indicates that country music is reflecting trends in the broader society. It may, of course, also be influencing those trends, the matter of causal direction posing one of the most important as well as most refractory questions in the study of popular culture.

While anti-cheating songs may be found, they are outnumbered by lyrics which, in their celebration of "illicit" sex mark a startling break with the predominant values and taboos of older country music. Even regrets were largely practical—the cheater had been caught and was suffering the consequences—rather than moralistic. Only six of the editorial-type songs clearly and simply condemned cheating, and guilt was a scarce commodity.

Whatever one may think of the social trends these lyrics trace, there is a new freedom from restrictions in country music that indicates clearly that the people who use these songs in their daily lives have moved from the old taboos; they have undoubtedly replaced those with new ones, as is the nature of people in connection with taboos. Charting and analyzing the taboos, and the changes in taboos provide significant indicators of the movement of a society.

Notes

[1]Bill C. Malone, *Country Music U.S.A.: A Fifty-Year History* (Austin: Univ. of Texas Press, 1968).

[2]Paul DiMaggio, Richard A. Peterson and Frank Esso, Jr. "Country Music: Ballad of the Silent Majority," in *The Sounds of Social Change*, ed. R.S. Denisoff and R.A. Peterson (Chicago: Rand McNally, 1972), pp. 38-55.

[3]For sources and other information about early country ballads referred to here only by title, see Malone.

[4]Malone, p. 25. For a discography of Jimmie Rodgers' songs, see Nolan Porterfield, *Jimmie Rodgers* (Urbana: Univ. of Illinois Press, 1979), pp. 386-424.

[5]. Malone, p. 163.

[6]Dorothy A. Horstman, "Loretta Lynn," in B.C. Malone and J. McCulloh, *Stars of Country Music* (Urbana: Univ. of Illinois Press, 1975), pp. 309-25.

[7]Horstman, p. 311.

[8]Teddy Bart, *Inside Music City USA* (Nashville: Aurora, 1970); John Hartford, *Word Movies*

(Garden City, N.Y.: Doubleday, 1971); John Grissom, *Country Music: White Man's Blues* (New York: Paperback Library, 1970).

[9]H. Paul Chalfant and Robert E. Beckley, "Beguiling and Betraying: The Image of Alcohol Use in Country Music," *Journal of Studies on Alcohol* 38 (1977), pp. 1428-33.

On Feeling Blue:
Sex, Reagonomics, Violence and Taboo

Jerry Herron

"The battle for the mind of North America will be fought in the video arena," or so said Dr. Brian O'Blivion—his electronically preserved image, at any rate—to the protagonist of *Videodrome*, not long before that unfortunate young man was ingested by an anthropomorphosed, console TV set, winningly, and convincingly, played by Deborah Harry, of Blondie fame. That cathode degustation punctuates a great, if short-lived, tradition in American cinema: the tradition of the domestic splatter movie, which has produced such enduring classics as *Prom Night, Terror Train* and *Sweet Sixteen*, to name only three. From the late 1970s to the early 80s, there seemed an endless supply of, and desire for, these stories about nice, middle-class kids getting hacked and punctured, when they were least expecting it, by darkness-dwelling crazies.

But no more: now, through the ministrations of some stunningly nauseating visual techniques, the film medium has, with *Videodrome*, devoured its own subject, thereby transforming that subject, both literally and figuratively, into something new and different: the first fully video-based actant. James Woods, who plays the leading role in *Videodrome*, changes visibly from filmic character into a kind of organic VCR—a high-tech special effects ensemble—capable of loading content directly, "naturally," through a cassette-ingesting orifice in his abdomen. This produced transformation of the subject from character into video projection—from source of action into locus of effects—marks a generic self-consciousness that cannot help but provoke nostalgia. Gone is the innocent unawareness out of which the domestic splatter film was born, with its unique combination of visual technology, voyeurism and revisionist morality. There was a simpler time when we might confront the mutilation of nubile teenagers with a measure of affective innocence, even horror. But that time is past; we have grown up into the self-ironic meditations of *Videodrome*. If, as

Professor O'Blivion maintains in one of his post-McLuhan aphorisms, "TV is the retina of the mind's eye," then we have come of age visually; we have been delivered up, like James Woods, as clients to the variegated stimulation and control of a mature, service-based technology. And with that delivery, the classic splatter movie succumbs to an inevitable, generic exhaustion.

This journey from innocence to nostalgia hasn't been for nothing, of course. Careers were launched, along the way; some considerable profits have been made. And though the domestic splatter film itself may have passed from currency—along with certain powerful if sanguinary titillations—Americans have, best of all, become the subject of a new, and perhaps even great, awakening. We find ourselves again under the gaze of those sacred truths, and taboos, which have proved the guardian of our national life, the source of our historical greatness: " ... America is in the midst of a spiritual awakening and a moral renewal."[1] That is how President Reagan stated the case last spring, soon after the release of *Videodrome*. As he pointed out then, the exposed, and therefore responsible, individual remains the crucial monad of our national moral life: " ...we must never forget that no government schemes are going to perfect man; we know that living in this world means dealing with what philosophers would call the phenomenology of evil or, as theologians would put it, the doctrine of sin."[2] Such a statement would have made little or no sense, formerly, to people out of touch with our historic rituals, who had forgotten the true meaning of Halloween or Friday the 13 lost as they, or we, were in a still lingering hope of getting ourselves collectively born again. Now that our flirtation with populist politics and perfectible morality has come to a timely if expensive end, the threatened individual once more emerges as the authentic subject of that moral narrative which is America.

As such, it is the individual—we now realize again—who must be held accountable, philosophically and theologically. But there is no such thing as a fixed individuality, nor can there be in a society whose basis is growth. That is the fateful truth which devours James Woods, in his own livingroom. The constitution of the individual subject, just as the categories of sin and evil which are used to characterize that subject, makes sense only in relation to something else: sin as opposed to salvation, evil as opposed to good. The true subject, the protagonist, of our moral narrative emerges, then, as a product of difference—difference from the proscribed Other, the taboo dark option, which each of us, moment by moment, might be devoured by. And we needn't travel intergalactic distances to know the dark side of this force. Evil has shown that it can wear a hometown face, which is the powerful truth of domestic splatter filming. Fortunately, however, we have our national memory to save and preserve us as we try to make our way toward the future. "I'm sure you must get discouraged at times," as the President said, "but there is a great spiritual awakening in America, a renewal of traditional values that have been the bedrock of America's goodness and greatness."[3] Here the voice of tradition teaches us how to remain different from the Other, at least potentially.

But we must watch ourselves, and we must watch one another, because the times are full of dangers and surveillance has become essential, as the teenagers of splatter-America discover only too late. At night all cats look gray, as Benjamin Franklin used to say, in prophetic anticipation of our late, moral dusk. At least we have learned, finally, what John Carpenter was trying to teach us: that difference deferred invites destruction. *E pluribus unum* is no joking matter, in other words, nor can we allow it ever to become one. "Modern society aspires to equality among men," as Rene Girard first, regretfully, observed in 1972, "and tends instinctively to regard all differences, even those unrelated to the economic or social status of men, as obstacles in the path of human happiness."[4] That observation comes in his book *Violence and the Sacred* (now in its third English-language printing), where he investigates and cautions against "the violent abolition of distinction—the major cause of cultural disintegration" (p. 98). Book sales and Reaganomics aside, it is obvious that we have begun once more to take seriously, even if perhaps ironically, the making of traditional differences—witness no less an authority than Paul Fussell, Reagan Professor of English at the University of Pennsylvania (Donald T. Reagan, that is), who has confirmed, with considerable scholarly authority, the personal "awakening" which is the immediate and sanguine result of the domestic splatter film. "Despite our public embrace of political and judicial equality," Professor Fussell points out in his book *Class*, "in individual perception and understanding—much of which we refrain from publicizing—we arrange things vertically and insist on crucial differences in value .... It's as if in our heart of hearts we don't want agglomerations but distinctions. Analysis and separation we find interesting, synthesis boring."[5] Ronald Reagan appropriately acts out, and out of, our heart's desire, as analysis and separation take on a special, moral imperative. The triumph of populist equality—

metaphorical if not actual—brought with it the erasure of differences, the willed violation of taboos, up to and almost including the ERA; and that in turn produced the guilty nightmares which became splatter violence. Once we were lost, but now we are found. The question, then, is who precisely has found us, and to what end? That, I believe, is what the rise and demise of the domestic splatter genre are all about.

The form has a distinguished pre-history, dating back perhaps to Edison's *Mary Queen of Scots* and Melies special effects films, both of which evince a fascination with technology and chopping women into pieces. More immediately, Tobe Hooper's *Texas Chainsaw Massacre* and Brian DePalma's *Carrie* demonstrate a newly sophisticated visual competence and an affective willingness or even need to invite that competence to perform, to violate our collective expectations of what can, or ought, to be seen. In neither case, however, did the performance lead to self-replication. Splatters's truly classic and self-perpetuating era didn't begin until 1978, when John Carpenter released the first of his *Halloween* trilogy and introduced audiences both to the high-tech Boogie Man and to Jamie Lee Curtis, the actress who would preside as the Helen Hayes of her post-pubescent genre.

In rapid succession, both the *Halloween* and *Friday the 13th* cycles appeared, together with numerous spin-offs, each one reenacting a by-now familiar pattern of trauma, isolation and violent retribution: *Prom Night, Terror Train, Mother's Day, My Bloody Valentine, Happy Birthday to Me* and others. In each case, a holiday goes wrong: a group of celebratory adolescents violate traditional taboos—especially sexual ones—and in so doing invite the wrath of a traumatized, stalking Nemesis, who is never far to find in the splatter-era darkness. There will, perhaps, be further incarnations of domestic splatter, but the two matrix cycles are done, with the exhaustion of the genre itself having been produced visually, as James Woods is engulfed by the electronic kiss of Debbie Harry. Hereafter, splatter films, if they exist, will at best be a nostalgic exercise, dependent upon reminiscence rather than immediate affective engagement.

This is so because the genre was born of a precise need, on the part of certain cultural and technological already-givens, to be discovered as the synthetic answer to a nascent question, which prior forms could only realize in indirect and imperfect ways. It is a measure of domestic splatter's success—and of the changes which have occurred—that this once crucially posed question has grown superfluous to the now-autonomous authority of a powerfully invoked answer. Tradition—"the bedrock of America's goodness and greatness"—has found a way to dwell profitably in the future; it has taught the future how to need the past, just as we of the Pepsi generation have been "taught" to need the executive services of the oldest man ever to hold the office of President. Splatter did not, on its own, of course, make this possible, but it was surely among the cultural overdeterminers without which any such change would have remained inconceivable, and therefore unattainable.

The origin of the splatter film, as well as its recent exhaustion, have to do with an historic—and carefully publicized—shift, which has demanded a new—and even more carefully, if not explicitly, publicized—language of subjects.

During the 1970s Americans moved rapidly toward and have now achieved a radical alteration in our collective economic lives: we used to be (and had always been) a nation of producers, with the majority employed in making *things*, from raw materials to finished products; we have become, since mid-1982 (according to the U.S. Bureau of Labor Statistics)[6] a nation of *providers*, with the majority called to work now by the insubstantial errands of "service." We are approaching jointly what *Time* referred to recently in its cover story as "The New Economy."[7] Indicative of what is about to come, the "weekly newsmagazine" chose as its "man of the year" for 1983 not a man at all but a computer, a "machine of the year," as quintessential symbol of the service culture that is about to be."[8] "A New World dawns," we are told: "What's all this got to do with computers? you ask. They reopen the territory, that's what they do.Not the land, of course. That's gone like the topsoil, with the wind. But the land was never our real territory anyway. It was the dream, my friends; the territory was always the New World ideal. We don't want to run out of that. Goodbye Land. Hello space."[9] We stand, then, like Huck Finn—according to *Time,* that is—poised before the proffered freedom of this new territory, "our real territory." But if we're going to find homes in Tomorrowland, we'll first have to master the space—the inner space of self—that changing conditions have now exposed. And when the going gets tough, the tough are the ones who show real class.

America will surely continue to consume the products of industry, but increasingly our livelihood, in fact our very survival as a nation—so the "media" frequently remind us—will depend upon our mastering that new language of self, by which the individual exists not primarily as a collection of objects, a mere narrative of consumer purchases, but as a non-narrative instantiation of services, particularly those traditionally regenerative services associated with high-tech fitness: "So, move over, Jane Fonda, here comes the Ronald Reagan Workout plan."[10] This new subjectivity constitutes the culturally and economically privileged answer, whose value remained incompletely realized until splatter technologists—among other New World-makers—came up with the right form of question. Americans need to learn how to make themselves need the future, in other words, but need has to be so instanced—as a language of subjects—that investors in the about-to-be can retain imaginative control over their projection of self into an incompletely realized future. We've been taught to feel anxious about growing up, which is the defining feature of the splatter experience, so that the dependable past becomes a necessary, and profitable, palliative: ideological dramamine, for the cancellation of cultural motion sickness.

Quite properly, *Newsweek*, the other supermarket arbiter of American experience, celebrated its first half century by turning from object to subject: from production to service. "For fifty years *Newsweek* has covered the people who make news," their golden-age cover proclaims; "Our anniversary issue celebrates the men and women who live the news, the unsung people who make our country."[11] There is a crucial distinction being established here, in the discourse of popular experience, between a narrative of *production*—the traditional out-put of those few people who make the news—and the non-narrative *service* of those traditionally invisible individuals whose job it is to make up the country. Enough of old-news stories; the challenge now is figuring out a language fit for future-world analysis. This is a win-or-lose, high-stakes game, as we are rarely allowed to forget: "...a sweeping transformation...is creating a New Economy .... While traditional smokestack industries are reeling from foreign competition, surging high-technology companies are leading the world in innovation .... The winds of economic change are swirling in different directions across the U.S. ... The accelerating pace of technological innovation threatens jobs in old industries even as it creates work in new fields."[12] Both exhiliration and devastation await: "Can technology create as many jobs as it destroys? How difficult will it be for workers to move from the jobs of the past to the jobs of the future?"[13] Out of our general uncertainty as to what is in store for us, and how we should prepare ourselves, the domestic splatter film was born: a genre rich in tension and surprises if there ever was one. The enormous popularity of splatter violence, particularly among the same "nice," white middle-class teenagers who are its primary subjects, and therefore victims, attests to the anxiety attendant upon our collective entry into the technological adulthood that microchips will provide. No more beach blankets and no more Beaver; contemporary adolescence appears to have turned into a long and not-so-good Friday the 13th.

In this context, then, domestic splatter violence has become the psycho-social R & D for post-industrial capitalism. As forms occupied crucially with renegotiating the subject, these films foreground the body, particularly the undraped body, as both the most potent and the most titillating heiroglyph of the self. Despite the graphic annihilation of virtually all the subjects in these films, bodies are rarely violated without first being revealed, the revelation and the violation being portrayed more or less as cause and effect. In terms of censorship standards, we've been able to look at both violence and naked flesh for some time now, but only recently have we, especially the adolescents among us, become so enthusiastic about seeing the two brought together in particularly graphic forms.

The body, as subject, in these films is made vulnerable in an intense, personal way superfluous to an object culture, and there is good reason for this. The body remains in itself incidental to the culture of products, of material consuming: in terms of profit, it makes no difference who does the buying, so long as the buying gets done. The economic health of a product culture depends upon discipline, of course, and upon consumers who have been taught, as subjects, how to act. But subjectivity itself is not the on-going focus of transactions; instead, it is external objects that make up a life: "Goods assembled together in ownership make physical, visible statements about the heirarchy of values to which their chooser subscribes. Goods can be cherished or judged inappropriate, discarded and replaced."[14] As this passage from Mary Douglas' "anthropology of consumption" suggests, object culture is based on a cumulative version of identity, a narrative materialization of what a person amounts to.

The media, or "publicity," of such a culture, as John Berger calls it, provide the narrative *langue* essential to Douglas' "physical, visible statements": "Publicity is, in essence, nostalgic. It has to sell the past to the future. It cannot in itself supply the standards of its own claims. And so all its references to quality are bound to be retrospective and traditional. It would lack both confidence and credibility if it used a strictly contemporary language."[15] So when Ralph Lauren, for instance, talks about "the essence of the American lifestyle ... intregrity and a respect for tradition," American consumers have, traditionally, been ready to listen,[16] and to buy, just as when President Reagan invokes the same traditional authority for the market positioning of his own narrative products. The "New Economy" of service, however, and the subjectivity that provides its basis, are precisely antithetical to these nostalgic, narrative appeals. The profitable exploitation of the future depends upon non-narrative forms of subjectivity, paradoxic though this may at first appear, relative to Americans' current veneration of "traditions." But—as will become clear shortly—there is a difference between *being* traditional, which comparatively few people are, and *hiring* the temporary service of professional traditionalists, such as Messrs. Reagan and Fussell. Only the latter promises much in the way of return.

This is so because the consumables of future-tech are not goods at all but services which can themselves neither be displayed nor usefully narratized; service becomes visible, and therefore capable of articulating "crucial differences in value," only as function: as an effect invited and subsequently absorbed by a subject. It is the subject, then, rather than an ensemble of objects, that realizes the meaning, the "value," of consuming. Services produce an anthropological discourse, in Douglas' terms, they become capable—and therefore profitable—as "visible statements about the hierarchy of values to which their chooser subscribes," only when the subject himself or herself is revealed as the immediate expressions of functions that necessarily disconnect themselves from narrative chronologies of accumulation.

Unlike products, the ideal environment for service is neither past nor future oriented, but an endlessly renewable present where time remains forever swallowing its own tail. Fitness, for example, rather than accumulation becomes the idealized referent of service-culture class, and once you are in shape, you garner the value of having gotten there by exposing yourself, not by showing off your exercise equipment. The point, as most fitness hypes make clear, is to nullify both the pre-fit past and the post-aerobic future, with its ultimate and inevitable assault of decay, so that the subject dwells forever in a renewably articulate present. The body must now be expressed as visibly fit, either directly, as auto-valorizing surface, which is the case with splatter films, or else indirectly, as exhibitionistic, micro-chip performance, which becomes the concern of such films as *Tron, Joy Sticks* and *Wargames*. The last has now generated the successful TV spin-off, *Whiz Kids*. Here, as on the jogging track, performance is indistinguishable from self. You are what you can do, and those who can't simply become pathetic, or else middle-aged, which is virtually the same thing. The now "look," particularly as chronology begins to threaten the body, is the eternal, get-physical present of the firm-fleshed and quick-reacting adolescent. The future belongs to the hackers and joggers: to the young at heart and synapse. Age, then, becomes a reverse sign of status, a taboo as daunting as communism, or cellulite. Visible deterioration, such as Soviet leaders are, not incidentally, prone to, communicates a moral failure, an inability, to consume, to become subject to, the desired ensemble of future-culture competencies. The over-forty woman, for instance, may have come into her own—as we are often told, via Joan Collins, Raquel Welch, Linda Evans and friends—but only when she can demonstrate visibly how little she looks like what she "really" is, and how she can still perform just like a kid. The aim of service, therefore, is the specific denial of time: the body that never ages, the instincts and reflexes that never dull, an a-chronology of renewable function, rather than the linear pavement of history.

Of course traditional material-consuming will still be involved in the post-world of service culture, as I have suggested: the crucial pursuit of difference-making, or purchasable "class," will no doubt continue in the common spaces of spa-America. As any knowledgeable service subject already understands, packaging is essential to the proper display of the newly toned self—witness, for example the amount of magazine space and television time devoted to "active wear" fashion, and to the advertisement of expensive exercise equipment and fitness programs, which make well-being appear unobtainable—though not, of course, less desirable—to the other than fiscally fit. And that is the point, so that we may "arrange things vertically and insist on crucial differences in value," such as those that comprise Professor Fussell's serviceable instruction manual.[17] The problem, then, is not that service-culture obviates consuming. On the contrary, service opens whole new and unexpected markets. But in every case these vast new economic zones remain dependent upon a need structure which is alien to traditional consumer narratives.

Thus the seeming paradox of recent market reversals: at the very dawn of the computer age, a large number of computer companies are in trouble financially, with two industry leaders,

Osborne and Texas Instruments, having either folded or else gotten out of home computers entirely. Or there is the unexpected and seemingly atavistic revival of the recording industry, which most analysts had assumed to have taken a permanent second place to video and arcade games as the consumable of choice for adolescent America.[18] Neither instance is proof of high-tech service culture's having been a hoax, a trendy idea whose time is now gone. On the contrary, we will remain a service culture whether we want to or not, since the production facilities which were once ours have been permanently exported to foreign countries.

The problem now is trying to reinterpret the post-industrial subject so as to assure a disciplined supply of needs for those services and service-based commodities which the economy is presently capable of delivering. Andrew Pollack, for instance, recently pointed out in the *New York Times* that it's not the computer which has failed but the imaginations of those who serve it. They have failed to institute a sufficient population of subjects capable of needing micro-chip servicing; as he said, "a compelling use has not emerged that would make the computer an essential purchase."[19] If Texas Instruments were as clever as Vic Tanny, they would still be in the computer business today. That they are not says more about the difficulty of imagining the future in an other-than-traditional way—particularly for those whose service remains tied to a tangible product—than it does about the viability of a post-narrative world. As the President remarked, however, we are in the midst of a revival, the whole point of which is to purge the past of chronological impediments, so that the utility of tradition need not be limited by actual memory.

If they are to succeed, revivals such as ours must always confront the inconvenient and perhaps even incapacitating fact of there having been a time when the thing being revived was thought unnecessary—else there would be no point in reviving it. The effective recuperation of a discarded or perhaps even alien *then* within a forgetful *now* depends upon the motivation of an appropriate attitude toward the signs of "classic" difference. Mr. Reagan—or his presidency—offers tangible proof that a class attitude has at last won popular acceptance, and in that he has proved genuinely prophetic, even trendy. He is among friends.

The *avant* of our pop-cultural *garde*, for example, has demonstrated an astute promotional instinct for future-need; it has doubled back to devour that problematic chronology which is currently protracting our entry into the un-historical about-to-be. In effect, our cultural birthdate is being erased, so that we can claim whatever age we feel fit enough to become. Formerly, a particular fashion or style might have become popular by way of mimicry: a Doctor Zhivago look, a Gatsby look, a Chariots of Fire/Brideshead look. In each case, the look was associated with, and originated by, an "authentic" narrative text, painstakingly recreated, right down to the license plates and cigarette packs. By buying the look, consumers bought for themselves "physical, visible statements about the hierarchy of values to which they subscribe"—values that took on meaning by virtue of precise chronological fidelity. Current pop culture is concerned with looks too, and particularly with "vintage" affectation, but rather more in terms of cultural cannibalism, or historical dismemberment, than nostalgic rehabilitation: "Just yesterday, it was enough to be hip. These days, you've got to have attitude .... Attitude is a self-consciously styled variant of camp, an aesthetic based on ripping images out of the past and presenting them out of context—usually deadpan and always with irony. Like market positioning, it is a way of projecting identity, of packaging, but always with a twist."[20] Thus opines *New York* magazine on the nouvelle subjectivity. The article describes a number of attitudinally illustrative subjects, who conjure the past only to dislocate and thus historically to de-value it in non-sequiturs.

The point is to trivialize the sacred privileges of time: "The benchmarks of the sixties—Vietnam, the Kennedy and King assassinations, Bob Dylan and the Beatles, psychodelia, the drug culture, the anti-war movement—were meant to be taken seriously. It can be perplexing—and almost sacreligious to some—to see them lumped into a pop collage with Ozzie and Harriet as if they were equivalent."[21] In each case, the new subjectivity instances itself by foregrounding, and then deconstructing—in a sense, metaphorically stripping away—a formerly privileged relation between signifier and signified. The arbitrary nature of the sign is thus rendered ironically, as an essential "truth" of pop-consciousness, just as the post-splatter self, or subject, emerges directly for view, no longer hiding behind outdated culture narratives of the past. So pervasive has the attack on chronology become that all good neighborhoods now have their own vintage clothing boutiques, where buyers can obtain wardrobes expressive of their temporally detoxified lifestyles. Or failing that, there's the Salvation Army story, where attitude has long been in style, though only recently obtainable on Visa or Mastercard.

In this context, America's recent, backward-looking revival no

longer appears anachronistic, but inevitable, even practical. Service
culture offers nothing new, at least at the level of labor. If current
projections hold, participants in the high-tech future are much more
likely to be sales clerks, janitors or waitresses than engineers or
computer programmers. We appear headed back toward a labor
intensive job market, with the majority of workers concentrated in
familiar, relatively low-paying positions, which afford little
prospect for advancement.[22] The global syndicalization of
technology here places under erasure the character types, the
"lives," called into being by the traditional consumer narrative of
upward mobility. Far from inventing something novel, therefore,
the attitudinal *avant garde* is merely acting out the recent
experience of a great many Americans who have had forced upon
them the ironic arbitrariness of history. The old forms of sense-
making no longer work—the characters and plots that people
formerly lived and believed in—so that time has left the individual
exposed, bereft of an explanatory "role" to fit him or her for present
contingencies. "You can't fake fitness," as Jaclyn Smith warns
from atop her "Lifecycle" in the Vic Tanny ad; "Either you're in
shape or you're not."[23] As things have turned out, a great number of
people have been exposed, individually, as unfit. And the truth,
within this discursive environment, is that those who fail deserve to:
they simply have the wrong stuff, and rather too much of it.

Under these conditions, the "renewal" of traditional class
distinctions makes a great deal of sense. People's attitudes have
now been adjusted in such a way that they are willing to affiliate
with the institution of un-historical values, which were never
necessarily their own. The irony of history, the de-constructed
ending of our collective narrative, has turned the markers of class
into magical signs. It's not the upper class who failed, after all, but
those without class, so that "traditional" signs become consumable
talismans for warding off the bad stories of failure; just as newly
appropriate life-cycles burn away the superfluous tissue of memory.
Unhampered by a potentially interfering chronology, the
arbitrariness of the past now expresses itself as both profit and
control.

This adjustment of attitude would probably remain impossible,
however, or at least less completely so, if it were not for the presence
of a threatening Other to motivate the ironic transformation of self
which is involved. Without a maniac lurking in the darkness, that is
to say, post-splatter discipline would surely seem and feel a less
pressing issue to young adults on the day after Halloween. Likewise,

without the God-less Russians, we wouldn't have to be so concerned with our own morality of fitness. Perhaps the most vital service provided by Mr. Reagan in his presidency is the production of a discursive Other capable of preserving the authority of belief while presiding over the disintegration of those truths which large numbers of Americans have traditionally believed in: "All the moral values which this country cherishes—freedom, democracy, the right of peoples and nations to determine their own destiny, to speak and write, to live and worship as they choose—all these basic rights are fundamentally challenged by a powerful adversary which does not wish to see these values survive."[24] By instituting the figure of an oppositional Other in this way, the presidential discourse assures that the focus of hostility will remain coherently fixed on a foreign site. It is healthy and patriotic to hate the Soviets; it is shameful and un-American to speak ill of IBM or the Almighty.

Opposition becomes especially meaningful to the present, uncertain market because it motivates, as moral imperative, the precise commitment to service-culture values that individuals must undertake if the post-industrial future is to find a home among us. It is altogether fitting and proper, then, that the chief executive—on a visit last spring to the Magic Kingdom (Orlando branch)—should declare video gaming to be an essential part of America's national defense: "Watch a 12-year-old take evasive action and score multiple hits while playing 'Space Invaders,' and you will appreciate the skills of tomorrow's pilot."[25] Walter Cronkite shares this conviction. "I always thought one reason we were so strong as a nation, up to and including World War II, was that we could mobilize so quickly," he said recently; "We had a nation of young people who ... understood how to make things work .... Well, today we're living in a high-tech society and our people are going to have the same advantages because they've grown up with those [computer] games."[26]

Here proper insight—a true reading of the Other—transforms the apparent triviality of computer gaming into the act of national preparedness which it actually is. The advent of high technology has not cut us off from the past; rather it has presented us with a challenge which merely serves to restore a sense of national identity that might otherwise have been lost. Of course we may be called upon to make sacrifices, just as we were in the previous war, but no sacrifice surely is too great for the preservation of our way of life—a way of life now violently threatened by "theirs."

In this connection, splatter films do not function autonomously to produce their looked-for, traditionalizing result; they are only half of a larger ritual process. Jamie Lee Curtis's heroines—who become mundane sacrifices to high-tech subjectivity—depend equally upon the idealized and precisely differentiated heroines of such films as *Blue Lagoon, Summer Lovers* and *Paradise*. If *Halloween I* dates the outset of domestic sacrificial rites, perhaps Cheryl Tiegs' near simultaneous appearance on the *Sports Illustrated* swimsuit issue marks the beginning of see-through ideality, although the pervasive and presiding presence of this fantasy-form, at least as it gets translated into film, is Brooke Shields. So potently fit, in fact, is the flesh of this blooming adolescent that once divested of her famous Calvins, only her mother Terri—as per proud insistence—has witnessed the perfection that lies beyond (excepting, of course, the unfortunate episode in the bathtub at age ten). Even when Brooke's flesh seems to present itself in person, as in *Blue Lagoon*, we are actually beholding only a pubescent fill-in, which fact the beamish parent has been quick to publicize. But this is just as things should be because the affective power of an ideal can be preserved only so long as its mythic unavailability remains intact. The image, the idealization, becomes viable precisely because it exists just out of reach: it is crucial to know—to see—that perfect fitness might indeed be possible, at least in the perfectible medium of film, but it is equally important to realize that no real-world consumer could ever be expected actually to possess it. For the ideal movie girl, there's an ideal movie boy, both of them visually tantalizing—images of what bodies *ought* to be—but substantively, generically untouchable. They get away with their perfection because they are protected by the medium they're in.

Unlike the quotidian world where Jamie Lee Curtis and friends come to their physical awakening, and frequently untimely demise, nudity and sexuality remain safe, "natural," in the idealization films because a certain prophylactic distance is established: a kind of bluish once-upon-a-time, which derives from a self-deconstructing use of genre conventions, expressive of an appropriate "attitude" toward service. In *Blue Lagoon*, for instance, chance maroons two virtuous and genetically middle-class cousins, Richard and Emmaline, on a typically Edenic island, where the weather is never bad, the fruit and fish never in short supply and where the restless, drum-beating natives never venture onto the beach to see what the beautiful people are up to. Everything in Never-Never Land remains just as it's supposed to, and with the exception of bodily exposure, more or less as it had in the first *Blue Lagoon* of 1949. The present day film evokes a complete range of set-piece markers. But, it seems, only to forget, or else trivialize, them once they've been carefully presented.

The opening and closing sequences provide tall-ships evocations of nineteenth century ocean travel, for instance, and for a time the children are looked after by the ship's cook, Paddy Button, who is the very model of a pre-modern salt. But Paddy passes away unaccountably (and early) in a drunken stupor one night, and the two children are left to themselves. They become back-to-basics enthusiasts, caring little for the proprieties of their native time and place. Instead, they spend most of their on-screen moments either without clothes altogether or else clad only in a Tarzan-like jock for the boy, and an always-fresh ensemble of frilly underwear for the girl, who will grow up into Brooke Shields. The historical setting has apparently become superfluous, so that attention shifts, naturally, to the developingly fit bodies of the young people, whose maturation is spent almost entirely under water, swimming with, and presumably "relating to" the other timeless creatures that dwell there. The underwater sequences are really quite beautiful: they translate jail-bait tantalizing into "art" through the careful application of medium, so that the final product has the look of a Jacques Cousteau documentary shot, by accident, at a nude beach. We are being offered a carefully managed invitation to get— guiltlessly—up close and personal with two idyllic young bodies. Richard and Emmaline leave behind the vocabulary and speech patterns of the nineteenth century, if they had ever assimilated them, and adopt an idiom that sounds indistinguishable from contemporary American English. The film might appear, then, to have grown unaware of its own anachronism, so powerful does the appeal of exposed, and naturalized, flesh become.

This, however, is pointedly not the case. Rather than mishandling its own materials, the film works carefully to construct, or more aptly to de-construct, a new relations between signifier and signified. *Blue Lagoon* is an "attitude" film; it foregrounds history and filmic conventions only to use them in a self-consciously "deadpan," fictional way. This becomes most apparent as Richard and Em grow up. Some of the set-piece trappings, most notably their clothes, fall away, so as to accommodate a maximum of contemporizing star exposure, which is essential to the "market-positioning" of the ideal. But the plot never allows a total abandonment of conventionality. Aided by a vast store of stereopticon plates, which they have preserved from their shipwreck, the pair learns how to grow up into the nice middle-class couple they innately yearn to become. The slides illustrate and comment paradigmatically on the transit to adulthood, showing scenes of courtship, marriage and family life. From the slides, the maturing adolescents learn how to form their own sexual and domestic yearnings so as to end up thoroughly, if prematurely, bourgeois: first they fall in love, then they get married and have a baby; the man works as provider, while the woman tends hearth and home.

The point all the way through is not realism but attitudinal surveillance. The didactic stereopticon plates, just like the other historical trappings, are made to look silly, in their stylized difference from the beautiful, "natural" world of the lagoon. Their conventionality, their fictional status, gets foregrounded in an ironic way: "Attitude is . . . an aesthetic based on ripping images out of the past and presenting them out of context—usually deadpan and always with irony." At the same time, it is the willingness of the film's Adam and Eve to be conventionalized that earns them the right to display and enjoy their bodies. Unlike the other pair, Richard and Emmaline don't abandon God's edicts; on the contrary, they seek him out, directly, in one of the film's more overtly outlandish sequences. But the arbitrariness, the made-up character, of the sign is the precise point here, so that propitiation and obeisance are in themselves sufficient warrants of appropriate, paradigmatic behavior—the submission to culturally privileged icons—regardless of how transparent or ridiculous the actual icons may appear. Richard and Emmaline—though naked and visibly active sexually—remain "nice kids." They have earned their right to undrape the future-self of a-temporal fitness, just as the film has earned the right to depict, or more properly expose, them by having already naturalized—via the mock-subversion of attitudinal irony—the basic discipline of neo-conservatism. In this way, the film preserves the function of authority while at the same time admitting the necessary arbitrariness of the particular forms that authority may take. *Blue Lagoon* represents, then, the guiding impulse which informs Reagan-era revivalism.

Much the same thing happens in two subsequent spin-offs, though neither one has achieved the box office success of the original. In *Paradise* an evil Arab prince, circa 1823, chases two Richard and Emmaline clones across the desert and into each other's arms. Again, most of the period props, clothing included, are discarded early on, along with the female body's English accent, which never really exists anyway. What we *do* get is a lot of "beautiful" bathing sequences, ala Richard and Em, as the currently nubile young man and woman move through a string of three-star oases. They don't have a stereopticon, but luckily, they bring along a pair of chimps and an old medical book to guide them through dawning adulthood's predictable conundrums. Evil Arab princes or no, both chimp and human couples "discover" each other, fall in love, complete their pair-bonding and conceive. And both idylls end happily, with the founding of two nuclear families.

Summer Lovers provides a contemporary, though no less carefully administered, setting for its account of familial genesis. In this film, however, alternate lifestyle arrives in the lagoon. The main cast members—a trio of slightly older, scrub-a-dub post-graduates (two women and a man)—investigate three-way sex and tentative lesbianism, in addition to the more familiar permutations of hetereosexual encounter. But their investigations never turn threatening, or perverse, because they are carefully supervised, just as the pubescent mingling of their somewhat younger progenitors. To begin with, the film draws upon the same Never-Never Land motif, with the menage setting up in the apparently endless summer of the Greek islands: that ageless, mythical site where anything becomes possible. They come together through the now familiar ritual of a nude dip in a travelogue beautiful lagoon. The "lovers" here have also all made proper, middle-class career choices, with the most frequently and fully revealed of the three being the woman archaeologist, a contemporizing reader of the past, who is demonstrably the furthest along with her career, which just goes to show that body and self have become indistinguishable in the blue world of future-tech.

What these movies hold in common—and what makes them new—is the graphic foregrounding of adolescent, entry-level sexuality: the subject matter of choice for service-culture fantasy. The films are about "going all the way," and they go all the way in visually producing that content, with more or less equal portions of male and female nudity, explicit depictions of masturbation, menstruation and intercourse, culminating in conception and childbirth.

In this way, they are different from films that deal with "adult" sexual materials, using "mature" actors—films such as *An Officer and a Gentleman* or *The Postman Always Rings Twice*. Here eroticism is not so egalitarian or so fully available visually; and it is surely **not meant** to appear innocent or "natural"; it is also—

crucially—positioned as subversive. In both instances, sex gets in the way of characters' lives; it makes them behave counter to the established values of those around them, whether this behavior ends up being judged good or ill by the film itself. In the Lagoon movies, however, sexuality leads always to the complete internalization of recognized, respectable values: everybody who sleeps together "gets married" and starts a family, virtually at the point of their first kiss. "Goodness" appears to be hormonally inscribed in the glands of Brooke and her friends, who are even less like their more immediate contemporaries in *Porky's* and *Ridgemont High*. In these, and similar films, the fictional gaze is almost always male and sexuality is confined to an arrested, masturbatory voyeurism. As Janet Maslin has recently pointed out, pairing off and going all the way are out: "...the mating dance [takes] precedence over mating itself. Real sex is probably more grown-up than any of these movies care to be, and it would call for distinct and individual characters."[27] By comparison, the blue-genre films deal with two or at most three characters, who are brought together specifically for the depiction of consummated sexual relationships. As to how "real" these consummations are, they are at least as real as the (formerly) brown-wrapped magazine sources from which their fantasy content derives. They, unlike the locker room peek-a-boo films, allow full access to the bodies of subjects: they validate visually, rather than emotionally, the authenticity, the "real" status, of chosen sexual content, however idealized and hyper-fit it may have been necessary to make that content appear.

Idealization films have appropriated a taboo content and reproduced it so as to gain entry to the shopping-mall audiences of Middle America: the very people who must first learn how to submit to the future if they're ever going to live there. To begin with, the production values of these films remain invariably high, so that they don't look like the x-rated smut. But most of all, they are packaged according to the throwaway standards of attitude/revival: the fantasyland images of fitness all submit to some form of generic discipline. The conventions of a highly conventionalized genre assume a parental role, reminding, and assuring audiences that only nice kids will be allowed to "do it"; and once they do, they will begin behaving like ideally responsible adults. Here, desire and the need for service become one: the content of desire becomes obtainable only when serviced by the conventional forms of traditional culture. "In a way," Michel

Foucault has said, "we can see the state as a modern matrix of individualization or a new form of pastoral power .... It is no longer a question of leading people to their salvation in the next world but rather enduring it in this world. And in this context, the word 'salvation' takes on different meanings: health, well-being ... security, protection against accidents."[28] In order to ensure the salvation of the subject, then—as America moves from the past of production to the future of service—subjectivity itself must be renegotiated. But while the content of subjectivity must necessarily change, the supervisory function of traditional, "historical" forms must be maintained, and projected into the future. The lagoon movies have ritualized this confrontation of management and desire, at least in part. Their ritual processing of content would remain effectively meaningless, however, without the complementary rendition of Jamie Lee Curtis' dark side of the post-industrial force.

The discourse of subjects, with which these movies are profitably preoccupied, is more than a local, filmic matter, however, just as contemporary demographic transformations involve more people than the teenagers onto whose shoulders, or other bodily parts, the future must inevitably descend. Both idealization and domestic splatter films are parts of and concurrent with a generalized renegotiation of the subject, one of the most prophetic instances of which is Rene Girard's *Violence and the Sacred*. Girard doesn't really explain the connections between *Halloween* and *Blue Lagoon*; as a matter of fact, he isn't interested in these films at all. What he does do, however, is provide the affective technology for installing an appropriate attitude toward the past. This is the providential discovery of his study, but for whose graceful insight, none might have escaped unharmed from the post-structural dark. The thematic power of synchronic violence—of the stalking, potent Other—becomes a kind of mnemonic suppressant for cancelling appetites that might prevent the subject from getting into shape. But given a properly motivated attitude, *then* and *now* become interchangeable, so that everybody can fit once more into their prom-night clothes. And that, really, is the truth that the domestic splatter film works so powerfully to motivate.

The idealized *Blue Lagoon* subject is transformed into the sacrificial victim of *Halloween* and *Friday the 13th* by means of alternate, generic appropriation. The anxiety engendered by the ideal—or rather by the viewer-subject's inability to possess ideal levels of visual and performative competence—provides the affective material necessary for motivating a new subjectivity. Once again, the undraped body figures centrally, as generalized reference to the desirable self. As it happens, splatter film teenagers are not less toned, tanned and attractive than their lagoon-dwelling contemporaries. But lacking the prophylaxis of a functioning value system—a managerial, moral "attitude" appropriate to young Americans of their "class"—they come to a very bad end indeed. Their willful profanation—the collapsing of those "natural" distinctions of morality and sexual propriety on which a profitable service environment depends—calls down the wrath of the ever-present maniac, whose genesis is never madness but a ruthless insistence on rectitude. As a punishment for their sins, the willingly immoral victims "get what they deserve," and in the process, the formerly unapproachable text of desire—the perfect body—gets read in a new and culturally overdetermined way, so as to transform anxiety into an alternate agenda of need, a synthetic subjectivity based on a powerful, technological idiom. The six films comprising the most famous domestic splatter cycles illustrate the working-out of this schematic.

The films of the *Halloween* and *Friday the 13th* cycles might be thought of as splatter violence at home and abroad, respectively. The *Halloween I* and *II* characters are high school students primarily, middle-American hometown kids; the *Friday the 13th* characters their slightly older, summer camp counselor clones, on an excursion into the countryside. In both cases, young people isolate themselves in pairs, so as to act out the now archaic, declasse, and dangerous lifestyle of sexual liberation.

In *Halloween* this begins at home, while the parents are away; in *Friday the 13th* it happens out in the country, after a group of urban characters returns to nature. Clothes get removed, bodies are revealed with some considerable abandon and enthusiasm, just as in the *Blue Lagoon* idealization, except that here, in the mundane world, punishment follows necessarily and swiftly upon the unmediated violation of taboos. Brooke Shields could not be expected to know any better; and given a chance, she and her sisters demonstrate an innate urge for middle-class propriety. But the same cannot be said for the overstimulated friends of Jamie Lee Curtis, who have had all the advantages of a traditional up-bringing, which they seem to value very little. In each case, the characters not only seek to escape supervision, which is the only sure safety in this filmic world; in their excesses, they threaten the very social institutions that have provided their comfortable lives and which they are subsequently charged with protecting.

These unfortunate, though culpable, victims are operating under an historically identifiable bad faith—a faith antithetical to the "traditions" of service-culture revivalism. The *Halloween* and *Friday the 13th* characters believe in, and act out a recognizably old fashioned narrative of "liberation." But as Donald Pleasance, the psychiatrist and normative source in *Halloween I* and *II* explains, there is no such thing as liberation, because the Other from whom we seek to free ourselves has a powerful, internal double, against which only traditional social forms can protect us, no matter how unconventionalized, how much and necessarily subsumed by attitude. The Soviet menace here discovers a powerful ally in this updated version of original sin. Just to make the message clear, Michael Myers, the *Halloween* maniac and Pleasance's lifelong patient, scrawls the Celtic word *samhain* on a wall. The doctor explains that *samhain* was the old Druid holiday, now become our Halloween: the time of ritual sacrifice and appeasement. Then, being a man of science, as well as a psychiatrist, he up-dates the meaning of the holiday: "*Samhain* isn't evil spirits, it's the unconscious mind. We're all afraid of the dark inside ourselves." And at least according to these films, we have good reason to be afraid.

The inner darkness, if not carefully managed and contained, will erupt in terrible and violent ways. "The disintegration of myths and rituals," as Rene Girard has said, "and indeed of religious thought in general, leads not to genuine demythologizing, but to the outbreak of a new sacrificial crisis .... The holiday-gone-wrong serves nicely to symbolize decadence .... Instead of holding violence in check, the ceremonies inaugurate a new cycle of revenge."[29] In this way, tradition appropriates violence thematically, reading its presence in a culture as visible evidence for the failure of liberation narratives, for the imperative need of managerial controls, even if in the fictionally demythologized forms of post-ironic attitude.

The *Halloween* and *Friday the 13th* young people act out Girard's bad holiday in an almost programmatic way, which ends with their becoming the high-tech victims of "a new sacrificial crisis." *Halloween I* begins with Jamie Lee Curtis (Laurie Strode) and two of her high school girlfriends, Annie and Lynda, discussing sex and the good life in their hometown, Haddonfield, Illinois. Lynda and Annie are both active and enthusiastic sexually, while Laurie remains a "nice girl": she doesn't smoke or drink; she does her homework; she is shy and demure when the conversation turns to talk of "boys." By her friends' standards, Laurie is old-fashioned, though we now recognize her to be a forerunner of the moral new wave. On Halloween night, 1978, Laurie is babysitting chastely while her friends Lynda and Annie play an evening of sexual adventures: they invite the boys over, neglect their own babysitting responsibilities, drink, take off their clothes and invite sex openly. Clearly they are not properly fearful of "the dark inside ourselves." In this world where the parents are permanently out, they let themselves go, and in return they fall victim to Michael Myers. Only Laurie survives his repeated attacks, preserved apparently by her seamless virtue and her solicitous care for the two small children who are in her charge.

In *Halloween II* Laurie arrives at the town hospital to be treated for the injuries she received in *I*. Here the same cycle of dereliction and libido works itself out. The doctor is drunk, the functionaries are all more interested in their own desires—either for TV, or each other—than in patient care. What this film depicts is a "disintegration of myths and rituals" just as in the original: people—many of them—just don't seem to care any more; the ties that bind the culture together are shown to be in a dangerously weakened state. This again renders the figuratively, if not literally, exposed idividuals easy prey for the miraculously revived Michael Myers, who likewise stalks this film, executing the incompetent and careless. Once again, however, the virtuous and—even with a broken leg—industrious Laurie Strode survives, though by the arrival of *Halloween III* there would be no further need for her services.

Almost the same pattern obtains in *Friday the 13th*, *I* and *II*, except that there is no genuine "good girl" here; there is only a survivor who makes her way from one film to the next, where she is promptly dispatched by Jason, the stalking Nemesis of Camp Crystal Lake. In this case, the sequel is even more precisely a replication of the first film. In each, the main characters are camp counselors, vastly more concerned with sexual development than with their own real work, which is the proper care of impressionable Americans. As role models, these young people are simply unfit, and in the splatter world, fitness is decidedly more than skin deep, though the nicely toned surfaces of most characters get at least a cursory examination. But their good looks do not protect them. They seek out darkness and isolation for their coupling, drinking and drug-taking, which is why they come to the woods in the first place.

Decadence, however—no matter how much concealed—does not go unpunished here any more than it did back in town. First Betsy Palmer, an employee of the camp, and then her quasi-supernatural son Jason stalk the woodsy territory turning this wistfully liberated Walden into horrid Red Death.

In both sequences, *Halloween* and *Friday the 13th*, the "message" is clearly and unmistakably the same: the sexual fantasies engendered by highly idealized images become punishable offenses if acted out in the real world, unmediated by those traditional sanctions which prevent the inner darkness from getting out of control, and thus demolishing the culture. Lest this point be missed, the provenance of each "maniac" is clearly and—by the film's standards, at least—reasonably established. Michael Myers does what he does because at age six he got a look at his teenage sister's too-quick entry into the sexual revolution, with her boyfriend one Halloween night. In his parent's absence, he stabs his sister to death, in the name of traditional propriety. Then, after spending fifteen years in a mental hospital, where Donald Pleasence's "cure" has been wholly ineffective, he returns home to Haddonfield to kill his sister all over again, and again, wherever he encounters her traumatizing type of behavior. In *Friday the 13th* camp counselors who are supposed to be watching Betsy Palmer's son opt instead for sex. While they are closeted together, the son drowns, which turns the doting mother into a stalking psychopath, who gets even with Jason's "murderers," and all their subsequent imitators, by dispatching them promptly at the first evidence of hanky panky. Then when the mother is decapitated herself, by one particularly resourceful counselor, Jason returns from his watery grave—now full grown—to carry on his mother's work in part two.

The morality of both film sequences is as relentless as it is singleminded. What makes these formulaic enactments viable as instruments of social management and leads to the culmination of both trilogies is the application of technology to the task of radically re-textualizing the subjects—both "characters" within the films and spectators who watch them. At the sacrificial "crisis," as Girard might call it, the Nemesis figure confronts a, usually, undraped body. The "reality" of this subject has been established visually: we get to see adolescent fitness, exposed, and often performing sexually, thanks to our own relaxed standards of screen morality.

Then, at the moment of crisis, when the body is violated—thus breaking one of the oldest taboos known to man—most often by penetration or dismemberment, we too are punished—affectively—

for our voyeur's participation in the carnality of the subject, just as the subjects themselves are punished for their profanation. People who watch such things—without the proper attitude—deserve to be scared, in other words, and so they will be. To begin with, at least, most of the people who watched splatter violence occurring were the same adolescents whose stand-ins were being graphically brutalized on the screen, which says a great deal about the level of anxiety induced culturally among adolescent subjects as they contemplate entry into the world of elective—and potentially service-able—adult sexuality.

What happens on the screen is both startling and upsetting, then, because of the extraordinary realism that these films achieve. Surprise, of course, is always a part of the sacrificial process, but more than that, splatter films take advantage of a highly developed special effects repertory, though the *Halloween* films do this to a lesser extent, at least initially, than those of the *Friday the 13th* sequence. Strangulation is the typical mode chosen by Michael Myers in *Halloween I;* by *Halloween II* he becomes more inventive, dispatching his victims by drowning them in boiling water, injecting their eyeballs with air bubbles, or slitting their throats with a surgical scalpel. This is followed in *Halloween III* with "sacrifices" based on decapitation (in which the victim's head is yanked off) or the crushing of the skull, effected by the insertion of fingers into the eye sockets. *Friday the 13th*, interested from the very start in graphic and highly inventive violence, tries not to liquidate any two characters in exactly the same way. Some have arrows thrust through their throats, others are impaled with spears or pitchforks, or get meat cleavers in the chest or hatchets in the head, or have their heads crushed so that their 3-D eyeballs pop out into the faces of the audience. What happens, with increasing frequency as the cycles go forward, is that we don't see the results of violence merely—a character's reaction shot, a cut, and then an already dead victim. We see a live character, without obvious cutaways, receiving some very special and disturbing effects.

But at this precise point, the subject, as image, takes on a new value, in relation to the real. What had been an actual body becomes a service-able surface, which is then appropriated for reading by the special effects creator of the film. Character dissolves, or gives way to technological actant. The viewer-subject assimilates the hyper-realism of horror by radically and powerfully reinterpreting the body and its inhabiting self: what had previously been an object now becomes an assembly of potential, filmic special services, one complexly overdetermined by a combination of desire, anxiety and hatred. The viewer desires his object visually, and hires the "right" to see the undraped character performing the tabooed acts—acts which would doubtless bear a special charge for adolescents who come to their first knowledge of sexuality through film images. But insofar as the object of desire remains within a mundane setting, not tabooed by generic packaging of *Blue Lagoon*—that object engenders anxiety in the viewer over his or her inability to have, or be, the "real" thing. The actors, however, do actually know each other's real flesh; we can seem them. And as their quotidian success, or access to reality, measures the spectator's distance from it, anxiety turns to hatred, which the maniac conveniently acts out in a kind of brutal, parodic rape. In each of the films, the attack is portrayed from the maniac's viewpoint, it is witnessed through his eyes.

His desire for violence is offered up to the spectator as the privileged reading of each sacrifice scene, and it is this desire which makes for the coherence of the film. "In the midst of the sacrificial crisis," as Girard has said, "there is no point in attaching desire to any one object, no matter how attractive, for desire is wholly directed toward violence itself."[30] Thus the film depends upon high-resolution violence for its power over the subject, both character and spectator, just as Girard must originate the Other of violence in order to preserve the attitudinally arbitrary conventions of culture.

The question is not what will happen, because everybody knows what's going to happen. Splatter films methodically trivialize the conventional reality of both narrative and character, so that the only meaningful question becomes one of technique. Character gives way to function; plot degenerates to cyclical rehearsals of effects. How will they—that is to say the special effects technologists represented by the maniac—do it next time? Structurally, each of the films instances this question as the real point of the representational crisis. The visceral power of sacrificial scenes is displaced; the affective crisis is appropriated, or serviced, by renewable processes, as the horrible becomes a field of technical discourse and curiosity. In order to "understand" his chosen film genre, the splatter fan doesn't read film criticism, but studies special effects techniques.[31]

Appropriately then both the *Friday the 13th* and *Halloween* cycles conclude with the foregrounding of technology itself; they lose a great deal of their power, though not without producing a certain deconstructive intelligence. *Halloween III* abandons

Michael Myers and the Mid-west entirely; it takes place in northern California and centers around the techno-syndicalism of Conal Cochran, a Druid toy manufacturer who has planted little chips of Stonehenge in each of his fabulously successful Silver Shamrock masks. On Halloween night all the children will be wearing their masks and watching the big giveaway on TV. A signal will be transmitted secretly to the lethal masks, in which micro chemistry will activate the Stonehenge chip, and the children of America will become a terrible sacrifice, a recuperation of the bloody rituals that started the old Celtic new year. "It's not so different now," as Cocharan explains; "it's time again." Here nudity is held to a minimum; only the hero's girlfriend reveals herself, for which she pays not with dismemberment or puncturing but with her being turned into one of Cochran's high-tech robots. The hero, even without her help, prevents the apocalypse—or most of it—and we are left to assume that the world is substantially safe once more and incapable, probably, of producing a *Halloween IV*. The film is interesting at the level of its own self-awareness, with the foregrounded metaphor of the high-tech automatons—the perfect service subjects—as the ultimate progeny of holiday violence. But affectively it is puny when compared to the first two episodes, which no doubt explains its general lack of box-office success.

Similarly *Friday the 13th III* makes technology the central topic of concern. Here the film is shot in 3-D so that a great deal of time is devoted to scenes that have virtually nothing to do with the plot or characters, but rather with the exploitation of technical medium. Yo-Yos, clothesline poles and popcorn, for example, all become as important to the film as actors: anything that can be made to come off the screen and into your face. Like *Halloween III*, the film is attempting to show that it knows what's going on; just as the special-effects explicators do, it is trying to produce a concurrent reading of itself. Again, actual nudity plays a relatively smaller part, with visual titillation giving way to more overtly suggestive dialogue. But unlike *Halloween III*, which merely thematizes service, in *Friday the 13th III*, the technology of 3-D takes over, so that plot and character become trivial adjuncts to the "real" action. Although there is an attempt to establish a connection with *I* and *II*, the connection is never coherently worked out. Nor is the ensemble of characters, who have nothing in common aside from their stereotypical flatness. This is not to say that prior splatter films define a rich tradition of characterization, because they obviously don't. Generally, however, there is an attempt to produce a coherent group identity by assembling characters that typify—or ought to typify—the values of middle America. It is those values, after all, which are being attacked and then variously defended. But in *Friday the 13th* there is no such group; the organizing idea of the summer camp, with its libidinal counselors, has been abandoned. Now the characters are assembled in apparently random fashion. Like the clowns who arrive packed in the circus car, they come to be here (in their holiday van) not as members of a cast, but because each of them can do a trick. Each one generates a bit of stage business which will then facilitate the application of visual technology. Again the film did not become so successful as its predecessors, thanks to its probably misunderstood attempt at deconstructive self-consciousness.

At the same time, however, both *Friday the 13th* and *Halloween III*, in their comparative failures, are in a sense the inevitable products of prior generic success, and in their self-conscious preoccupation with technology, they announce their own antequation, as a form. They invite the self-devouring of *Videdrome*, which is shortly to come. If the ideal service subject is a self of performative competencies—either more or less awakened—rather than one of acquisitive desires; and if the optimal service space is the non-narrative, forever-now of spa-America, then the splatter filming of both part *III*s has reached its final destination. There are no more stories to tell, because the point all along was to exhaust narrative and character alike as available sources of meaning. Instead, the viewer subject was "taught" to read the self in ways that deliver him, willingly, as a matter of desire, into the hands of technological administration.

At the last, then, the technical competencies of filming succeed at exhausting the screen space of usable content, which was the point from the very beginning. It was not Michael Myers or Jason and his mother who were really attacking the plot-bound characters of domestic splatter; rather, it was the technological imperatives of the genre itself. And finally the real protagonist emerges. The soundtrack, the "musical" score, has been the violent hero all along, though this fact remains largely obscured until the foregrounding of technology focuses attention on the "role" being played by "effects." This role becomes especially, and debilitatingly, clear in *Friday the 13th*, where the collusion of sound and visual technology completely overpowers the remaining content, thus making obvious the pervasive role played by audio cues. Just as the maniac wears a disguise—a mask which is discarded in Part III of both sequences—

so has sound kept secret the now revealed "scandal"[32] of its administrative competence and omnipresent control. The earlier films work, as this one does not, precisely because the true subject remains a mystery. As Girard has pointed out, "We, the spoiled children of privilege, consider the god's anger as something illusory. In fact it is a terrible reality" (259). Only in the surrender to mystery does the ritual power of violence become available. Similarly, it is only by granting technology its necessary disguise that the films can be expected to teach us what we need to know.

All along, then, the soundtrack was the actual predator—the insubstantial, technological protagonist who can see in the dark and who knows what is going to happen. The viewer of these movies soon "learns" how little he can trust the credibility of characters and narratives; they are disposable here, just as they have become in "real" life, which point the final films of both the *Halloween* and *Friday the 13th* cycles make clear. Knowledge now exists exclusively at the level of technological subjectivity. In order to "understand" the film, the viewer must ultimately, however knowingly, de-value the narrative, objective surfaces of representational characters. The only remaining source of authority is the audio track, which services faithfully the viewer-subject's anxious need for reliable guidance. Neither set of films has a fully developed soundtrack; what each has instead is an electronic sounding motif which is used over and over again, and which travels from one film to the next, to administer an appropriate subjectivity. The unmusical "score" of both *Halloween* and *Friday the 13th* comments on the action within the frame, announcing—and casting into ironic perspective—the impending attack of the maniac. At the sacrificial crisis, when the multiple determinations of the film converge, it is the unseen omniscience of sound which is always already aware of, and in charge of, the resolution that the viewer-subject must work affectively to achieve. And in almost every instance, the sound can be relied upon not to take advantage, not to "lie" about what is going to happen. Through the application of a repetitive, electronic cue, then, each of these films establishes service as the now inevitable need of choice for the future-consciousness being administered.

We are here being taught, in an extraordinarily forceful way, the arbitrariness of the visual sign—the object self—because once this proposition becomes a lived, affective reality, the ideal environment for future-tech will have been achieved. By ideal, I mean an environment that operates on the post-historical cycles of electronic gaming: endless functioning without linear reference. I mean an environment that defines the subject not as a cumulative narrative product but as a re-cyclable source of desire for service. The consciousness of the video gamesman, then, is the ideal toward which the domestic splatter film has been working and which we, collectively, are approaching closer all the time: here the player buys the right to have his or her subjectivity variously, electronically, administered. For hire, the player is given an arbitrary cipher self, which purchasable technology then inserts into a variety of repeatable and usually threatening situations. Success consists in staying alive, in the continued competence of the proxy subject to consume more service; failure—death—is the inability to be serviced: a failure to need the right things. And those who fail deserve to, because they are simply not fit. The need engendered here is not so much to get somewhere as it is to maintain and to renew a repeatable range of technical functions.

The splatter film appeared just at the point when high-tech subjectivity arose, as a potential and potentially profitable question, and now the form appears to have passed from among us. The developed, technical competence of the genre has exhausted that content on which it depended—a content of narrative plots believably objective characters, which was old-fashioned from the very beginning because it played on ancient taboos. And this is just how things were meant to happen; the imaginative space claimed by domestic splatter first had to be cleared of such archaisms before the viewer-subject could be properly exposed to the parental guidance of futurity. That exposure, and the resulting sense of post-sacrificial "renewal," are everywhere in evidence, as reinstituted families gather before their viewing screens—the cathode hearth of service-America—to observe the common rituals that bind us as individual subjects to the syndicalized technology which makes us whole.

This renewal, of course, would have remained impossible without a technologically updated appreciation for the Other: the proscribed presence of taboo, which if embraced will overwhelm us in a violence even more terrible than we can imagine. And as the recent past has shown, our imaginations are pretty good. But we have come through, a free people—free after the day's serviceable labors—to commune through the screen-based functions of video subjectivity. From the *Twenty-Minute Workout* in the morning, to *Halloween* or *Texas Chainsaw Massacre* (in video game reincarnations), to Music Television for the wee hours of the night, we have constantly available the newly fit images that lead us to desire those time-denying stimuli which will keep us free.

Through that surrender we achieve our renewal and fend off the Other, the most recent celebration of this achievement being ABC Television's *The Day After*, which topped the fall ratings sweeps with a 43 percent audience share.[33] In that film, which announces itself generically as a standard disaster piece, the usual consolations of plot and character are threateningly withdrawn. Things visibly don't work out right; as a matter of fact, they don't work out at all. The "people" we get to know—even Jason Robards—don't make it to safety. Instead, they just look worse and worse until they die. The telic consolation usually promised by narrative conventions here withers into disturbing, quasi-documentary flatness. But that is not where *The Day After* ends, as anybody knows who watched it.

The generic disintegration of the film, from disaster piece into July Fourth gone wrong, gets recuperated by the arbitrary institutions of electronic authority: the talking heads of the epilogue who appropriate to their post-narrative supervision the affective by-products of video imaging. It doesn't matter, really, whether one "side" or the other won the debate. The point here is that both sides, together with the television network, agreed ahead of time that there should be a debate. And America responded; we kept on watching, as if we'd now mastered the lesson of post-splatter darkness: that only the affiliated will survive the shocks which are to come, and it doesn't matter, particularly who we affiliate with, because it is the function—the service—of authority, rather than its substance which has been made attitudinally desirable.

The Reverend Jerry Falwell was right in explaining to Phil Donahue, soon afterward, that the program didn't do the nuclear cause any harm, because it didn't, nor was it intended to. The "issues" are not presently at issue; it is the subjects, rather than the objects, of control which must now be properly negotiated, as the carefully noncommital packaging of the evening's "entertainment" makes clear. What the film does, then, is to instance the need for service: it performs a paradigmatic divestiture of those imaginative archaisms which might interfere with the direct exposure of "individuals" to the surveillance of post-contemporary desire. Thus, the political "double bind," as Michel Foucault calls it, "which is the simultaneous individualization and totalization of modern power structures."[34] Even so, we are not now falling into the unfeeling coldness of 1984, regardless of what Foucault's tone, or the calendar, may imply.

There's a cup of kindness yet, for actants prepared to drink it. As we have been powerfully taught, our memories may no longer serve us as they once did, in the pre-ironic past, but that doesn't mean we must live without solace. What it does mean is that solace must become attitudinal and post-ironic, as it seems already to have done: a matter of traditions no longer affiliated—necessarily—with actual belief or remembrance; of signs that become no less significant because of their visible arbitrariness. So, the battle for the mind of North America, as Professor O'Blivion called it, appears to be over, and we have won. The Other has been successfully, and violently, revived and in that revival we become subject to the beneficent attitude that will save us. "Violence will come to an end," as Professor Girard has said, "only after it has had the last word and that word has been accepted as divine. The meaning of this word must remain hidden, the mechanism of unanimity remain concealed . . . . The only barrier against human violence is raised on misconception."[35] That the fit have prevailed is clear: we take satisfaction in the youthful look of Mr. Reagan's dyed hair, in the vigor of his rouged cheeks, in the sincerity of his reading of the presidential script. Thus we become individually, electively, the clients of an attitude which only just yesterday, it seems, hardly any of us would, or could, have imagined needing. Progress is still our most important product.

Notes

[1]"Excerpts from President's Speech to National Association of Evangeliicals," *New York Times*, 9 March 1983, p. A18, col. 4. Hereafter all references to the *Times* are to the edition available outside the New York area.

[2]*Times*, 9 March 1983, p. A18, col. 4.   [3]*Ibid.*, col. 3.

[4]Rene Girard, *Violence and the Sacred*, trans. Patrick Gregory (Baltimore: Johns Hopkins Univ. Press,1977), p. 49.

[5]Paul Fussell, *Class: A Guide Through the American Status System* (New York: Summit Books, 1983), p. 21.

[6]"Changes in the U.S. Work Force," *New York Times*, 6 July 1982, p. A11, cols. 2-3.

[7]*Time*, 30 May 1983, cover.   [8]*Time*, 3 Jan. 1983, cover.

[9]Roger Rosenblatt, "A New World Dawns," *Time*, 3 Jan. 1983, p. 13.

[10]Ronald Reagan, "How to Stay Fit," *Parade*, 4 Dec. 1983, p. 4.

[11]*Newsweek*, Special Anniversary Issue, Spring 1983, cover.

[12]Charles P. Alexander, "The New Economy," *Time*, 30 May 1983, pp. 62-3.

[13]Alexander, pp. 63-4.

[14]Mary Douglas and Baron Isherwood, *The World of Goods: Towards an Anthropology of Consumption* (New York: Norton, 1979), p. 5.

[15]John Berger, *Ways of Seeing* (1973; rpt. Harmondsworth: Penguin, 1977), p. 139.

[16]*Vanity Fair*, 46 (March 1983), 14.   [17]Fussell, p. 21.

[18]Jon Pareles, "The Pop Record Business Showing Recovery Signs After 4-year Slump," *New York Times*, 28 Nov. 1983, p. 20, cols. 1-3.

[19]Andrew Pollack, "Finding Home Computer Uses," *New York Times*, 11 May 1983, p. 25, col. 3.

[20]Craig Unger, "Attitude," *New York*, 15 (26 July 1982), 24.

[21]Unger, p. 31.

[22]Alexander, p. 64. See also William Serrin, " 'High Tech' Is No Jobs Panacea, Experts Say," *New York Times*, 18 Sept., 1983, p. 1, cols. 2-4.

[23]*Detroit Free Press*, 31 May 1983, p. 16A, cols. 1-6.

[24]Ronald Reagan, "Nuclear Weapons: An Interim Agreement," *Vital Speeches of the Day*, 49 (15 April 1983), 391.

[25]"President Gives Video Games a Qualified Seal of Approval," *Detroit Free Press*, 9 March 1983, p. 6A, col. 1.

[26]Kenneth R. Clark, "Pac-Man? Cronkite Approves," *Detroit Free Press*, 9 March 1982, p. 8C, col. 1.

[27]Janet Maslin, "Under the 1983 Chic, Movies Still Leer At Women," *New York Times*, 22 May 1983, p. 21, col. 3.

[28]Michel Foucault, "The Subject and Power," *Critical Inquiry*, 8 (Summer 1982), 783-84.

[29]Girard, p. 125.   [30]Girard, p. 145.

[31]See, for example, the fine study of this topic by Harold Schechter and David Everitt, *Film Tricks: Special Effects in the Movies* (New York: Dial, 1980).

[32]For a suggestive study of the role of sound in relation to the visual aspects of film, see Rick Altman, "Moving Lips: Cinema as Ventriloquism," *Yale French Studies*, No. 60, pp. 67-79.

[33]Sally Bedell Smith, "CBS Tops Fall 'Sweeps' Fifth Time," *New York Times*, 3 Dec., 1983, p. 14, col. 4.

[34]Foucault, p. 785.   [35]Girard, p. 135.

Loggers Can't Cry:
And Other Taboos of the Northwest Woods

Jack Estes

On the annual Logger Appreciation Day in Port Angeles, Washington, hundreds of real men drive their big shiny log trucks through this northwest city, horns blaring and noisy diesels revving. The 1982 Grand Marshall, an old-timer named Guy Decker, led the parade in the back seat of a new Chrysler LeBaron convertible, smiling and waving to onlookers in spite of the buckets of rain falling on his eighty-year-old head. Like any honest northwest logger, Guy Decker appeared undaunted by the rainfall. After all, he'd spent a good part of his life working in such conditions and he'd be damned if he'd let a little rain stop him this time, either.[1]

In the woods there's a story of a logger who became known as "The Silent Man." He simply never spoke to anyone, except once. He ate by himself, worked by himself, and sat alone at night staring off into space. No one ever saw him write a letter and no one reported that he ever exchanged words. Apparently after a couple of weeks, someone dared to strike up a conversation, asking him how long he'd been out on the Coast. His response was, "My friend, I have been on the Coast a good many years, but I want you to understand that I am not going to undergo any cross-examination." He quit the camp the next morning.[2]

A logger's widow reported that her husband had suffered from cold hands and from sleepless nights for a couple of days before he was killed. The day of his accident was scheduled to have been his last working day in the woods. When his widow disclosed that he'd had cold hands and sleepless nights, no one was surprised at his death. People's only surprise was that he went to work in spite of the "signals," known commonly among loggers as portentous.[3]

Back in the late sixties, in Forks, Washington, a remote logging town in the wettest corner of the United States, a long-haired biker stopped in one of the local taverns for a beer. In a true-life parallel of *Easy Rider*, so the story goes, this biker just didn't look quite right to the loggers in the bar, loggers who at that time (it has since changed) were all quite short-haired. This biker—some say he was even a member of the Hell's Angels gang—fought hard, but left town after a beating and, most importantly, a haircut. (The legend continues, by the way, that he returned with his friends and wiped out the folks in the tavern.)

A logger doesn't let rain affect his objective; a logger doesn't pry into the personal affairs of others; a logger doesn't ignore the superstitions; a logger doesn't readily accept "strangers" who seem to be antithetical to the logger's way of life: These are a few of the taboos that circulate among northwest loggers and against which they lead their way of life. In this danger-filled, inter-dependent society, codes of dress, language, behavior and morality are quite strictly adhered to. Taboos—socially impressed restrictions which have no apparent logical base—run rampant in these communities.[4] Taboos do not include the dozens of safety rules: not standing in the bight of a cable, for example, or not going into the woods without a hard hat. These types of rules are logically imposed and can be easily defended. A double-bladed axe can't be left buried in a tree, for instance, because of the danger. A story circulates of a crew's dog, Shorty, that loved to frolic on fallen trees—until he ran into the exposed blade of an axe and was split right up the middle.[5] But why can't a logger wear a "Phillips head hat" instead of a standard hard hat? Why can't a logger refer to his boots by their proper name— "caulked boots"—rather than the mispronounced "cork boots"? Or why can't a logger, a "real" logger, drive a logging truck?[6]

This society seems more concerned than most about image. This is ironic, actually, since one description which the logger holds most dearly is that he is independent, rugged, unaffected by the opinions of others. In reality, of course, image is of major significance: There is a strict status system, a strict seniority system, and a strict competence system. As a result of such images, part of the logger's difficulty lies in the overlapping of these same systems: A "horn" (or greenhorn) can be at the bottom of the status and seniority systems and still be well respected in terms of his competence *so long as he passes the tests.*

One example of this is that among some crews a "woodman's test" is sometimes ceremoniously given to a young logger. After telling him he must hit a log dead center with his axe, the veterans will blindfold him and, unbeknownst to the initiate, put his gloves and hardhat on the spot. An accurate shot will therefore destroy two of the young logger's most needed implements.[7]

On the other hand, a veteran might very well have little respect from others because of his own repetitive failing of the tests—his careless treatment of a chainsaw, fraternization with the U.S. Forest Service workers, poorly timed jokes about a fellow logger's wife or girlfriend, or, perhaps most importantly, his ignorance of the basic rules of safety, like passing a log directly over the head of a fellow worker.

In fact, the tests never really end. For example, in terms of status, driving a truck is at the bottom. A log truck driver is *not* a real logger, and even the lowest logger is higher than any trucker. However, if the trucker isn't afraid to get out of his truck and to give the landing crew a hand now and then, he can elevate his position remarkably fast. He can, in effect, pass the trucker test: Does the man know how to work? Without having proved himself, the trucker actually becomes taboo and is avoided. Some truckers even try subtle bribes to win a crew's favor, buying a six-pack of Coke, for instance, and placing it in a cold stream for the men to share.

A logger who fails the various tests is also taboo: Can he drink beer all night and still get up in time to catch the crew bus—the "crummy" (sometimes by four o'clock)? Does he have the proper attire (stagged pants, cork boots, hickory shirt, long woolies, Logger World suspenders, and metal—not plastic—hard hat)? If he's been to college, does he keep his education to himself? If he's a Christian (and, yes, there are some in the woods, often a whole crew of them, in fact), does he avoid trying to convert others or to criticize others for any un-Christian habits? Does he know the language—the jargon, the slang, the rhythms—which are compatible with the profession? Can he chew tobacco (and does he call it "snoose")? Is his tobacco Copenhagen, or is it some "pussy brand"? Does he go for hours in the field without needing a drink, or is he known for "loving the water bottle?"[8] Does he seem to have too high an opinion of himself, or does he keep his accomplishments quiet? Any of these areas is significant enough to create an ostracism of even a veteran logger.

A logger might read the book *Real Men Don't Eat Quiche* the way the unsophisticated teen-ager reads *The Preppie Handbook* or *The Valley Girls' Guide to Reality;* it could be a guidebook to his behavior (although he'd never admit to using any form of guidebook). On the other hand, a logger wouldn't actually be seen reading anything except the newspaper *Loggers' World* out of Chehalis, Washington, the latest Max Brand western, or a hard-core "crotch" novel (often reading the juicy parts over the CB). It is also taboo to read anything that hints of intellectual stimulation. Would they vote for the ERA? No, of course not. Women have a specific place in the life of a real logger, and that place isn't as an equal, particularly in the woods.

Loggers don't listen to classical music or to jazz. Such music is taboo, and a person who did listen would definitely be someone who thinks he's superior. Loggers do listen to country-western music or, recently, to rock. When they go to a dance, loggers like to drink a lot of beer. They don't sit around in the dance hall and talk to their dates, either: They dance, and they sit with other loggers (and their women); they laugh and cuss and laugh some more. And when they dance, they dance with their own and, occasionally, with their friends' women; but if they don't know you, don't ask their women to dance. That is forbidden. They also like to wear their logging clothes to the dances, a practice that is now outlawed in most establishments due primarily to the effects of corks on the floors, but due also to the general desire of proprietors to clean up their clientele[9] (Without corks, of course, the rest of the outfit looks a bit silly.)

Certain ideas have traditionally been taboo for loggers, but these ideas are changing somewhat. Political liberalism is definitely taboo. They believe that abortion is wrong, that families need to be strengthened, that the U.S. of A. must be preserved as it is. They are also anti-union, not because they trust management so much as because they trust themselves. They figure on earning their jobs. They are definitely opposed to Indian fishing rights and to any form of gun control: These men are fishermen and hunters and supporting such pinko positions is taboo, absolutely. They can accept the Indian—as long as he proves himself—but they can't accept his getting any special privileges just because of his race.

Across cultures, taboos are traditionally associated with death. There are things that simply must not be done in this world where death is a companion. Loggers themselves seldom talk about the danger, preferring to think that they're "too tough to die."[10] Also, unless his wife or child dies, a logger doesn't cry. Loggers are tough; they epitomize the American male role: Show no emotion. One logger's wife, in fact, recalls her husband's having smashed his thumb with a hammer and not even saying "Ouch!"[11] Loggers are so tough that they don't take toilet paper into the woods with them. They'd rather tear off a chunk of their shirts or grab a handful of leaves than be caught with such a sissy convenience.

Interestingly, in spite of their close relationship with nature, loggers are not known for their ecological conscientiousness. Believing in what some call "the myth of perpetual yield," loggers seem willing and eager to get as many trees cut down as quickly and as cheaply as possible. The clear-cut, they say, can always be re-planted with fast-growing Douglas Fir and the region will be reforested before a person can even count his money. At least that's the logger's position. Environmentalism has become a dirty word, a taboo. The term is defined among loggers as no-work, and—in days of nearly 40% unemployment among these men—no-work is the nemesis of all loggers. One former Forks resident, referring specifically to the log trucker, put it this way:

> The truck driver is dreaming while he wears ruts in Highway 101, dreaming of fucking that little redheaded barmaid, dreaming of cashing his paycheck, dreaming of putting another six-pack down, of bowhunting on Sunday, of decking some dude in Art's Place on Saturday night. He possesses zilch appreciation of watershed process and farm; but infinite bullshit about log exports, those damn crazy Japs, and why all the black bears oughta be shot![12]

Freud (called a "jerk" by one interviewee) suggested that taboos reflect "emotional ambivalence," even neuroses and psychoses. If so, he might well have examined the logger culture and emerged with the idea that masculinity and status are heavily emphasized among members of this group because of the logger's insecurity in these very areas. Certainly the logger's often violent antipathy toward homosexuals would contribute to this interpretation. Even acknowledging that he was acquainted with the company's male nurse drew jokes and catcalls to one logger.[13] The slightest sign of "swishiness" will make a logger taboo. (Monty Python's popular "I'm a Lumberjack" song actually derives its humor from this dichotomy, the funniest lines being, "I put on women's clothing and just hang around the bars.") A standard view of such attitudes is that latent homosexuality exists just beneath the tough exterior. The culturally impacted Super-ego overpowers any suggestion whatsoever of "aberrant" sexuality. The topic is so much a taboo that one interviewee told me that "no logger is going to let you walk away with all your teeth if you keep pushing your latent homo thesis."[13]

Freud's theory appears to be overly simplistic. In the case of the logger it may be carrying the stereotyping too far. Part of the reason for this highly macho society might be attributable to the type of work itself. With danger being part of each logger's daily life, a person needs to know exactly whom he can rely on. He has to have a great deal of trust in those who work behind him. Carelessness is a threat not only to the logger but also to his co-workers. Accidents are common, and the men in the woods live with the risk of death every day. Taboos that prohibit certain dress, language, behavior and morality help to unite a group. In the woods, strength is a virtue, and so strength is admired; working in adverse situations is a necessity, so ruggedness is admired; knowing one's job perfectly is required, so language and dress—the signals of one's know-how—are very important. In the woods, a man wants to know, without a doubt, that he can trust his life to this eighteen-year-old kid, this kid who may not even know the difference between a logger and a lumberjack.[15]

Notes

[1]"Logger Day Celebration Goes on in Spite of Rain," *The Port Angeles Daily News*, Oct. 24, 1982, p. A3.

[2]Richard L. Williams, *The Loggers,*

[3]Barre Tolken, *The Dynamics of Folklore* (Boston: Houghton Mifflin, 1981).

[4]See especially Sigmund Freud, *Totem and Taboo* (originally published in 1913), trans. James Scrachey (New York: Norton, 1950), pp. 18-36.

[5]Interview with Brian Doherty, Port Angeles, Washington, Oct. 29, 1982.

[6]Interview with Craig Switzer, Port Angeles, Washington, Oct. 10, 1982.

[7]Doherty.   [8]Switzer.

[9]Telephone interview with Bonnie Nelson, Oct. 28, 1982.

[10]Telephone interview with Cathy Logg, Nov. 4, 1982.

[11]Nelson.

[12]Anonymous interviewee.

[13]Switzer.   [14]Switzer.

[15]The difference, by the way, is somewhat regional: West Coast loggers would consider being called a lumberjack an insult to their masculinity whereas east coast and midwest loggers seem to accept the designation.

Speak No Evil:
Word Taboos Among Scottish Fishermen

Edward E. Knipe & David G. Bromley

In all societies there are expectations of what people ought and ought not to do. Associated with these expectations are sanctions which either reward or punish people for conformity to or violation of these expectations. Normative prescriptions and proscriptions vary in terms of to whom they apply, the types of situations in which they apply and the time period for which they apply. The strongest norms are those which apply to all persons, in all situations, for all times. It is for this reason that normative proscriptions like, "Thou shalt not kill," are held in such awe; at least in theory there simply are no exceptions.

Although we shall be concerned exclusively with taboos here, it is useful to distinguish between strong positive and strong negative norms. James Frazer (1922: 22) observed:

Positive magic or sorcery says "Do this in order that so and so may happen." Negative magic or taboo says "Do not do this lest so and so should happen." The aim of positive magic or sorcery is to produce a desired event; the aim of negative magic or taboo is to avoid an undesirable one.

The term "taboo" now is often used to describe behaviors which are universally forbidden within a given social group. Sexual intercourse between individuals defined as relatives, speaking the name of the group's deity or eating of a clan totem except under certain ritual conditions constitute traditional anthropological examples of taboos. In its original usage drawn from anthropological field studies of homogeneous, native cultures, however, there was an additional element which separated taboo from other prohibitions—the notion of automatic punishment. Engaging in taboo behavior would result automatically and inevitably in punishment. So, sexual intercourse between relatives would result in deformed children and eating the clan totem would result in famine. As Margaret Mead put it (Steiner, 1956: 22): "Tabu may be defined as a negative sanction, a prohibition whose infringement results in an automatic penalty without human or superhuman mediation."

Taboo behaviors by their nature are dangerous both to individuals who engage in them and to others, for the automatic penalties which result from taboo violations often have social effects which extend beyond the individual violator. The establishment of taboos thus constitutes a way for social groups to identify dangerous behaviors and, having identified them and the misfortunes which will result from them, to establish grounds for controlling those behaviors.

In this paper we will offer an explanation for a continuing reduction in the number of words which are proscribed as taboo among Scottish fishermen while at sea. In seeking to fashion an explanation for the erosion of historically important taboos, it will be important to understand both the symbolic significance of particular words and structural changes in traditional village life and in the fishing industry. The data for this paper are drawn from a larger study conducted by the senior author (Knipe, 1984) on the impact of changing fishing technology on a small fishing village, Gamrie, which is located on the northeast coast of Scotland.

Gamrie

The village, officially named Gardenstown, is called by the villagers by the parish name Gamrie. It is located on the Moray Firth about 40 miles north by northwest from Aberdeen. Although the harbor is too small to accommodate modern commercial fishing boats and there is no fish market, it is, nevertheless, a fishing village. With the exception of a few local service occupations and a transporting firm, over 90 percent of the working males are engaged in fishing. The fishermen commute either to a number of nearby harbors with fish markets or, more frequently, to the west coast where they fish for herring.

The village was founded in 1720 by the landowner, Alexander Garden of Troup, but historical and archeological evidence indicates a continuous occupation since the late Neolithic-early Bronze Age. From available data the village had a population of 300 in 1780, increased to over 1,400 by 1900 and is presently between 800 and 900. For a number of reasons, primarily related to changes in fishing technology, the village population appears to be steady or in a slight decline over expected natural increase.

The village is relatively isolated from other towns and villages along the coast. There is only one road in and out of Gamrie, and it dead-ends in the village. As a result, there is none of the through traffic which might have created a continual infusion of outside influence. Recently some of the older fishermen's houses have been purchased by non-residents for vacation homes, but there are only a handful of these "outsiders" who spend more than a few weeks per year in these homes. Thus, Gamrie may be characterized as a small, isolated, single-industry community with a high concentration of persons who have spent their entire lives in the village.

Traditional Fishing Taboos

There is no practice so universally observed in fishing communities like Gamrie as some form of what might be called "fishing magic." Some type of proscriptive or prescriptive practices relative to the abundance of the catch or the weather or personal safety have been recorded among fishing peoples in all parts of the world. For example, Cove (1978) observed that the tabooed words among Cornwall fishermen were clergy, women and rabbits. Poggie and Gersuny (1974), in their study of Rhode Island fishermen and lobstermen, found that the three most standard customs were: "Don't turn hatch cover upside down"; "Don't whistle because it whistles up a breeze"; "Don't mention pig on board." Similar practices are reported by Lofgren (n.d.) for Swedish fishermen in Noorland and Scania.

Peter Anson (1950) reported many activities of fishermen in Scotland and elsewhere that involved both taboo and sorcery. Activities thought to bring about good luck included sprinkling the house with salt water at New Year's, hanging seaweed over the front door of the house, and spitting on the hearth. Activities to be avoided included burning fish bones, and encountering "ill-fitted" persons (literally ill-footed, any person thought to bring misfortune). Counting boats at sea or counting nets on land or walking over them (especially if done by an "ill-fitted" person) were considered unlucky. When going out fishing, one should avoid women, cats, ministers, red-headed persons or people with flat feet. A number of words were to be avoided at sea. Depending upon the area, this list of forbidden words included minister, kirk (church), rat, salmon, pig, fox and rabbit. If these words were inadvertently used, the negative consequences could be averted if the crew would shout "Cauld iron" (cold iron) and grab the nearest piece of metal. When the forbidden word was needed in a conversation, it would take the form of a euphemism. Thus, pigs were "grumphies," or "the four-fitted (four-footed) beasties"; salmon were called "charlies" or "the big fish"; ministers were "the man wi' the black quyte (waist-coat) and the kirk was the "bell hoose." To this list Anson (1965: 131) added:

> On no account could reference be made on a Scottish fishing vessel to a minister, kirk, pig, salmon, trout, hare, rabbit or dog .... Before hauling lines it was strictly forbidden to mention a horse, cow, dog, pig, hare, rabbit, rat, and certain other quadrupeds.

Fishing Taboos in Contemporary Gamrie

Recent fieldwork in Gamrie indicates that a number of the traditional taboos remain. The most commonly recognized taboo words in this village were salmon, pig and rabbit or hare. There was also an avoidance of whistling on board ship and of ministers and "women of a certain kind" (i.e. unmarried mothers, the sexually promiscuous and those who were deemed peculiar or odd). However, even those few taboos are largely vestiges of past tradition, having lost most of their influence.

The senior author gained passage on two different fishing boats. The first was a small vessel by modern standards, that could remain at sea for a relatively short time and possessed a limited catch capacity. The skipper, a man in his fifties, had been a fisherman all his life and was one of three brothers who owned similar boats. This captain obviously continued to accept the traditional village values and lifestyle. For example, he was one of the few fishermen who still wore an earring. Earrings were believed to be protective in the event that a man fell overboard. According to lore, the earring provided a surface that could be gripped by those on board and thus save the drowning victim.

Given this skipper's traditionalism, it is not surprising that taboo words could not be uttered on board. When the senior author mentioned the word pig in front of crew members, their reaction was first to look at one another, then to laugh. They made it clear, however, that he should not say that word on board the boat or the skipper might get angry enough to steam back to port and put him ashore. While they regarded such prohibitions as silly, they were not willing to test the tolerance of the skipper and therefore avoided using taboo words.

The other boat was a larger, more modern craft capable of staying out on fishing expeditions for a week at a time and having a much larger hold capacity. The whole ambiance of this vessel was quite different—it was that of a modern commercial/industrial enterprise. When members of this crew were asked about tabooed words, they agreed that such words no longer were avoided. They pointed out that not only did these words have little significance to them but also that bacon was frequently served while they were out on the boat, and salmon, when they were occasionally caught, would be put on the menu. Rabbit and hare are not eaten by villagers, but this appears to be the result of an outbreak of myxomatosis in the area rather than avoidance of those foods because they were taboo. The difference in conformity to historical proscriptions between the smaller craft skippered by an older, more conservative fisherman and the larger craft where the old ways were given less credence is indicative of the continuing erosion of the traditional taboos.

Although the traditional taboos were either disregarded or assumed the quasi-humorous character associated with such contemporary American proscriptions as walking under a ladder and breaking a mirror, some idiosyncratic magical practices remain. One of these is what might be called "net magic." Most fishing boats carry a spare net that can be used if the net in use is badly damaged. On trawlers some damage occurs almost every time the net is drawn, and so between shots the net is mended. Occasionally the primary net is so badly torn that the spare net must be substituted. Some captains feel that one net catches better than another, even when those nets were made of the same material and by the same manufacturer. This belief can result in a great deal of time being spent mending the "lucky" net rather than employing the substitute net. The result, of course, is that an opportunity for a "shot" and hence a larger catch or more rapid achievement of the desired catch, may be lost.

In another case a boat captain refused to change his clothes after he had a successful catch. While fishermen often wear the same clothes for a week while at sea, they usually wash their clothes over the weekend. In this case, the skipper continued to wear the same clothes as long as the good fishing continued. This practice is akin to superstitious behavior by baseball players who refuse to change bats while on a hitting streak, anglers who have a lucky lure or investors who follow magical formulas in buying and selling activity. Finally, there were some magical practices related to

Forbidden Fruits

personal safety even among younger fishermen. In addition to the wearing of earrings discussed previously, there were cases of fishermen wearing religious medals. What makes this practice interesting is that the medals contained the figures of Catholic saints. There are no Catholics in this part of Scotland, and the wearers knew nothing about the saints whose protection they were apparently invoking. This practice would seem to be akin to contemporary Americans wearing a rabbit's foot on their keychains. These individuals believe, although usually not strongly, that the object is lucky. However, they typically do not know why the object is lucky, and their possession of the object can be attributed more to general cultural lore than to a belief in a specific magical relationship.

Explaining Content and Change in Word Taboos

Two sets of questions emerge from this patterning of word taboos among Scottish fishermen. First, how can we account for the creation and later the decline of these taboos. The best explanation for the construction of these taboos is the extreme danger and unpredictability of fishing as a livelihood. As Malinowski observed (Gmelch, 1971: 39):

We find magic wherever the elements of chance and accident, and the emotional play between hope and fear have a wide and extensive range. We do not find magic wherever the pursuit is reliable, and well under the control of rational methods.

Historically, commercial fishing incorporated precisely this set of ingredients. Early fishermen sought their subsistence against a constant backdrop of personal risk and an apparently whimsical mother nature. For these men the ocean posed a constant danger as the countless songs and stories of lives and ships lost to the sea dramatically attest. Their boats were small and completely dependent on favorable winds for mobility. These fishermen possessed a limited capacity to locate migrating schools of fish, were unable to accurately forecast changes in the weather, were easily incapacitated by fog and storms, and lacked the capability to communicate with other vessels or land in the event of mishaps at sea.

It is precisely this combination of danger and uncertainty that yields to magical solutions. With survival hinging on a successful catch, extreme danger associated with each fishing expedition, and, at least at times, an apparently random relationship between effort expended and successes attained, inescapably there is an individual and collective search for factors which might shift the locus of control from nature to man.

The advent of modern fishing technology dramatically altered the balance of power. True the sea remained a formidable, unremitting adversary. But contemporary fishermen do possess both greater actual control and a greater sense of control than their predecessors. It is this combination of lowered personal risk and a clear causal link between technology and fishing success which has eroded the influence of traditional taboos. Contemporary fishermen use echosounders to identify large schools of fish rather than watching diving Ganets, humpback whales or surface disturbances in the water to locate their quarry. Weather forecasts are obtained over the radio, and the incapacitating effects of fog on navigation can be neutralized by the use of radar and a direction finder. Now if a skipper is not successful in a fishing expedition, the explanation is formulated in terms of lack of knowledge or poor equipment. Quite simply, the changes in boat design and fishing technology have brought with them a greater degree of certainty in fishing, and with that increased certainty has come a decreased reliance upon the use of taboos.

The second question concerns the specific content of the taboo words. How and why were certain people, animals and objects associated with unfavorable fishing results? One possible explanation is chance. There doubtless was a good deal of accident involved in the attribution of causal relationships since these fishermen were confronting a complex situation characterized by flux and unpredictability. Under such conditions spurious causal relationships would be difficult or impossible to refute decisively. The belief in lucky nets and the refusal to change clothes while fishing is favorable on the part of some contemporary fishermen probably is illustrative of how chance relationships came to be reviewed as causal among earlier generations of fishermen. Only the regular, observable success associated with the proper use of modern fishing technology inhibits the institutionalization of some of these "magical" relationships as prescriptions or proscriptions. They still emerge spontaneously at an individual level, but they are not as readily incorporated into the cultural system.

There is, however, another more important dimension to understanding the content of taboo words among these fishermen. The tabooed words and practices, logically enough, reflect a concern with beings, objects and forces which impinge upon their survival and prosperity. Each of the words which has been proscribed is linked symbolically to those concerns. Taken together, these tabooed words and related practices comprise a set of symbols which metaphorically distinguish between fishermen and non-fishermen. This set of taboos symbolically creates a binary (we-they) world which reaffirms the common concerns and values of fishermen. The taboo is on mixing or linking that which is fishermen with that which is non-fisherman.

In a fishing village the fishermen are the primary producers of food and commodities for trade while, in commercial terms at least, women and ministers are nonproductive. The taboo on mentioning women and ministers constitutes a prohibition on mixing the productive and the non-productive. Fishermen naturally regard themselves as men of the sea. The taboo on mentioning pigs and rabbits constitutes a prohibition on mixing the land and the sea. The fishermen, while the productive center of the village, were not the center of power. The land on which Gamrie is located originally was granted to the Scottish equivalent of an English lord. The landlord also provided capital for and possessed control over the boats used by the fishermen; indeed, in the 1700s, fishermen indentured themselves to the lord. Salmon, which historically has been one of the most prestigious fish, long has been regulated by the crown or civil authorities. Such constraints on catching prized fish obviously antagonized fishermen. The taboo on mentioning salmon, then, constitutes a prohibition on mixing the fishermen with their rulers. Finally, wind traditionally has been a mixed blessing for fishermen. It was, when temperate, the source of power for sailboats but when excessive it was a highly destructive force. The taboo on whistling constitutes a prohibition on symbolically linking a human action with a potentially destructive outside force in such a fashion as to call for the latter.

From this perspective what all of these taboos have in common is a symbolic affirmation of in-group solidarity. It is clear that the particular words and actions which traditionally were proscribed symbolically represent these mutual concerns. In asserting this position it is important to recall that the taboos were not instrumentally effective. Avoidance of the taboos did not in fact ward off disaster or insure a good catch. The primary function of these proscriptions was strengthening of group cohesiveness, and this quality was particularly important for a group locked into a situation characterized by danger and unpredictability. Confronted with a lack of instrumental control, the group struggled to maintain symbolic control and internal cohesiveness.

Conclusions

In this paper we have examined the rise and decline of word taboos among Scottish fishermen while at sea. The emergence of these taboos can be traced to the danger and unpredictability accompanying commercial fishing in traditional fishing villages such as Gamrie. The erosion of the influence of these taboos was caused by advances in technology which reduced both the danger and the unpredictability associated with the fishing enterprise. The substantive content of the taboos reflected the various "outside" groups and environmental challenges vis a vis the fishermen's collective identity. The various taboos symbolically identify groups and forces which are not to be mixed with the ingroup. These avoidance practices helped fishermen maintain a sense of symbolic control in a situation in which they lacked instrumental control. As gains were made in instrumental control, the taboos lost much of their influence. Today Gamrie is gradually becoming a "modern" community, in which rationalism, technology and interdependence supplant ritualism, traditionalism and autonomy.

References Cited

Anson, Peter F.
   1950   *Scots Fisherfolk*. Banff: The Saltire Society.
Cove, John J.
   1978   "Ecology, Structuralism and Fishing Taboos." in *Adaptation and Symbolism: Essays on Social Organization*. Karen Ann Watson and S. Lee Seaton (eds.) Honolulu: The University Press of Hawaii. pp. 143-144.
Frazer, J.G.
   1922   *The Golden Bough* (abridged ed.) London: Macmillan.
Gmelch, George
   1971   "Baseball Magic." *Trans-Action* 8:39-41, 45.
Knipe, Ed.
   1984   *Gamrie: An Exploration in Cultural Ecology*. Washington, D.C.: University Press of America.
Lofgren, Orvar
   n.d.   *Fisherman's Luck: Magic and Social Tensions in Two*

Maritime Settings. mimeo.
Poggie, John J. and Carl Gersuny
  1974   *Fishermen of Galilee.* Kingston: University of Rhode Island Marine Bulletin Series, No. 17.
Steiner, Franz
  1967   *Taboo.* Baltimore: Penguin.